HUNTERS FROM THE SKY

The German Parachute Corps
1940-1945

BY

CHARLES WHITING

with a new preface

Cooper Square Press

First Cooper Square Press edition 2001

This Cooper Square Press paperback edition of *Hunters from the Sky* is an unabridged republication of the edition first published in New York in 1974, supplemented here with a new preface by the author and five new photographs. It is reprinted by arrangement with Leo Cooper, Ltd. and the author

Published by Cooper Square Press
An Imprint of the Rowman & Littlefield Publishing Group
150 Fifth Avenue, Suite 817
New York, New York 10011

Distributed by National Book Network

Library of Congress Cataloging-in-Publication Data

Whiting, Charles, 1926–
    Hunters from the sky : the German parachute corps, 1940–1945 / Charles Whiting.
        p. cm.
    Originally published: New York : Stein and Day, 1974.
    Includes bibliographical references.
    ISBN 0-8154-1145-6 (pbk. : alk. paper)
        1. Germany—Armed Forces—Parachute troops—History—20th century. 2. Germany—Armed Forces—Airborne troops—History. 3. World War, 1939–1945—Aerial operations, German. 4. World War, 1939–1945—Regimental histories—Germany. I. Title.

D757.63.W46 2001
940.54'4943—dc21   2001028491

Contents

Illustrations

The author and publisher would like to thank the following for permission to reproduce the above illustrations: The Robert Hunt Library, nos. 1, 2, 3, 5, 7, 9, 10, and 16; The Imperial War Museum, no. 8; and Bundesarchiv, nos. 4 and 6. Illustrations nos. 11, 12, 13, 14, and 15 courtesy of the author.

Maps

Acknowledgements

Many individuals have helped me in the writing of this book. Of the representatives of the various German parachute divisions, I should like to mention Herren Rupp (3rd Para), Gerstenmeier and Deep (5th Para) and Kroeger (2nd Para). Of the men who fought against the Hunters from the Sky and survived to admire them for their courage and ability, I owe a particular debt for information to General Farrar-Hockley, Squadron Leader Eric Taylor and Mr Bill Moore.

But my major debt is to that man without whom this book would not have been written, the 'Father of the *Fallschirmjaeger*' —General Kurt Student.

C. W.

Preface to the Cooper Square Press Edition

'It's either root-hog or die! Shoot the works! If those Hun bastards can do it, then so can we. If those sons-of-bitches want war in the raw, then that's the way we'll give it to them.'
General George S. Patton,
first order of the day, 24 December, 1944

By the morning of 24 December, 1944, Patton had a whole corps moving towards Bastogne. There the US 101st Airborne—'the Screaming Eagles'—were trapped. It was the task of Patton's three-division-strong forces (including his favorite armored division, the Fourth) to break through to the paratroopers before it was too late. On that snowy, freezing morning—nearly sixty years ago now—Patton's 50,000 men commenced the great counterattack.

Hours later, 10,000 teenaged German soldiers, most of whom had been in the infantry for only a matter of weeks or months, stopped Patton's army in its tracks. Before this battle even their commander, Colonel Ludwig Heilmann, had derided the young Germans: 'This division is fourth rate. It should not be allowed to cross the Reich's frontier.'

On the same day that Patton had issued his bold fighting order, German civilians led a posse of heavily armed US Military Police to a medieval house in the backstreets of picturesque Monschau, located at the end of the sixty-mile-long Ardennes front just across the German frontier on the Belgium border. The police were coming to arrest a 'very dangerous officer, Baron von der Heydte,' who had just made an appearance 'out of nowhere' and had begged for shelter in the ancient home.

The MPs knew the Baron well. He and his regiment had been a thorn in the Allies' side ever since that force had been formed. His 3,000 men had delayed the breakout of the 82nd Airborne and its sister division, the 101st, for nearly forty-eight hours on the beaches at Utah, back in June 1944. Now, for the last week, the

1,000 men under his command had wreaked havoc within the US lines on the Allied side of the front. The Baron's soldiers had created near panic everywhere, with GI doubting GI. An American MP shot out the tires on the vehicle of Field Marshal Bernard Law Montgomery, Patton's hated rival. Brigadier-General Bruce Clarke, leader of the US 7th Armored Division, which was defending St. Vith, had actually been arrested by his own police, who suspected he was a 'Kraut in a US uniform.' General Omar Bradley, his superior and commander of the US 12th Army Group, had himself narrowly avoided arrest.

Who were these men in camouflaged 'bone bags,' as they called their uniforms, these soldiers who contributed so much to the Allies' early defeats at the Battle of the Bulge debacle? They were German paratroopers who had preceded into combat both the American 'Screaming Eagles' and the 82nd Airborne's 'All Americans' squadrons. The German Parachute Corps pioneered air war, giving little heed to when the infantry—or the 'straight legs,' as they scornfully styled them—would finally catch up. In 1940 they conquered Holland. One year later, they captured Crete from the air, despite the fact that the British, tipped off by ULTRA, knew they were coming. In the year 2000, when American airborne forces celebrated their sixtieth anniversary, astute military men acknowledged that the early American heroes from Fort Benning had learned virtually everything they knew about the art of airborne war from their German opponents.

This book is a brief history of those daring German warriors, the *Fallschirmjaeger* (literally, 'parachute hunter'), or, as they were more commonly known, 'Hunters from the Sky.'

Foreword

The Red Devils, *Les Paras*, The Screaming Eagles—all names which make the hearts of their friends beat more boldly and those of their enemies jump with fear, names synonymous with tough reckless men, quite different from the common run of soldiers. They do not march to war as do the infantry. Nor do they ride there like the tankers. Instead they drop from the air into the midst of the enemy's defences, prepared to engage in individual combat as soon as their boots hit the ground.

Today the *élite* of every modern army from that of South Vietnam to those of the more obscure states of South America is composed of the 'paras', men alike in spite of their colour and language. Their uniform is distinctive and international—open-necked camouflaged coveralls—taken from the French *paras* who fought in Indo-China and North Africa; the red beret, the proud emblem of the British Parachute Regiment which has been in action continuously from 1942; and the brown, high-laced jump-boots adopted from the wartime US 82nd and 101st Airborne Divisions of Normandy and Bastogne fame.

All of them are volunteers, with a reputation for and an over-whelming pride in their unusual toughness. A deserved toughness too, for unlike the average soldier they have to conquer two fears. Not only have they to overcome their fear of the enemy, but also of that element into which they must launch themselves by an effort of will before they do battle—the air. They are, indeed, a *corps d'élite*, with their own customs, own traditions, own special methods of fighting—and of dying! The para-troopers, whatever their nationality, have their own particular *mystique*, composed in equal parts of boldness, bravado and an unbeatable professionalism.

Who were the men who started the whole thing? Those first 'paras' have been long forgotten. They never gained a nickname, although whenever they made an appearance their exploits filled the headlines. Their real war was over before the special *mystique* of the airborne soldier developed. Yet they went through their 'Sicily' before the 'Red Devils' were born; their 'Bastogne' four years before the 101st Airborne, the 'Screaming Eagles', did; and their 'Arnhem' was fought—*and won*—almost half a decade before that tragic British defeat.

Their power was broken as early as 1941 when they achieved the most outstanding victory of any airborne unit in the thirty-odd years that such soldiers have dropped into battle. Crete, the capture of an island from the air, was a tremendous victory, but it brought with it the seeds of their defeat; for their losses in the campaign were so heavy that, with certain exceptions, they were never to drop into battle in any large numbers again.

Yet they lived on to pass on their traditions to the new 'paras' who were to follow. A month after their first victory shook the world, Winston Churchill ordered the formation of a British parachute corps. Its first piece of equipment—one of their helmets captured on the battlefield. Later they were to hand on their jump-boots and camouflaged smocks to the American airborne divisions and later, when that war was over and a new one had started, their marching songs to *Les Paras*, in the jungles of Indo-China and the deserts of North Africa.

These men were known as the *Fallschirmjaeger*—the 'hunters from the sky'.

Section One

The Years of Victory

'This weapon has a great future.'
Field-Marshal Goering after watching the first
mass German paradrop, 7 October, 1938

1940—The Big Drop

'The paratroops are so valuable for me that I am only going to use them if it's worth while. The Army managed Poland without them. I am not going to reveal the secret of the new weapon prematurely.'

Adolf Hitler to General Student, October, 1939

One

Now there was silence. A moment before, the pilots of the cumbersome three-engined Junkers 52s had loosed the cables. There had been a slight jerk as the glider pilots had brought up the noses of their machines in order to brake. Now the 'Auntie Jus', as the paratroopers called the towing planes, were banking in a slow curve, making for their home fields outside Cologne to the south. All noise had died away. Everything on this May dawn seemed unbelievably calm and peaceful.

Below the paratroopers, Belgium still slept. In the pine-forests of the Ardennes the raw Belgian recruits called up so hurriedly a few months before might be already awake; and the pale pink glow of the huge steel furnaces on the horizon indicated that Liege's night shift was still busy. Yet to the south the great flat plain, the door to Belgium and Northern France, to which the 500 men in the gliders and the para transports hoped they held the key, lay silent and asleep. Neutral Belgium was enjoying—unknowingly—its last day of peace.

It was just before four and the night sky was changing to the dirty white of the false dawn. The remaining nine gliders, which formed the core of the attack, swung into battle formation. Somewhere to their rear their commander, Lieutenant Witzig, fumed as his plane made a forced landing on the German side of the border—as did another glider which came down at Dueren. But the eighty-odd men of the German 7th Parachute Division's specially trained engineer detachment did not know that. As the cream of Nazi Germany's glider pilots started to bring their planes down, they thought that everything was going according to plan.

A light mist was forming but they were able to make out the dim outline of their target—Belgium's most modern and most important fortress—Fort Eben-Emael, commanding the junction of the River Meuse and the Albert Canal, regarded by military specialists as the most impregnable fortification in Western Europe.

Stronger than both the French Maginot Line and the German West Wall (the Siegfried Line), it was constructed in a series of concrete and steel underground galleries, with its gun turrets protected by special Liege armour and manned by 1,200 picked soldiers. Now these eighty-odd paratroopers who, though they did not know it, were already leaderless, were going to crack this tough nut and by so doing open the door for the Führer's great drive to the West.

The fort loomed up larger and larger. The pilots were right on target and began to reduce speed. The first pilot applied his nose-dive brakes and the light plane shuddered under the strain. Inside, Sergeant Wenzel ordered: 'Helmets on!' Swiftly the paras strapped on their rimless, cloth-covered helmets and took up the prescribed position for a landing. The hiss of the wind against the glider's wings grew louder. The fuselage trembled violently and they heard the frightening crackle of small arms fire. Then came a rending crash, a tearing of canvas, and the shrill squeal of the skids as the first glider hit the rough ground. It slithered to the right and skidded to a stop. A moment later the next glider hit the ground behind it, and the next, and the next. At once the gliders' interiors were transformed into a frenzy of movement. Orders were rapped out. Men sprang to their feet.

The door of the first plane was flung open and the paras stumbled out, branching off instinctively to left and right as they had been trained. An ancient Belgian machine-gun began firing to their right and the air was soon filled with curses and orders in rapid French and the more guttural Flemish of the other ranks.[1] The battle had been joined. It was dawn, 10 May, 1940. The 'Hunters from the Sky'—the German *Fallschirmjaeger*— had begun the world's first large scale airborne assault.[2]

*　　　*　　　*

[1] In the Belgian Army at that time, 90 per cent of the officers were francophone.

[2] Reportedly the Russians dropped parachutists during the Russo-Finnish War but not on a large scale. German paras were also used in the 1940 Norway campaign, but only at company strength as reinforcements.

Operation Yellow, as Hitler's plan for the invasion of the West was called, dated back to the autumn of 1939. In essence it envisaged the German main assault at the centre of their front through the Ardennes. The German General Staff assumed that the Anglo-French forces rushing to the aid of neutral Belgium would not expect an armoured thrust through the hilly and heavily wooded Ardennes. Thus there would be only weak Belgian formations to oppose them until they hit the major Belgian defensive lines. These were deployed along the two parallel river lines formed by the Scheldt (Escaut) and the Meuse (Maas), linked by the Albert Canal. The canal, defended by pillboxes, its bridges ready for demolition, had been planned and designed with a view to military use.

Backed by the Liege fortifications, dating back to the seventeenth century, but now modernized by four new forts, including Eben-Emael, the position was regarded by both the Belgian and German command as virtually impregnable.

But the prewar engineers who designed the Fort had not reckoned with a new type of soldier, one who attacked from the sky. Thus the job of taking Fort Eben-Emael—and the conquest of Holland, whose vital airfields were coveted by the *Luftwaffe* for use against Britain—were handed to the Wehrmacht's newest formation—Reichsmarshal Goering's *Fallschirmjaeger*, commanded by General Kurt Student.

Just as Britain's own parachute troops came into existence at the express command of Winston Churchill, impressed by the success of the *Fallschirmjaeger*, so the German airborne troops had been born in 1935 when the German military attaché in Moscow had reported on a mass drop of Soviet paratroops, led by a full general, at the summer manoeuvres near Kiev. He sent a top secret signal to Berlin, which read with dramatic but startling simplicity:

'Russian paratroops indicate revolutionary change in the technique of war!'

The man who received the signal was Hermann Goering, head of the *Luftwaffe*. A First World War fighter ace, Goering was not slow in reacting. He decided to form his own paratroop formation, based on volunteers from his *Regiment Goering*, which up to then had been employed on airfield guard duties and similar 'housekeeping' tasks, giving the task of organizing the new formation to Major Bruno Bräuer.

The order reached the Major at his base at Stendhal, near Berlin, and it did not make him very happy. As he wrote later: 'When I received the command to form a para battalion in September, 1935, it seemed to me to be an unbelievably difficult task. I hadn't the slightest knowledge of flying or anything related to it. I had not even flown at that time, not to mention having never seen anyone use a parachute!'

But Bräuer was an obedient soldier and an excellent organizer. He discussed the surprising order with the CO of the *Regiment Goering*, who finally agreed to allow him to ask for volunteers, 'I thought,' Bräuer said after the war, 'that we might get thirty or forty volunteers whom we could train to become the teachers of the mass of volunteers following later.'

Major Bräuer was in for a surprise.

When the details started to come in, he found that every company had reported scores of volunteers for the new, unknown and exceedingly dangerous arm. At the end of that first afternoon, Bräuer called Goering and told the Marshal: 'In one go, we have a paratroop battalion of twenty-four officers and eight hundred men!'

And not one of them had even seen a parachute before!

Soon Bräuer was helping his volunteers through their training at Stendhal Airfield, improvising and inventing all along the line, from the type of helmet the men would wear down to their jump-boots. At the same time he kept expanding his new command at a fast rate.

First Lieutenant Schulz, who like Bräuer ended the war as a paratroop general, remembers how he was summoned to the latter's office at the end of 1935. Bräuer got down to business at once. 'I need a platoon of engineers for my battalion. I'd like you to ask for volunteers among your men. Perhaps we can get a platoon together, for a start at least.'

Again Bräuer was in for a surprise. That day Schulz called his company together and gave them a talk on the new arm, about which he knew as little as Bräuer had three months before, ending it with the words: 'Why don't you follow my example?' He had already told them that he was going to join the *Fallschirmjaeger*.

His sales-talk had had its effect. As one, they shouted, '*Jawohl!*'

Schulz said drily: 'Well, from today onwards you're paratroopers.' Bräuer had gained another company.

In 1937 the *Wehrmacht* formed its first paratroop battalion. It, too, grew quickly, under the command of Major Richard Heidrich, being trained by the *Luftwaffe* at the jump-school in Stendhal, until in July, 1938 the two units—Bräuer's Air Corps paras and Major Heidrich's Army ones—were merged to form the 7th Airborne Division, the first of its kind in the western hemisphere. Command was given to Major-General Kurt Student.

Kurt Student was forty-eight when he took over Germany's first parachute division, an old man by comparison with most of his men, whose average age was twenty-five. But if he was old in years, Student was young in heart.

He had started his military career as a cadet in the Prussian Army, transferring into the new Imperial German Air Force as a pilot in 1913. By 1916 he was commanding his own fighter squadron and in spite of the short life expectancy of the average pilot, he managed to survive the war.

Although there was little future in the beaten German Army of 1919, limited by the Treaty of Versailles to 100,000 men, Student decided to stay in the forces. From 1919 to 1928 he served as the sole member of the Aviation Section of the *Reichswehr* (the Army was forbidden to have planes), being 'responsible for two thousand individual items from raw materials to the finished aeroplane, so that in time of war or when Germany was again allowed to have an air force, the factories could start turning out planes immediately'. In Russia he also secretly trained 300 German pilots, although the Army possessed only a single plane.[3]

In 1929, Student returned to the infantry, taking over command of the 2nd Infantry Regiment two years later. In 1933, the year Hitler came to power, he was promoted to lieutenant-colonel and transferred to the new Air Ministry and returned to flying. Promotion thereafter was rapid and when the order came to take over the paratroops, Kurt Student was a major-general,

[3] These and other details were given to the author by General Student himself.

picked, as he believed, 'because of my experience in preparing for the formation of the *Luftwaffe* prior to Hitler's takeover'.

Student was impressed by the *Luftwaffe*'s jump school. His only complaint was that the training took too long—three months. He ordered it to be cut down to six weeks; if he were to create a division out of the existing two battalions, he would need a lot of men trained quickly. The jump school commandant protested that he could not take the responsibility for the drastically reduced training period. Student retorted: 'You don't need to. I will.' The Division started to take shape, but Student did not like the sabotage role that the High Command had assigned to it. He fought and won a battle to use his paratroops, not as saboteurs, but as an essential part of the new blitzkrieg tactics being developed by men like General Guderian. In the hustle and bustle of his new command, Student did not have time to complete his own jump training, so, ironically enough, the man the German Army acknowledged as the 'father of the paratroops' never once jumped out of a plane!

'Gentlemen,' Student addressed the assembled officers of the 7th Parachute Division and the 22nd Air Landing Division, 'our target is "Fortress Holland".' He pointed to the huge wall map of the Netherlands which decorated the wall of the conference room at the Handorf Air Force Barracks, just outside Munster.

'This "Fortress" stretches north as far as the North Sea. In the east it reaches to the Ijssel, where it is joined by various canals, lakes and the like. From there it stretches to the Waal in the south and the *"Hollandsch Diep"*.'[4]

Student was highly regarded for his ability to explain a situation and the officers present, who ranged from the Chief of the 2nd Air Fleet, Marshal Kesselring, through General Count von Sponeck, Commander of the 22nd Division, one day to be shot for cowardice at Hitler's own order,[5] down to the most junior officer present, First Lieutenant Rudolf Witzig, could follow his exposé without difficulty.

'This *"Diep"* is crossed at Moerdijk by the five-kilometre-long

[4] The *Hollandsch Diep* is the name given to the waterway which flows from the confluence of the Rhine (Waal) and the Meuse (Maas) to the sea.

[5] Von Sponeck withdrew his division against orders in Russia. Hitler had him stripped of his command and imprisoned. He was shot late in the war, probably by the Gestapo.

Moerdijk Bridge, which forms the most important link with Rotterdam, the heart of the "Fortress Holland".'

Student was an advocate of the 'short method', as he called it, the dropping of paratroops right on the objective, ready to fight as soon as their boots hit the ground. He went on, 'Like the Katwijk Air Field near Rotterdam and the fields at Dordrecht, Waalhaven and Maasluis, it [the Moerdijk Bridge] is vital. It is, therefore, our mission to take it and the others and hold them until the ground troops reach us.'

Student then sketched in the details. After a dive-bombing attack, the motor road crossing at the Moerdijk Bridge would be won by a *coup de main*, with paras dropping at both ends of it and overwhelming the Dutch defenders. Shock and surprise at this new form of warfare would make up for the attackers' lack of strength.

Naturally, Student knew that his 4,000 paratroopers would not be able to hold the bridges into the heart of 'Fortress Holland' for long. As a result he had been reinforced by a regiment of Sponeck's Division, commanded by Lieutenant-Colonel von Choltitz.[6]

The Regiment would land on the airfields captured by the paras and help to complete the success of the 'airborne carpet', which Student hoped he could unroll right across the Rhine delta, some sixty to a hundred miles ahead of the leading German ground troops. It was a bold plan and there were senior officers present in the conference room who thought it was much too bold.

Count von Sponeck was one. During a pause in Student's exposé, he asked drily, 'And how long do you think it will take for the tanks to reach Moerdijk and Rotterdam?'

Student looked at Air Marshal Kesselring. The Marshal, who had been an artilleryman before he had been transferred to the new *Luftwaffe*, cleared his throat. As he recalled in his memoirs: 'For my taste the signal arrangements (vital in such a link-up) were rather too complicated, especially as Student was reluctant to allow the 22nd Infantry Division much rope.' But Kesselring knew that Student had been awarded 'a privileged position by

[6] Von Choltitz was commander of Paris in 1944. He refused to obey Hitler's order to burn the city to the ground and saved his life by surrendering to the Allies.

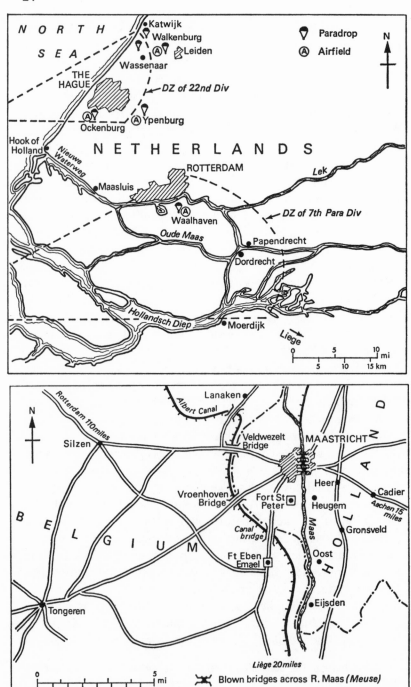

Top map:

N O R T H

S E A

THE HAGUE

Hook of Holland

Katwijk

Walkenburg

Wassenaar

Leiden

DZ of 22nd Div

Ockenburg

Ypenburg

N E T H E R L A N D S

Nieuwe Waterweg

ROTTERDAM

Lek

Maasluis

Waalhaven

DZ of 7th Para Div

Oude Maas

Papendrecht

Dordrecht

Hollandsch Diep

Moerdijk

Liège

Paradrop

Airfield

N

0   5   10 mi
5   10   15 km

Bottom map:

N

Rotterdam 110 miles

Silzen

Lanaken

Albert Canal

Veldwezelt Bridge

MAASTRICHT

B E L G I U M

Vroenhoven Bridge

Fort St Peter

Heer

Cadier

Aachen 15 miles

Canal bridge

Heugem

H O L L A N D

Gronsveld

Ft Eben Emael

Maas

Oost

Tongeren

Eijsden

Liège 20 miles

0   5 mi
8 km

Blown bridges across R. Maas (Meuse)

the Führer which the former had seized eagerly with both hands.'
He resigned himself, therefore, to accepting Student's optimism.

'Gentlemen,' he said, 'in my last conversation with Colonel
General von Bock,[7] I informed him of the organization and
combat tasks of the whole Air Fleet. I took up two points in
particular—firstly that the tanks of the 18th Army must reach
the paratroop forces in the Rotterdam area by the third day of
the operation; secondly that the Army must link up with the
gliderborne forces employed in the capture of the Albert Canal
bridges almost immediately.'

Von Sponeck seemed satisfied and Student continued with
his briefing, issuing orders to individual battalion commanders.
'Captain Schulz, you are in charge of capturing Rotterdam Air
Field with the 3rd Battalion of the 1st Para Regiment, so that
Colonel von Choltitz can land his men without opposition.
Captain Prager, you are in charge of the capture of the Moer-
dijk bridges. You must prevent any attempt to blow them up.
They are vital for our armoured troops. You understand?'

The CO of the 2nd Para Battalion understood.

One by one the officers of Bräuer's *Fallschirmjaeger Regiment
1* (Bräuer was now a colonel) received their detailed orders.
When Student was finished with them he turned his attention to
the two officers who were going to command the second part of
the operation. They were Captain Koch and his second-in-
command, First Lieutenant Witzig, who had been detached from
the 7th Para with 500 of the precious paratroopers[8] for the most
important assignment of all—the capture of the vital bridges
across the River Meuse and the Fort at Eben-Emael, eight kilometres south of Maastricht. Koch and Witzig had been training
for the operation at the *Luftwaffe* field at Hildesheim since
November, 1939. They had practised glider landings in the
smallest possible area under the most stringent security precautions, not even knowing the name of the fort they were
training to capture,[9] but Student knew that Koch's unit was the

[7] Commander of the twenty-seven-division-strong Army Group B,
to which the 18th Army belonged.

[8] Only about three-quarters of Student's men were completely
trained.

[9] After the war Witzig wrote of his unit: 'No leave was granted, nor
were we allowed out or to mix with men from other units. The sapper
unit was constantly moved around under different code names.'

best trained, most closely knit body of men under his command. Now he told the two officers the details of the task they had been training for: 'Your gliders will land on the surface plateau of the Fort and keep it occupied until Lieutenant-Colonel Mikosch can take it with his Engineer Battalion 51 in a ground attack.'

Witzig glanced at the special map of the Fort which hung on the other wall. It was bang up-to-date, the latest details having been supplied by Belgian deserters. It did not look good at all. The place bristled with light and heavy gun emplacements, but he comforted himself with the thought that once they had managed to get within striking distance, they could employ their 'secret weapon' which might well mean the success of the whole operation.

Then the meeting broke up. The battalion commanders crowded around the maps, chatting about their various assignments. Colonel Bruno Bräuer turned to Schulz: 'Well,' he said, 'now you know where you're going at last.'

'Yes, Colonel, now I know, but I'm glad to be taking part in the first combat drop.'

'It'll be no walk-over,' the Colonel warned.

At that moment Kesselring rose to his feet and walked to the centre of the room. 'Gentlemen,' he said, 'in the next few days the Air Force and, in particular, the Para Corps will be the centre of public interest. The success of our operational plan will depend on the realization of these very bold individual actions. The greatest factor in the success of our efforts is the condition and spirit of our paratroopers. The careful planning of the operation and the thorough training of our men are the basis of the whole of Operation Yellow. It is up to you to show that the paratroopers can fight—and win!'

Two

Captain Schulz positioned himself at the door of the Junkers transport, the wind whipping at his overalls. Like the men he commanded, he was jumping into combat for the first time and his mind raced with the frightening possibilities. Would he be hurt? Would the Dutch fire at him while he was hanging in mid-air? What if his chute were hit by flak?

The Ju 52 was down to just over 450 feet. The lower it got the less chance they had of being killed during the drop, but their casualties through broken bones and twisted ankles would be correspondingly higher once they hit the ground.

'Get ready,' Schulz bellowed over his shoulder, 'one minute to go!'

Holding on tightly with his left hand, he checked his parachute for the umpteenth time and felt his equipment pack. He took one last look behind him. Lieutenant Schuller was in the number two position. Everything was going according to plan.

Then he jumped. The weight of his pack and chute seemed to snatch him out of the plane and he started to drop at a terrifying speed. Then there was a loud crack and the great white cloud of parachute billowed free above him.

As he wrote later: 'While floating down I establish my position and note the heavy fire coming from all around the perimeter of the airfield. That's where the defences are and it looks as if they are strong. Even so, there are comic interludes. Some of my men land slap-bang on the backs of cows which up to that moment had been grazing peacefully.'

Schulz hit the ground hard. Rolling over in the manner taught at the training school at Stendhal, he felt himself submerged by his chute. Freeing himself, he slipped off the safety catch of his machine pistol and doubled for the nearest cover.

To his front a Dutch machine-gun started to hammer away, but for the moment the enemy fire was weak. Schulz raised his flare pistol and squeezed the trigger twice. Twin green flares hissed into the sky and hung there momentarily, Schullen spotted them and came running up to report that he had collected the machine-gun section.

'*Herr Leutnant!*' Sergeant Ahrens was gesticulating wildly. 'Over there!' he cried.

Three Dutch troop transports were racing towards them at top speed.

'Fire!' Schulz roared. The two German machine-gunners opened up at once and the trucks came to an abrupt stop. Dutch infantry poured out of them and fled for cover. Small arms fire started coming their way. The Queen's Grenadiers, as they later discovered the Dutch soldiers to be, were quick to react.

Fortunately at that moment the company runners from the three companies appeared and reported that all three were safely in their start positions. They were followed, moments later, by two of the company commanders, First Lieutenant Becker and First Lieutenant Ringlein.

'Ringlein,' said Schulz, 'you take the left. Engage the corner pillbox in the south and push on to the edge of the airfield. Becker, you take the flak position on the northern perimeter of the field!'

'And me, *Herr Hauptmann*?' asked Schuller.

'You follow me with the machine-guns. Head for the office of the station commander.'

Thereupon he raised his arm and jerked it downwards twice —the signal to advance.

Schulz sprang to his feet and headed for the Dutch positions. The enemy saw his intentions at once and concentrated fire descended upon them. A couple of paras stumbled, threw up their arms and fell heavily.

Schulz was already in the first ditch. He slipped on the muddy bottom and went down. Someone grabbed him by the collar. He struggled to his feet and ran on, followed by his men. Before them were the bulky, abandoned Dutch trucks.

He shouted, 'Schuller, up here with Ahrens. You, Kloppke, take the second truck! Mundelein, the third.'

Hastily three groups of men climbed into the abandoned vehicles. The men had been trained to drive enemy vehicles and seconds later they were racing across the field towards the station commander's office.

A burst of machine-gun fire hit Schulz's truck which lurched violently as a tyre exploded, and in vain the driver tried to keep control as it spun wildly round. Schulz sprang out of the cab and threw himself into the knee-high May grass.

From both the south and the north ends of the perimeter there came the steady hammering of machine-guns, punctuated every few seconds by the sharp crack of a 20mm cannon. Obviously his two other companies had reached their objectives. Now it was up to him to do the same.

'Company forward!' he bellowed as the men clambered from the damaged truck. They ran forward, under covering fire by Ahrens' machine-guns on the flank. Again they did not get far. An Oerlikon caught them in the open and the Germans dropped to the ground, a few of them never to rise again. Schulz cursed and shouted for Sergeant Ahrens. Ahrens crawled forward.

'Listen, Ahrens,' Schulz said, 'get the men with the two machine-guns to give me covering fire. You follow me. I'm going to silence the Oerlikon.'

The two men started to crawl forward, their rumps rising and falling ludicrously above the grass. A handful of paras followed them to where the cannon was located in a small concrete bunker. The Dutch failed to spot them and Schulz could see the ugly red spurts of the cannon quite clearly through the slit.

They reached the dead ground in safety and Schulz knew it was up to him to make the last effort. He had to take the chance offered him. His body bent double, he ran forward, clutching the two smoke bombs Ahrens had given him. Behind him his men started to fire at the pillbox's slits. Forty yards—thirty—twenty—then Schulz threw himself down at the base of the pillbox. With trembling hands, he drew out the smoke grenades and thrust them through the nearest slit, following them with a stick grenade. There was a muffled explosion within the bunker and smoke started to pour from the slits.

Suddenly the pillbox's iron door was flung open and a group of blackened, bleeding men in tattered uniforms staggered out, their hands already raised in the gesture of surrender.

Schulz had won. He raised his flare pistol once more and fired a single red flare into the sky to indicate that the bunker had been taken. The fire from his own positions stopped and his men came running across the fields and took over the prisoners.

'Within thirty minutes of the start, the field was firmly in our hands,' Captain Schulz wrote later. 'Apart from a battery of four 75mm Skoda guns sited outside the perimeter and still firing, the entire defence had been wiped out or taken prisoner. The Dutch had fought very bravely, harder in fact than one would expect from a people which had not waged war for over a hundred years.'

A little while later Schulz and his men captured the station commander, a Dutch Colonel. During the surrender formalities, the German's eye fell on a silver cross on the Colonel's desk. In its centre it bore the number forty, also in silver. 'Does that mean forty years?' Schulz queried.

The Colonel nodded. 'Yes, I am celebrating my fortieth year in the Army today.'

Schulz was moved. Forty years in the Army and the man had lost his first and last battle within half an hour! 'Let me offer you my congratulations on your anniversary,' he said hastily.

The Dutchman shrugged. 'I'm afraid my thanks for your congratulations do not come from a grateful heart,' he said. 'After all you've taken my station from me.'

Schulz shrugged and got down to business. 'Is your field mined?'

'No,' the Colonel answered.

But Schulz was taking no chances. He ordered the Dutchman to accompany him in the latter's own car. While Schuller squeezed behind the wheel, First Lieutenant Becker hung on to the door. Thus the four of them sped back and forth along the runways and hard pads, testing for mines in the fastest, yet most dangerous, manner possible. Once the car hit a shell-hole and bounced high in the air. From the petrified looks on the others' faces, Schulz could see they thought they had hit a mine. But the Colonel had told the truth: his field was not mined.

Schulz then ordered Schuller to drive over to the Battalion's signal detachment which had already set up its equipment on the southern perimeter and radio to von Choltitz's airborne force that the field was ready to receive them.

But the message was never sent. Before Schuller reached the

signals detachment, the air was filled with the sound of approaching planes and then the first Junkers appeared on the horizon.

Suddenly a squadron of Hurricanes zoomed into view heading for the defenceless German transports at over 300 miles an hour. Horrified, Schulz watched their progress. The transports hadn't a chance against the British fighters. The two groups grew closer and closer. Where were the German fighters? Where was the fighter cover Kesselring had promised them at Munster?

Then just as it seemed inevitable that von Choltitz's force was doomed to destruction, help appeared on the horizon. A squadron of Me109s roared into battle. The Hurricanes zoomed upwards to meet the new danger and the sky was instantly transformed into a roaring, snarling mess of individual planes, weaving and turning desperately, their white-tailed loops and turns punctuated by the chatter of machine-guns and the grunt of cannon.

But Schulz had no time to watch the fighter battle as the first heavily-laden transport came into land. Springing into the Dutch colonel's car, he raced across the field to where it had come to a stop. The corrugated door was flung open and Colonel von Choltitz appeared. He spotted Schulz and dropped to the ground, a smile of relief on his face.

'My God, Schulz,' he said. 'I'm glad you made it!'

'We . . .' Schulz shouted, trying to make himself heard against the noise of the air battle. But he never finished his sentence. There was a thick crump of heavy anti-aircraft fire and a moment later another gun, located somewhere on the other side of the perimeter, joined in.

As the Germans watched in horror, another transport coming into land received a direct hit. Flames streaming from its rear, it hit the tarmac at full speed and burst apart. No one got out.

Now the Dutch set about the transport fleet with a will. A third plane was hit and a fourth. As Schulz wrote later: 'The sound of battle was deafening. The howl of aero-engines and ammunition, exploding in the hangars, was joined by the crash of mortar fire and the rattle of machine-guns plugging the planes. Speed was the thing!'

Leaving von Choltitz to look after his command, he jumped back into the Colonel's car, shouting at Becker to take his men and attack the battery which seemed to be firing from near the

Waalhaven. A voice behind him stopped him for a moment, 'Captain, take me with you'.

It was the Dutch Colonel.

Schulz realized that he might be useful in obtaining the surrender of the remaining enemy positions and flung open the car door. The Colonel jumped in and they were off, heading for the enemy guns.

Suddenly a couple of Messerschmitts broke away from the dog-fight and zoomed down over the Dutch positions. Cannon fire crackled along the line of their wings. Behind this cover, the newly landed infantry and a handful of paras ran forward. Schulz braked hard. The Dutch had spotted them and a rapid burst of machine-gun fire threw up a line of dust and pebbles just ahead of them. He jumped out and the Colonel panted after him. But instead of following Schulz into the nearest ditch, the Colonel ran towards the nearest Dutch battery, both hands above his head, crying, 'Don't shoot . . . Stop firing!'

When he was only a hundred yards from the Dutch positions, a burst of machine-gun fire struck him in the chest. He threw up his hands and fell—dead.[1]

The Dutchman's death seemed a cruel waste. Within minutes it was all over anyway and the battery was taken for a handful of German casualties. Now the airport was completely in German hands and von Choltitz could land the rest of his Regiment 16 without further trouble.

[1] After the war, Dutch papers maintained that Schulz had forced the Colonel to try to make his comrades surrender. Major-General Schulz has always denied this.

Three

The capture of the airfield was only a preliminary to the vital task of capturing the bridges needed for the follow-up ground troops. Without the bridges, some of them among the longest single-span bridges in the world, the myriad Dutch waterways could be held even by weak enemy forces, against everything that General Hubicki's 9th Panzer Division could throw at them.

As Student had planned it, one of Choltitz's battalions would move north from the airfield towards Rotterdam, while the other two battalions would push south to Dordrecht. Thus it was that as soon as von Choltitz had his men safely on the ground, his battalions, supported by those of Schulz's paras who could be freed from guard duties, started their push north and south.

Choltitz's III Battalion had the toughest assignment—to fight its way through the miles of surburban Rotterdam, where even the rawest Dutch recruit could hold up a company with a machine-gun. In order to reduce this risk, Student had designed a highly novel form of support for the III Battalion. Under the command of First Lieutenant Horst Kerfin, fifty paras of Schulz's battalion had been dropped over South Rotterdam's football stadium, which lay directly on the main road into the heart of the city. At the same time twelve ancient Heinkel 59 seaplanes, carrying a mixed group of 120 infantrymen from Choltitz's command plus engineers from the 22nd para engineers, commanded by First Lieutenant Schrader, landed on the river on both sides of the great Willems Bridge.

It was a bold plan and it came off. The Dutch workmen were amazed by the sudden appearance of the antiquated seaplanes just after dawn. As they taxied slowly up to the northern bank of the river, not a shot was fired at them! Nor did the infantry meet any resistance as they inflated their rubber dinghies and started to paddle uneasily to the edge of the bridge. Indeed the very boldness of their plan helped them. As Lieutenant Bruns of the Paras remembered after the war: 'Workmen, crossing the big bridge on their way to work, had mistakenly decided that the seaplanes were English and *so they helped the soldiers to climb up the river bank*!'

Hardly had they taken up their positions around the bridge, waiting for the Dutch attack, when they were alarmed by the roar of engines and the clanging of bells. A streetcar followed by half a dozen cars of different shapes and sizes came racing towards them, scattering Dutch cyclists to both sides. They were filled with heavily armed men!

A nervous para took aim. Just as he was about to fire an NCO knocked his rifle up. 'They're our men!' he cried.

They were. Kerfin's paras had simply commandeered one of the local trams, kicking out the surprised Dutch workmen and flinging their briefcases after them. Then Kerfin had set off, the tram crowded with boisterous *Fallschirmjaeger*. Those who couldn't get on grabbed cars and followed.

The black-coated police, who were armed with heavy revolvers, standing at busy cross-roads directing the traffic, were too surprised to stop them, as were the odd soldiers, guarding the dock installations. Dressed in their coal-scuttle helmets and puttees, they watched the Germans' progress open-mouthed, without firing a single shot.

With the tram bells ringing madly, the paras passed every obstacle without being even challenged. Thus they roared through South Rotterdam until they reached the Willems Bridge.

Soon, however, their laughter changed to sorrow. For although Choltitz's III Battalion fought its way to the southern bank of the river, it never got across. Schrader's and Kerfin's company-strength force was cut off for the whole course of the battle, subject to the full weight of desperate Dutch counterattacks, supported by both water and air-borne forces. Only half of them ever saw their homes again.

That morning the Dutch had awoken to find that, after one hundred years of neutrality, they were at war. And it was war of the most horrible and modern kind—not on some distant front, but right in their own backyard, directed at both civilians and military alike. As one eyewitness remembers that terrible dawn: 'There were great flames shooting up into the sky and beams of light from the searchlights and the sirens were going very loud ... We could see bullets from our guns going up ... The air raid shelter was full of people, all our neighbours and some people I didn't know.

'They were all talking loudly and no one was dressed, just coats over their nightclothes ... At first most people thought the noise was only practice. All the time people kept running outside and coming back with news. It was war all right and the radio was giving the alarm and calling all the time for all men in the reserves to report for duty to the nearest place. The radio said this over and over again.'[1]

But in spite of the initial chaos caused by the suddenness of the attack, the Dutch now started to react. The Commander-in-Chief, General Winkelmann, threw in his best troops, the Dutch Marines, nicknamed the 'Black Devils', to recapture the all-important Maas bridges. At the same time he contacted Navy Chief Admiral Fuerstner and asked for his assistance. The Admiral responded promptly. He sent the patrol boat *Z–5* up the river with orders to take the Maas bridges under fire. She was supported by the torpedo boat *TM–51*. At the same time three auxiliary mine-sweepers were ordered to patrol off the Waalhaven to prevent any kind of relief force trying to link up with the besieged paratroopers.

At eight o'clock that morning the patrol boat and her companion started to shell the Germans at a range of one hundred yards. Their fire was murderous at such short distance. The German machine-gunners, guarding the bank, scurried for cover. Now the Dutch gunners began to direct their fire at the seaplanes. One after another they were hit and burst into flames. Then the Dutch switched from the planes to the paras, whose position grew worse by the minute.

By eleven the *Z-5* had expended her ammunition and followed the *TM–51* back up the river, her superstructure riddled with German bullet holes. The Germans had a few minutes' respite.

Then Admiral Fuerstner, happy with the success of his naval attack, ordered three much larger ships into the narrow channel to tackle the enemy. This time he was determined to wipe them out before they linked up with von Choltitz's infantry moving

[1] *My Sister and I: The Diary of a Dutch Refugee Boy*, D van der Heide (Harcourt, 1941).

up from the south. Hastily the destroyer the *Van Galen* and two gunboats—the *Johan Maurits van Nassau* and *Flores*—slipped their moorings at the Hook of Holland and started to steam up the ever narrowing channel. But by now General Student had arrived with the second wave of the *Fallschirmjaeger*. He had landed with his aide, Trettner, without casualties and had just taken charge of the operation at his HQ near Waalhaven when the first shells from the gunboats struck the ground 200 yards away.

He took them calmly. 'Watch it,' he said to Trettner, 'the English will be here soon as well.'[2]

He was not to be disappointed. At noon, six twin-engined Blenheims came in at about 200 miles an hour in ragged formation, machine-gunning the field at treetop height. Student was not impressed.

They were easy meat for the German flak gunners. Sticking to their light, multiple-barrelled 20mm guns in spite of the British tracer—the War Cabinet had refused to let the crews use bombs in case they hit civilians—the gunners knocked them out of the sky one by one while Student watched with professional interest.

Three came down in sight of the airfield. No one got out. Another burst into flames in mid-air and a single crew member bailed out, his parachute a mass of burning silk. The fifth plane roared over the heads of the German gunners, smoke pouring from it. It flew the length of the Waalhaven and finally crashed into the Rotterdam motor road with a tremendous explosion that sent exploding tracer zig-zagging crazily into the sky. The last plane fled.

Student knew that they would be back, but he had other problems on his mind; he would tackle that problem when it came up. He knew from the reports of his subordinate commanders that Dutch resistance was stiffening by the minute. Already the Dutch Air Force was beginning to bomb the bridges in his hands. If the infantry could not retake them from the German paras, then it was obvious that they were prepared to destroy them. Now the Dutch Navy was joining in. Yet, as he

[2] Student first set up his HQ in a Dutch schoolroom, with the General sitting at the teacher's desk and his staff officers in the ancient benches, like a 'group of overaged schoolboys', as General Student described it to the author.

told the British military historian Sir Basil Liddell Hart after the war, 'We dared not fail. For if we did the whole invasion would have failed!'

While Student tried desperately to bring order out of chaos, the *Van Galen* was steaming up the Nieuwe Waterweg. Fuerstner had ordered the destroyer's captain to bring indirect fire on the Waalhaven and the airfield in German hands. But the skipper was a bold man in the van Tromp tradition. Like his seventeenth-century predecessor who had sailed right up the Thames with a broom tied to his masthead to indicate how he would sweep the Royal Navy from the seas, the *Van Galen*'s captain intended to sail on until he was facing the German positions. Then he would let them feel the weight of his 4.5 inch guns. But the *Van Galen* never reached the Waalhaven.

Suddenly the air was filled with the sound of Stuka dive-bombers. Although he had never been in action before, the Dutch captain knew the sound from the newsreels, and it was as frightening in reality as it had been in the cinema. Instantly he ordered his anti-aircraft gunners to open fire. The multiple machine-guns, arranged in banks on both sides of the ship, cracked into action.

The Stuka dive-bombers came on. Diving at almost impossible angles, they roared in for the attack, sirens screaming. The noise was ear-splitting. When it seemed they would crash directly into the ship, they broke off. Their bombs came whistling down. Frantic manoeuvring in the narrow channel prevented any one of them hitting the ship directly, but there were too many near misses.

A steampipe burst; then another and the helmsman felt his power go. They managed to get her into the Merwede Harbour, but the *Van Galen*'s battle was over before it had started. The naval attack had ended in failure.

Now the Dutch Air Force took over. For the rest of that confused afternoon they bombed the Waalhaven area continuously while the Dutch Marines prepared for their counter-attack.

General Winkelmann calculated that if he broke the German hold on the centre bridge at Dordrecht, which was a key point on the road the German relief forces must use if they wanted to link up with the paras in Rotterdam, he could deal with their resistance to the north and south of Dordrecht at his leisure.

Thus at dark he sent in his 'Black Devils' to attack the paras under Lieutenant von Brandis occupying the centre bridge. Their attack was successful. They killed the young officer, flung his handful of men from their positions, and started to dig in on the long railway bridge, now littered with dead and the debris of war.

Von Choltitz reacted quickly to the threat to his rear and ordered his II and III battalions to speed up their advance. At the same time he asked for air support.

Lieutenant Bruns, who belonged to the 1st Battalion as a company commander, somehow or other found himself in the van of this attack with two truckloads of infantry. He did not stop to argue that he was not supposed to be there. Instead he drove at top speed to the scene of the action and captured the 650-metre-long swingbridge across the Old Maas, but the Dutch were still in charge of the ferry which barred his progress.

Bruns at once ordered his two mortar crews to soften up the hundred-odd Dutchmen, armed with heavy machine-guns, who held the ferry. The Dutch took cover and Bruns gathered his men and rushed forward, firing his machine pistol from the hip. To left and right came the awesome whoosh of his flame throwers. This was too much for the Dutch, who soon began to surrender. Here and there a man still held out, but a bullet or a stick grenade put an end to such individual stands.

The Germans pressed on, and their counter-attack at the centre bridge succeeded. Thus as 10 May, 1940, came to an end in central Holland, 5,000 Germans were firmly established on all three major bridgeheads being supplied from the airhead at Waalhaven. Student's plan had succeeded.

Now over the battered Waalhaven area, its ruined streets filled with the sporadic crackle of close combat, parachute flares began to drift down, bathing everything in their unnatural light. Captain Schulz, still holding the key airfield which was the main-spring of the whole battle for 'Fortress Holland', knew that they meant more bombers. All day they had been coming—British, Dutch and French light and medium bombers. Now it was the turn of the heavies.

Thirty-six twin-engined Wellingtons came in in the ponderous formation of 1940—the individual stream attack with one bomber roaring in to drop its load every five minutes.

'They dropped their bombs any old where and from barely fifty metres up,' Schulz said later. 'They fired their machine-guns at anything. The light flak soon drove them higher, but six of my men were wounded and a building full of ammunition received a direct hit. The whole lot blew up, together with stacks of signal flares, making a terrific firework display.'

In the middle of the attack, Schulz was ordered to report to Colonel von Choltitz. The infantryman was taking the whole business admirably calmly, but his apparent calmness at that moment must have concealed a mind full of doubts, for he was well aware of their exposed position. He also knew from Student that, although they were in relatively firm control of the three key bridges, nothing had been heard of his own divisional commander, General von Sponeck, who had been given the task of capturing the Hague area and the Dutch royal family.

Since Student's paras had captured the fields at Ypenburg, Ockenburg and Valkenburg for them, nothing more had been received from the Count's HQ. Had his many friends and comrades in the Division been wiped out?

And what had become of the 500 paras who had been dropped on the Albert Canal bridges and Fort Eben-Emael? Had their mission, upon which depended the whole success of the drive west, failed? But most of all he was worried about his own relief force. Where were General Hubicki's tanks? As 'Day One' of Operation Yellow gave way to 'Day Two', in the embattled bridgehead von Choltitz asked himself these questions.

Four

In December, 1939, Belgian police made a surprising arrest—a young man of indefinite nationality, trying to escape across the border into Germany with a collection of stolen Belgian Army uniforms. The puzzled police tried to find out from the thief why he wanted the clothing. But he stubbornly refused to talk. In the end he wandered off into jail and after a Flemish paper published a cartoon of a fat-faced Goering, who was well known for his delight in uniforms, admiring himself in the mirror, dressed in a Brussels tram conductor's uniform and remarking, 'This *does* suit me well', the whole incident was forgotten. No one in Belgium or Holland (where similar thefts took place) could know that the sneak thief had been acting on the orders of Adolf Hitler himself!

Five months later those stolen uniforms were put to use with startling success.

Just before dawn on the first day of the great attack against the West, an oddly assorted group of Dutch military police and roughly dressed civilians approached the lock-bridge at Heumen on the Waal-Maas Canal, one of the many small bridges which barred the progress of any invader coming from Germany five miles to the east.

The sentries of the Dutch 26th Infantry Regiment guarding the bridge watched as the group approached. They knew that an alert had been called for that morning—there were rumours going around of a local German attack, but the thirty civilians coming towards them seemed to be under the guard of a handful of military police, armed with rifles. Still they knew that they were not supposed to take any chances.

Thus when the strange group came to within a hundred yards of their positions, the closest sentry ordered them to halt. They did so obediently. While three of the Dutch MPs kept the civilians under control, a sergeant approached the sentry, showed his ID card and explained that the 'civilians' were really Germans, deserters from the *Wehrmacht*.

The sentry checked the sergeant's ID card and nodded to the men behind him. Idly they began lowering the lock-bridge so that the group could cross to the other side. It wasn't the first time that German deserters had passed this way in the eight months or so of the *Sitzkrieg*. Somewhere to the rear there was supposed to be a whole internment camp full of them.

Sullenly, the Germans began to tramp across the bridge. The sergeant of the guard approached the MP sergeant and suggested he guide them to where he could lodge his captives. The MP thanked him gratefully. Then, as the last German crossed the bridge heading for the uncertainty of the internment camp, it happened. The captives sprang into action. Fumbling in their clothes they brought out machine pistols and grenades. Like a well-trained soccer team they surged back towards the Dutch sentries, as if they had been involved in surprise actions like this a dozen times before. Before the startled Dutch knew what had happened, they were themselves prisoners, lined up against the wall by one of their fellow 'Dutchmen'.

The Germans, all members of Canaris' special Brandenburg unit, a group of paratroop-linguists trained for such Trojan horse operations as this, stormed the Dutch pillboxes. Then they headed for the local military HQ. Firing from the hip as they ran, they soon overcame the slight Dutch resistance.

In a matter of minutes it was all over. The senior Dutch officer was dead, along with several of his men. The bridge was in German hands and the demolition charges removed. The operation, the success of which was so vital to the paratroopers now landing in Holland and Belgium, had got off to a flying start.

All along the Dutch–Belgian–German border that morning, groups of 'Brandenburgers' and SS men tried to take the vital bridges needed for the ground troops if they were to link up with the paras. Aided by renegades from the Dutch Fascist Movement, the Germans seized the bridges or lost their lives if the guards were smart enough to see that they were not genuine Belgian or Dutch soldiers.

But even where they failed, as was the case with the three

bridges at Maastricht needed for the attack on Eben–Emael, their sudden appearance in Dutch and Belgian uniforms created an unprecedented spy scare. 'Fifth column phobia' broke out everywhere that morning, a phobia that was only paralleled by the events on the same frontier four years later at the onset of the Ardennes Offensive.

Innocent people were arrested everywhere. Nuns, policemen and Allied soldiers were particularly suspect. The Paris press reported that 200 paras had landed in British uniforms near the Hague, a report which was followed a little later by the announcement of the Dutch Minister of Foreign Affairs, E. van Kleffens, that parachutists had landed 'by the thousand'. The Fifth Column was here, there, everywhere and nowhere.

Lars Moon[1] recalled later: 'We began to have some idea of the scope and importance of the German parachutists' activities when the police came around to remove from the hotel all advertising signs for 'Pacha' Chicory, a step being taken all over Belgium at that moment. As the police officer explained, it had been discovered that the 'Pacha' signs bore on the back information for the use of German parachutists; this was later confirmed by repeated radio warnings. Chicory is widely used on the Continent as a coffee substitute and 'Pacha' was the most widely used brand of chicory in Belgium. As a consequence every little food shop in the country had signs advertising 'Pacha'. These signs had been printed in Belgium, but complicity on someone's part had permitted the Germans to put on the back of them indications useful to parachutists landing in the locality where the particular sign was to be used. Thanks to this arrangement a German parachutist needed to carry on his person no incriminating maps or addresses; wherever he might land, he needed only to find the nearest 'Pacha' chicory sign, which might be in a grocery shop or along a public highway and on its back he would find the cryptic indications giving him the location of the nearest German agent and how to find him.'[2]

*   *   *

[1] A European research worker who was one of the first to tackle the question of whether the Germans had employed a 'Fifth Column' in their surprise victory in the West.

[2] *Under the Iron Heel*, Hale, Lippincourt 1941.

While all this was going on Captain Koch's force of 500 engineers were trying to take the bridges across the Albert Canal at Canne, Vroenhoven and Veldwezelt. Once these had been captured, the leading German ground troops now approaching Masstricht could hurry forward to support their comrades under First Lieutenant Witzig, whose gliders had come down directly on top of the great fort of Eben-Emael.

The first of Captain Koch's men, 'Assault Group Concrete', under Lieutenant Schacht, came down right on target. The action at the Vroenhoven Bridge was short and sharp. For the loss of seven dead and twenty-four wounded, Schacht took the bridge and gained himself the Knight's Cross. Behind him, his CO, Captain Koch, set up his CP and started directing the operation.

First Lieutenant Altmann, commanding 114 men, was equally successful and took the Veldwezelt Bridge without casualties, but First Lieutenant Schaechter, commanding 'Assault Group Iron', was not so lucky. It was his mission to capture the Canne Bridge, directly under the guns of Fort Eben-Emael, the bridge which was earmarked for the crossing of the 151st Infantry Regiment. As the gliders began to land at about 5.30 a.m., Major B. Jottrand, the commander of Eben-Emael, gave the order to destroy the bridge. It went up in a great sheet of flame, but Schaecter still rushed forward only to be felled by a Belgian infantryman, concealed somewhere in the smoking ruins of the bridge. He was badly wounded.

At his CP near the Vroenhoven Bridge, Koch read the first reports with satisfaction. Even the report from the Canne Bridge —'Objective reached. Opposition rather strong. Bridge blown, but can be used with the aid of engineers'—did not worry him unduly. The problem now was what had happened to 'Assault Group Granite', led by his second-in-command, Lieutenant Witzig, which had landed directly on top of the fort.

When Witzig's glider failed to land with the first wave on the top of the fort, Sergeant Wenzel had taken charge and with his small force of eighty-odd men, had set about putting Europe's greatest fortification, staffed by a reported 1,200 men, out of action.

Rallying his paras, he sent them off to tackle the various retractable gun turrets which dotted the surface of the fort. The para engineers had not trained for so long in vain. In four-man teams they rushed their objectives, nursing their secret weapon —100 lb cavity charges carried in two parts in the shape of hemispheres. While the flame-throwers kept the Belgian machine-gunners at bay in their turrets, the engineers fixed their charges. The explosive could penetrate armour to a depth of ten inches and even if the Belgian armour were thicker, the resultant explosion would cause enough splinters to put the turret's crew out of action.

They were not disappointed. Within the first ten minutes, Sergeant Wenzel's men put of action installations 3, 4, 5, 6, 7, 8, 9, 10 and 11. Five 75mm guns were destroyed and 12cm twin cannon were put of action by paras jamming charges down their barrels.

Wenzel was overjoyed by the success of the initial attack, but now the Belgians were beginning to react. Their machine-gun fire grew heavier and although most of the fort was now shrouded in the smoke of battle, he could see Belgian infantry forming up in the south for a counter-attack. Major Jottrand, utterly surprised by the novel form of attack and the impact of the Germans' secret weapon,[3] had called up a nearby infantry regiment to counter-attack. But before they went into action, he decided on a desperate measure to reduce the strength of the enemy on the roof of the fort.

Confident in the strength of his concrete and armour plate, he ordered a support battery to bring fire down to bear on the daring 'hunters from the sky' before the infantry attacked. Like some irate elephant, he was going to swat them off his thick skin with a heavy swipe of his own tail.

Meanwhile Wenzel, on the roof of the fort, was suddenly alerted by one of his men, 'Sergeant', the para called, 'a glider!'

Wenzel sprang to the slit of the pillbox he was using as a CP. A glider—one of their own DFS 230 assault gliders—was coming in through the smoke and small arms fire at a steep angle!

[3] The use of the special charges was kept secret throughout the war. In 1941 a US magazine quoted a Dutch captain as saying that the men who had originally built Eben-Emael had been part German. They had married local girls and stayed in the district, growing chicory in underground caves and using the activity to plant explosives under the fort which they detonated on the day of the great attack.

A moment later, it landed less than a hundred yards away and overalled men started to clamber out. It was Lieutenant Witzig and his missing platoon!

Wenzel shouted at the top of his voice. The new arrivals, crouched in a defensive position around the tilted glider, searched the war-littered area in bewilderment. Then they spotted the white faces peering from the pillbox. 'Over here, 'Wenzel shouted in German. 'Over here.'

Witzig and his men needed no urging. They doubled across to the others to be greeted with much back-slapping and breathless explanations of what had happened. Witzig cut them short. After his glider had made a forced landing in a field, he had rushed to the nearest telephone and demanded another Junkers from the airbase at Gutersloh.[4] While the Ju 52 had been hurriedly alerted and rushed into the air, he had worked frantically with his men to clear a flight path through the ploughed field. In spite of the seeming impossibility of his situation, he had managed to get airborne again. But he was still three hours late and he knew that the mass of the ground troops must have reached Maastricht by now and that he had to work fast if he were going to pin down the fort's garrison so that the advancing 51st Engineer Battalion could take it by storm.

But before Witzig could do more than detail a couple of men to find the rest of the paras now scattered into small groups, attacking individual gun cupolas, the weight of the Belgian artillery descended upon them. The pillbox shook under the impact. Witzig realized that they were sitting ducks on the top of the fort. The enemy artillerymen, located on the heights above Canne, probably knew every inch of the terrain. They could hardly miss. It would not be long before they had zeroed in on the pillbox and all the other strong-points, obviously well-marked on their fire map, held by the paras.

He made up his mind. They would blow their way into a howitzer casemate below them and find shelter there. It was a risky business. God knows how many of the enemy might be waiting for them in the dark concrete corridors below, but Witzig knew he had to take the risk, hoping that the Belgians, as he

[4] Today the runway from which the transport took off is used by RAF Lightnings attached to NATO.

wrote later, 'felt captives in their own fortress' so that 'their fighting spirit was stifled'.

Thus as that first day in Belgium ended, the Germans—like their fellows in Holland—had had their share of victory and of defeat. In both cases, the 'hunters from the sky' had reached their objectives; yet the follow-up forces had failed to reach them.

Everywhere in the Rhineland, Goering's air fleet was flying mission after mission in an attempt to dull the enemy's counter-attacks on the hard-pressed paras, while division after division piled up at the border waiting for the command to advance.

In Maastricht, now in German hands, the centre of the town was a scene of unbelievable chaos: horse-drawn artillery mixed with the panzers of the tank divisions; Dutch prisoners thread-ing their way through the unshaven exhausted German infantry; civilians trying pathetically to rescue what little they could from their burning houses. Steadily the cobbled, war-littered streets piled up with unit after unit while angry senior officers shouted at red-faced MPs, who were trying to sort out the mess, but could not, because the St Servatius and Wilhelmine Bridges across the Maas were down.

Although there was no longer any fire coming from the west bank of the river, since Captain Koch's men had taken the two Albert Canal bridges to the rear of the Maas, Sergeant Portsteffen, in charge of one of the leading sections of the 51st Engineer Battalion, knew it was going to be a tough proposition to cross. They had no bridging equipment and all they had at their disposal were their rubber dinghies. Once they had crossed the river, they would have to break through any possible Dutch last-ditch resistance between the Maas and Koch's men on the Canal, dragging their dinghies with them. There they would have to repeat the same procedure. This time, however, they would make an assault crossing under fire from those of Fort Eben-Emael's guns which Witzig's men had failed to put out of action.

Five

Punctually at one o'clock on the morning of 11 May, 1940, Portsteffen's platoon started to throw their rubber dinghies into the Albert Canal. Everywhere along the steep bank other units of Colonel Mikosch's 51st Engineer Battalion did the same, springing after the swaying craft as best they could.

Portsteffen had just managed to struggle aboard with his men when a searchlight clicked on somewhere in the dark mass of Eben-Emael. A long finger of light swept the dark water. Portsteffen and his men held their breath. But the Belgians had spotted them.

The enemy machine-guns opened up. The noise was magnified tenfold by the high concrete walls of the canal, as if they were in some deep mountain canyon. Portsteffen cried at his men to start paddling. To try to scramble back the way they had come would have been suicide and the only thing to do was to seek the safety of the dead ground on the other side of the canal. Furiously they began paddling. While Colonel Mikosch supervised the loading of the second wave of boats which was to carry the battalion's anti-tank guns, the Belgians swept the canal with a bitter hail of fire. Everywhere men were hit. Some slumped over their paddles. Others fell over the sides into the dark water. And now the Fort's heavy guns—those that the paras had not been able to knock out—added their fire to that of the machine-gunners. The crossing of the Albert Canal threatened to become a massacre.

Witzig, still on top of the Fort, realized the danger. In particular he knew that the big gun in Emplacement 15, located by the side of the Canal, had to be knocked out if the sappers were ever going to get across to relieve them. He could hear it thumping away below him, and although he could not see the effect it was having on the crossing, he could well imagine it. But how the devil was he going to knock it out?

Suddenly he hit on an ingenious solution to the problem. If he could not knock the gun out, he would blind it. He shouted an order to Wenzel, whose head was now decorated by a dirty bandage, and they ran to the edge of the Fort, above where the big gun was located far below; every time it fired, they could feel the ground shudder under their feet. But it was not the gun they were after—it was the look-out slits of the metalled observation dome which guided its fire on to the Canal.

Witzig knew that he would be unable to knock out the dome. But at least he could blind it. Rapidly his men tied charges to the ends of ropes and then, lying flat on their stomachs, they stretched over the edge of the Fort and lowered them down. Charge after charge was exploded in front of the observation slits and for a while the gun continued to fire, as if nothing had happened. Then its salvoes began to grow more ragged as the intervals between each round became longer. Witzig could just imagine the Belgian observers cursing him somewhere far below, blinded by the constant smoke and dirt. Finally the gun stopped firing altogether and the paras could rest for a moment. They were completely worn out. As Witzig wrote later, 'The detachment lay exhausted and parched, under scattered fire from Belgian artillery and infantry outside the fortification; every burst of fire might have signalled the beginning of the counter-attack we expected, and our nerves were tense.' Relief would have to come soon. . .

Sergeant Portsteffen, at the head of the 51st's leading platoon, had been making his way through the darkness ever closer to the massive outline of the great Fort. Now it was nearly dawn and all that separated him and what was left of his men from the trapped paras was a steep-walled, concrete-lined ditch guarded by a bunker. The bunker had at least two machine-guns and at regular intervals they swept the ground in front of the ditch, as if instinctively sensing that the enemy was hidden somewhere out there in the darkness.

Portsteffen, his clothes torn by the barbed wire and covered with mud from the Canal crossing, studied the situation, as the darkness began to soften before the dawn. He and his men would have to rush the ditch, but as they clambered up the other side, they would be easy meat for the machine-gunners.

At that moment Colonel Mikosch's anti-tank gunners came to his aid. The Colonel had finally got them across the Canal and now he used them to take the remaining bunkers.

While the small 37mm anti-tank gun kept the bunker occupied, aiming as best it could at the slits, Portsteffen ordered his survivors forward for one last desperate effort. Wearily he started to crawl towards the ditch. The others followed, working their way forward through the damp grass under the cover of the cannon.

Portsteffen and his men crossed the ditch safely. Now they were about ten yards from the bunker. The anti-tank fire had ceased and the vicious red spurts of fire from the bunker indicated it was back in action. Portsteffen turned to the private just behind him. The man was burdened with an oddly shaped round pack. '*Los*,' he hissed, 'get going!'

The private rose and ran forward at the double. The machine-gunner swung round to meet him. The private pressed the trigger of the hose he was holding and a long spurt of oily-red flame shot forward and enveloped the bunker. Abruptly the machine-gun stopped firing.

Portsteffen gave an order and the engineers rose and pressed on.

Suddenly one of the men shouted: 'Sergeant, there's a German flag!' A tattered red swastika flag hung from a bunker to the left. The engineers rushed forward and the sound of their boots woke the defenders, who rushed to the slits, but the cries in German made them lower their weapons. Sergeant Wenzel threw himself out of the door and ran shouting down the slope to the advancing engineers. Behind him came the other paras, their battle discipline thrown to the winds.

Portsteffen also forgot his years of training. He rose and ran towards the paras and flung his arms around the wounded Wenzel. Together the two men performed a little dance on top of the Fort, oblivious to the Belgian machine-guns which had begun firing again from the direction of Canne. The link-up had been achieved. Now it would only be a matter of hours before the greatest fort in Europe would surrender to the 51st Engineer

Battalion. The para operation in Belgium had ended in a tremendous success![1]

*   *   *

But what of Student's men still trapped in 'Fortress Holland?' 11 May was a day of disaster for Count von Sponeck's force. On that day elements of three Dutch divisions attacked his 22nd Division and inflicted heavy losses. All three of his airheads at the airfields in Ypenburg, Ockenburg and Valkenburg had passed back into Dutch hands on the previous evening and he was now completely cut off from his home base.

Still he fought back grimly with the tenacity that one day was to bring him both honour and dishonour in Russia. The Dutch flung in air and ground forces. At The Hague and Katwijk the fighting was particularly severe, the Dutch losing a whole battalion and the Count half his NCOs and officers. But by now the Luftwaffe had gained air superiority and although the Dutch Air Force gained the 'Militaire Willemsorde' (the equivalent of the Victoria Cross) for its self-sacrifice that afternoon, it did not succeed in preventing the Germans from resupplying the Count with food and ammunition by parachute.

All the same it was obvious to both the Dutch and the Germans that the Hague operation of the 22nd Airlanding Division had failed badly.[2]

Student, at his command post in the Waalhaven, knew nothing of von Sponeck's defeat. He was too concerned with his own problems. His men now held an area of some ten miles by five between Rotterdam and Dordrecht, and although his command was bordered by the great water barriers of the Old and New Maas, it was under continual attack. To the north, the 'Black Devils' were steadily whittling down the paras' defence. In the south the Dutch were equally aggressive, constantly counter-attacking the lost bridges. Student flung in what was left of

[1] Just before Lieutenant Witzig withdrew his men, he was a spectator of the surrender of Major Jottrand, which took place at noon. 'According to a Belgian source,' he wrote later, 'there had been about 750 men present ... They had lost 23 dead and 59 wounded. Of the 85 German sappers who had set out on 10 May, six were killed and, apart from injuries caused by the hard landing, 15 were wounded.'

[2] Count von Sponeck's 10,000-odd men did, however, keep three Dutch divisions of some 50,000 men occupied at that critical period of the Battle for Holland—a victory of sorts.

Captain Schulz's IIIrd Para Battalion to try to redress the situation, but Schulz didn't get far. His advance party hit a line of Dutch motor cyclists, he was hit by a sniper and that was the end of his part in 'Operation Yellow'. (When he came to he was in Rotterdam's General Hospital being treated by a coloured Dutch doctor.)

Schulz's fate in the battles for the bridges was typical of the confused actions of 11 May, with Student fighting frantically to retain his toe-hold in Holland, losing more and more of his best officers and NCOs, being sustained only by the efforts of Kesselring's Stukas and Heinkels. The eleventh gave way to the twelfth and then finally the 9th Panzer Division broke through, reaching the Moerdijk bridge that same evening. The link-up had been achieved, although Dutch artillery was still maintaining heavy fire on the bridge.

French tanks coming up from the south tried to attack and Student called for the Stukas. Below, the German radiomen directed them on to their targets. The French tanks in the streets of Moerdijk did not have a chance. They were trapped between the houses and the Stukas could not miss. It was all over in a few minutes and when the Stukas departed, the silence echoed the defeat of the French hopes. As one German witness recalled later: 'All that's left of the village is one house—not in enemy hands—and the church. A completely shattered French tank of the latest Panhard type, with a 3-centimetre gun and a machine gun, blocks the main street, with all its crew dead.'

But although the link-up had been achieved, the Dutch still refused to surrender Rotterdam. Von Choltitz asked the Dutch emissary, Colonel Scharroo, to give up the port but he refused. He knew of the failure of von Sponeck's landing and reckoned that Student was only able to maintain his position by air support. Von Choltitz pressed him but the Dutch Colonel was adamant. It was a strange forerunner to the role Choltitz was himself to play when asked by the Allies to surrender Paris in 1944.

Student sweated out the rest of the day, his position becoming more and more critical, in spite of the apparent Dutch desire at least to discuss terms. On the morning of the 13th, the decisive date, he decided he could wait no longer. As Kesselring recalled in his *Memoirs*: 'On the morning of 13 May, Student kept calling for bomber support against enemy strongpoints inside Rotterdam and the point of main effort at the bridges where the parachutists were held up.' Then suddenly Student's radio went off the air and a worried Kesselring was left to draw his own conclusions. He decided to attack, though he was careful to warn the commander of the 100-bomber group which he dispatched to attack the beleaguered city to maintain a careful look-out for signal flares; he did not want his own troops to be bombed by mistake. A lesser consideration was that by the time the operation was launched, the Dutch might have surrendered. As Colonel Lackner, the CO of the 54th Wing which was to do the job, recalled later, 'On our approach we were to watch out for red Very lights on the Maas island. Should they appear we had orders not to attack Rotterdam. Instead we had to bomb the alternative target of two English divisions at Antwerp.'

Red was an unfortunate colour to pick in a battle where the dominant colour was the red of anti-aircraft guns and tracer, the only one which would penetrate the thick haze of combat which hung over Rotterdam!

The Heinkels were airborne by 1330 on 14 May. They approached their target in two streams—fifty-four planes under Colonel Lackner coming in from the east and forty-six under Colonel Hoehne from the south-west. Time over target was estimated to be 1500 hours. Hoehne's group arrived first, flying in close over the paras' positions. The Colonel in the lead saw the target first and informed the bomb aimer. The aimer released his load, followed moments later by the two planes behind him. Then, to his horror, Hoehne saw the red flares indicating that the raid was off and hurriedly radioed the rest of his flight to turn about. The Heinkels wheeled round, forty-three of them still carrying their bomb load.

Colonel Lackner was not so sharp-eyed. His fifty-four planes dived in to release ninety-seven tons of bombs on a tightly packed area of Rotterdam. Lieutenant Bruns recalled later, 'We tried desperately to make it clear by Very light signals that the pilots were to return, but the pilots did not see them, and thus our commanders found themselves right in the middle of the German hail of bombs.'

The results were devastating. The old town, particularly the warehouses packed tight with petroleum products for the docks, went up in flames at once. Fires started everywhere. The inhabitants, many with their clothes aflame, ran into the streets in panic. Refugees started to pour out of the suburbs. And in the hotel where Colonel von Choltitz had already convinced Colonel Scharroo to surrender the city, the German officers raged at the fools back at headquarters who had spoiled their victory in this inhuman manner.[3]

Rotterdam had been bombed after the fighting had ended!

But the German defeat (for the bombing of Rotterdam was a tremendous Allied propaganda victory) in their moment of victory did not end there. For hours confusion reigned. Von Choltitz recalled after the war the relief of Oberleutnant Kerfin's battered force of paras of whom there were only sixty left. After four nights and five days of fighting they came out of their shell-shattered houses near the river. 'A young paratrooper grasped the flag which he and his comrades had displayed on the foremost house to identify themselves to the bombers. He came up like a lost soul, the other warriors of the bridgehead behind him. Many were missing and the survivors were dirty and worn, some without weapons other than hand grenades in their pockets.' He wondered if men like these would ever be useful in battle again.

Scattered shooting continued all that day while both Germans and Dutch tried to extinguish the flames and cope with the mass of panic-stricken civilians seeking to flee the city, running away from the fires and the great clouds of thick oily-black smoke now blotting out the sun.

Sometime that afternoon Student and von Choltitz found themselves in a Dutch block of flats negotiating the terms of the surrender with their Dutch opposite numbers. Student had just remarked to the Dutchmen that 'in every battle there is a victor and a vanquished. On this occasion you have lost gentlemen, but your Dutch troops have fought well and bravely', when there was the sound of small arms fire outside.

[3] Dutch refugees spread the rumour that 30,000 people had been killed in the raid; in fact the number was less than 1,000, naturally a terrible enough figure. But the Rotterdam raid, like that on Coventry in which 554 men and women were killed, helped to further Britain's cause in the still neutral USA.

The Dutch looked at Student, who strode to the window and stared out. A newly arrived squad of the premier *Waffen SS* division, *die Leibstandarte* (the Hitler Bodyguard Division), which had seen little fighting up to now, had panicked when they saw a company of Dutch soldiers loom up out of the murk. The Dutch were armed too! Immediately they had started firing. The confused Dutch did not know what to do. They had come to surrender. Some raised their hands. Others, in desperation, began to return the German fire.

Student shouted at the SS men to stop firing. The result was a sudden burst of machine-gun fire in his direction. The slugs pattered against the brickwork and before he could duck a bullet struck him in the forehead. As he recalled many years later: 'I received a terrific blow on the head as if someone had struck me with a sledgehammer. I sensed a strange disgusting noise in my skull. It was the friction, breaking and splintering of my bones ... I had been hit in such a manner that the hole in my head was as big as a saucer. I knew I had been very seriously wounded. But all my will to live started up within me. With the last of my strength, I tried to hold on to the edge of the table. Then I lost consciousness.'

The man who had planned and executed the world's first mass combat paradrop fell back, a victim of his own forces.[4]

---

[4] But Student did not die. For over two hours he disappeared from sight, while a frantic divisional medical officer searched for him through the Dutch civilian hospitals. Finally he was found, still unconscious, with a strange metallic lump under his eye. Dr Langemeyer, the para surgeon, thought that the lump indicated that the Dutch had attempted to assassinate him and kept guard all night over his CO. When Student finally came to he explained that the lump was from an old hunting accident.

1941—Crisis on Crete

'The name of Crete is for me—the man who conquered it—
a bitter memory. I made a wrong decision when I suggested
this attack, since not only did it mean the loss of so many
paras who were my sons, but also the end of the Luftwaffe,
which I created myself.'

General Student after the war

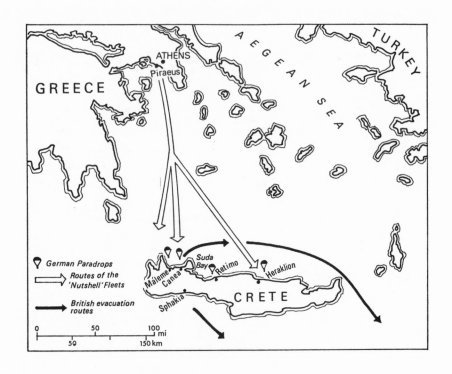

GREECE

ATHENS
Piraeus

A E G E A N   S E A

T U R K E Y

German Paradrops
Routes of the 'Nutshell' Fleets
British evacuation routes

Máleme
Canea
Suda Bay
Retimo
Heraklion
Sphakia

C R E T E

0   50   100 mi
    50   150 km

One

By the spring of 1941, Hermann Goering, one of Hitler's oldest associates and a man who had done much to establish Hitler's power in the old days of the National Socialist Party, was beginning to lose his influence. The honeymoon between the two most important men in Nazi Germany was over and now the period of marital strife which was to end in divorce was beginning.[1]

Eight months earlier Goering had confidently predicted that the *Luftwaffe* would win the battle for air supremacy of the Channel which was the essential prelude to any invasion of Great Britain. All summer his planes had battled against the RAF but in the end they had failed. Now, although it was still a year before the RAF could launch its first 1,000 bomber raid on the Reich, more and more British bombers were making their appearance over Germany. No doubt Goering often wished that he had never made the foolish boast that he would change his name to 'Meier' (presumably a Jewish name) if a British plane appeared over Germany. Now it was too late.

In the spring of 1941 he knew that the *Luftwaffe*, of which he was pathologically proud, would have to do something to refurbish its tarnished honour; for he knew full well that, if it didn't, there were plenty of ambitious men in the intimate circle around the Führer who would use the *Luftwaffe*'s failure to their own advantage.

General Student, by now recovered from his head wound,[2] appreciated some of his master's difficulties. Although his opponents considered Student to be a somewhat slow thinker, it is clear from the General's actions throughout the war that he was well aware of one feature of modern society—namely that

[1] Indeed, in 1945, Martin Bormann almost succeeded in convincing Hitler that the Air Marshal should be executed.

[2] The scar is still visible today, after thirty-two years.

successful publicity is essential to success. The gaps in his para-troop formations had been filled—the unit had been swamped with volunteers after their success in the Low Countries—and although his men, especially his junior officers, had, as we shall see, not yet learned the lessons of Holland, he thought that the 7th Parachute Division was again ready for action.

Thus it was that, exactly one year after he had put the final touches to his plan for the drop over the Low Countries, he offered the *Luftwaffe* High Command a new and even more ambitious plan. On 20 April, 1941, Student suggested to the *Luftwaffe* Chief-of-Staff, Jeschonnek, that Hitler's proposed Balkan Campaign would only be a partial success if the Germans allowed the British to retain bases in the Mediterranean from which they could bomb the vital Rumanian oil fields.

Jeschonnek, a thin-faced, clever-looking man, nodded his approval and waited for Student to come to the point.

When he did, it shocked the usually imperturbable staff officer. 'My suggestion is to take Crete!'

Student was suggesting that German air-borne forces should seize an island about 160 miles long by 35 miles wide, cut off from the Greek mainland by a broad stretch of sea. If that were not bad enough, the terrain was extremely tough, dominated by four mountain ranges so that movement over the extremely bad roads would be slow and difficult. And finally, since the British Navy would ensure that any follow-up by water-borne troops would be difficult if not impossible, the whole success of the attack would depend upon the German paras capturing the island's four airfields quickly, and retaining them.

But in spite of his initial hesitation, Jeschonnek understood his master's position vis-à-vis the Führer; Goering needed a spectacular coup in order to reinstate himself in Hitler's favour.[3] Naturally the capture of Crete would be of undoubted military importance, not only as a defensive measure (the protection of the Rumanian airfields), but also as an offensive move. From Crete the *Luftwaffe* would be able to bomb Suez, 500 miles away, and Alexandria, the Royal Navy's harbour, less than 360

[3] Indicative of Goering's mood at this time is his statement to Student when the latter reported to him after leaving hospital. After telling Student to look after himself, he said: *'God help us, Student, if we lose this war.'* This in January, 1941, when Hitler was master of most of Western Europe!

miles. Yet it was probably his realization of Goering's anxiety to uphold the prestige of the *Luftwaffe* which caused Jeschonnek to take the suggestion to the former. The man, who was reportedly a drug addict, who rouged his cheeks and painted his toenails, seized upon the idea eagerly. Undoubtedly it was the spectacular kind of action which—if it were successful—would reinstate him in the Fuhrer's favour.

The following day Student and Jeschonnek were ordered to report to Hitler's HQ to discuss the proposal with him.

General Keitel, the wooden-faced head of the High Command, nicknamed '*Laikeitel*' (a pun on his name and the word 'lackey') because of his subservience towards Hitler, and Jodl, the Chief-of-Staff, did not like the choice of Crete. Their counter-proposal was Malta and after that Crete.

Hitler, as was so often the case, overruled his generals. He decided in favour of Crete. He went even further. Carried away by the very boldness of the idea, he gave Student detailed instructions on how he should attack, suggesting that he should land 'simultaneously at many places'—a suggestion which broke the cardinal rule of German traditional military thinking '*klotzen nicht kleckern*' (roughly—'don't spread your men out in penny packets'). He ended his suggestions by recommending that Student should also be supported by an amphibious force, adding in untypical fashion, 'After all you can't stand on one leg'.[4]

So the planning for the operation began with the blessing of the Führer himself. Jeschonnek and Student organized the forces available into two *Fliegerkorps*—XI and VIII. Together these two corps had 500 transports, about 80 gliders, 280 bombers, 180 fighters and 40 reconnaissance planes. These would be used to transport and protect some 22,750 men, of whom 15,750 would go into battle by air, with the rest following by sea.

The main attack—Group West—would come in at dawn to attack the chief airfield at Maleme. Here the Assault Brigade under the command of General Meindl would capture the field, vital for the second wave, and then attempt to link up with Group Centre, which would land at the same time and take

---

[4] In Germany drinking men say that 'one can't stand on one leg' i.e. stick with one drink, another is needed. For the anti-alcohol, virtually teetotal, Hitler, this was an unusual statement.

Canea, Suda Bay and Retimo Airfield. Seven hours later the second wave—Group East—would drop, its target the capital Heraklion. Thereafter the men of the 5th Mountain Division would arrive to add weight to the attack, coming both by air and land.

Admiral Canaris, the shy, white-haired head of the German *Abwehr*, of whom it was said that he had strangled an Italian priest with his bare hands when under sentence of death in an Italian jail as a First World War spy, using the clergyman's robe to escape, assured Student and the planners that they could expect little resistance on the island. The rocky, arid island, which Canaris had visited during his pre-war trips to Greece, was defended by a demoralized Greek regiment and a few battered Australian and New Zealand formations which, he claimed, would not put up too much of a resistance. As for the fiercely independent islanders, who had only come under Greek rule a half a century or more, his spies told him that they would probably welcome the German paras 'with open arms'.

Thus the veterans and the many recruits to the 'hunters from the sky' who had been attracted by the headlines detailing the brave deeds of Sergeant Wenzel and Lieutenant Witzig at Eben-Emael and the dramatic drawings in the German Army magazine *Signal*, illustrating the daring attack on the Meuse bridges, drilled and trained, their hearts full of impossible dreams of glory, while far away in Berlin their fate was decided.

One of those new recruits to the paras, Baron von der Heydte, who had asked for a transfer to the paratroopers after he had completed staff college, recalls that April prior to the Crete operation in almost idyllic terms:

'It was the end of April, 1941, in Germany. A bright spring day dawned over the moorland, and across the broad tracts of the artillery range the young grass sparkled in the morning dew. It felt like the first Sunday after the creation of the world: everything was new and clean and good.

'A group of young soldiers had fallen in, the early sunlight glinting on their fresh faces. They were wearing the rimless helmets and copious, apparently ill-fitting jump-suits of German parachutists and their variegated apparel—a mixture of green, grey, brown and black patches—gave them the appearance of harlequins.

'In my capacity as commander of the 1st Battalion of the 3rd Parachute Regiment, it was my duty on that beautiful spring morning to decorate each of the twelve young men in the group with a parachutist's badge, for they had completed their jumping course . . .

'The small black cases, in which the gilt bronze badges depicting a plunging eagle in an oval garland of oak and laurel leaves lay upon dark blue velvet, were handed to me one by one by my adjutant (who happened to have been a theology student in civilian life). When I had affixed the last badge, it was up to me to say a few words to the men. I spoke of the obligations which the wearing of this decoration entailed. "Our formation is young. We have not yet any traditions. We must create tradition by our actions in the future. It depends upon us whether or not the sign of the plunging eagle—the badge which unites us—will go down in history as a symbol of military honour and valour." '

Little did he realize that bright April morning that nearly half the men he would soon lead into battle would be killed or wounded on a barren island so different from those lush green German fields, that the traditions of the new formation would be born in blood and death. For in London that morning Winston Churchill signalled to General Wavell, Commander-in-Chief of all British Forces in the Middle East: 'It seems clear from our information that a heavy air-borne attack by German troops and bombers will soon be made on Crete. Let me know what forces you have in the island and what your plans are. It ought to be a fine opportunity for killing the parachute troops!'

*   *   *

General Wavell, who was one of the unluckiest of all British commanders throughout the war, in spite of his undoubted intelligence and ability, flew to Crete on 30 April. He did not like what he found. General E. C. Weston, who had taken over the defence of the island at the end of March—he was the fifth Allied commander since the entry of Greece into the war and the stationing of British troops in the area—had not lived up to expectations. The defences were in poor shape, and Wavell felt that Weston had not had enough experience to defend the island in case of a full-scale attack. As a result he offered the job to General Freyberg, commander of the New Zealand division which had been recently evacuated from the Greek mainland.

Freyberg, thrice-wounded in the First World War, a holder of the VC and an aggressive, pugnacious man, was surprised. He did not like the appointment either. As he told Wavell: 'Forces at my disposal are totally inadequate to meet attack envisaged. Unless fighter aircraft are greatly increased and naval forces made available to deal with sea-borne attack I cannot hope to hold out with land forces alone, which as a result of campaign in Greece are now devoid of any artillery, have insufficient tools for digging, very little transport and inadequate war reserves of equipment and ammunition. Force here can and will fight, but without full support from Navy and Air Force cannot hope to repel invasion. If for other reasons these cannot be made available at once, urge the question of holding Crete should be reconsidered.'

Wavell was adamant and so, reluctantly, Freyberg accepted the appointment and threw the whole weight of his tremendous personality and considerable energy into reorganizing his battered formations.

In the main they consisted of about 25,000 men drawn from the 6th Australian Division and the 2nd New Zealand Division, most of whom had little but what they stood up in and their personal weapons. Their artillery was virtually non-existent, consisting of a hundred damaged guns, which Freyberg reduced to forty-nine usable ones by 'cannibalization'.

He realized that he must get reinforcements of some kind, but Wavell was reluctant to throw away any more troops in the Greek fiasco, when they were vitally needed for the fighting in the Western Desert. In the end he agreed to send a battalion of infantry—the 2nd Leicesters—plus a troop of artillery and two squadrons of tanks from the 3rd Hussars and the 7th Royal Tank Regiment.[5] It was not much but it was better than Freyberg had expected.

For two weeks Freyberg worked feverishly to get the island into shape for the expected attack, writing to Wavell at the end of that period: 'Have completed plan for defence of Crete and

---

[5] All these vehicles were badly battered from the fighting in the Desert and half of the Royal Tank Regiment vehicles went straight into workshops and stayed there for the duration of the fighting.

have just returned from final tour of defences. I feel greatly encouraged by my visit. Everywhere all ranks are fit and morale is high. All defences have been extended, and positions wired as much as possible. We have forty-five field guns placed, with adequate ammunition dumped. Two infantry tanks are at each aerodrome. Carriers and transports still being unloaded and delivered and 2nd Leicesters have arrived and will make Heraklion stronger. I do not wish to be over-confident, but I feel that at least we will give excellent account. With help of Royal Navy, I trust Crete will be held.'

But in spite of his optimistic signal, one thing still worried him—the problem of air cover and support. Wavell had been unable to send him any aircraft and as the few planes that were already on the island were hopelessly outnumbered against what Intelligence predicted the Germans would be able to throw into the forthcoming attack, Freyberg decided it would be useless to sacrifice them in a one-sided struggle. On 19 May he decided to fly them out. Unfortunately on the same day he was ordered *not* to destroy the now deserted airfields, in case the RAF needed them later. Thus if the enemy managed to capture one of the vital four airfields, his only means of landing large numbers of men on Crete, he would be able to bring it into operation at once. It was a fateful decision on the part of the British.

The Germans had been dive-bombing the island for four days. During the daylight they swept the Royal Navy from the sea and thus were able to reconnoitre Crete from the air without hindrance. Their reports and those of Canaris' agents, plus the unopposed bombing raids, made Student confident that in spite of the apparent enormity of their mission it would not be so difficult after all.

At his last conference held on the 19th in a hermetically-sealed and shuttered room in the Hotel Grand Bretagne in Athens, his confidence showed through his normally reserved exterior, as he told the junior officers of the 7th Para what their objective was to be. His juniors, however, could not conceal their excitement when they saw the large relief map of Crete prominently displayed on the wall. There was an excited buzz of comment and chatter.

Student hushed the outburst with a soft '*Mein Herren, ich*

bitte Sie'. The young para officers contained themselves, as Student began his briefing. Baron von der Heydte who was present remembers him speaking in 'a quiet but clear and slightly vibrant voice', as he explained his plan of attack. As von der Heydte recalls: 'It was his own personal plan. He had devised it, had struggled against heavy opposition for its accept-ance and had worked out all the details. One could perceive that this plan had become a part of him, a part of his life. He believed in it and lived for it and in it.'

When Student had finished, the intelligence officer took over. He passed on the information which he had received from Canaris via Student. On the island there were remnants of two or three weak Greek divisions, supported by British Dominion troops 'under the command of the well-known General Freyberg'.

'We have reports,' he told the officers, 'that the population will not fight. In fact the big men on the island wish to fight with you against England.' As von der Heydte recalls, this secret resistance group 'would make itself known to us by the code-words "Major Bock".'

The conference droned on. Unnecessary questions were asked and unnecessary answers were given. Noon passed and von der Heydte felt angry at the time wasted; 'I was in Athens, no more than a few hundred yards from the foot of the Acropolis ... I felt like a child at the open door of a room full of toys but not allowed to enter!'

But there was no time for such self-indulgence that day. When the conference finally came to an end, the regimental com-manders called their battalion commanders together for oper-ational instructions. Those given, the para officers snatched a hasty lunch. Officers and men were then bundled into trucks to take them to their fields, sweating heavily in their thick woollen jump-pants and waterproof smocks (they called them, with macabre humour, 'their bone sacks'), their knees protected by rubber kneepads, machine pistol magazines strapped to their lower legs. No one had thought of providing a tropical uniform for the paras yet.

The airfields with their 500-odd Junkers were organized con-fusion. Hundreds of machines shattered the night as they raced their engines before take-off. Huge dust clouds were flung up, in spite of all the efforts of the fire crews to damp down the dust with their hosepipes. Officers and NCOs blundered back and forth, flashing their green torches, shouting themselves hoarse in the din, as they tried to make themselves heard.

As von der Heydte recalled: 'During the hours which precede a sortie everything seems to become bewitched. Arms containers being hoisted into racks spill open, aircraft are not where they should be and the most important machine is liable, for some reason or another, to pack up.'

But slowly as zero hour came nearer, the officers and NCOs brought the confusion under control. The men and their equipment were finally loaded. It was midnight of 19 May, 1941. The roar of the three-engined Junkers grew to a crescendo. Inside, the paras gritted their teeth. The first machine lumbered forward through the dust. The great adventure had started.

Two

The morning of 20 May, 1941 was calm and cloudless over Crete. Soon, the New Zealanders in their slit trenches knew, the morning 'hate' would start; the German Stukas would come in again, as they had for the last six days, and start pounding the island in readiness for the invasion which soon must come. Now, while the sun was still a red ball against the stark black of the mountain peaks, they trooped wearily from their trenches and started lining up for their breakfast.

Brigadier Kippenberger watched them as he shaved on the first floor of his HQ in the small town of Galatos. They looked pretty ragged and to his professional eye not very soldierly, but he knew they were good material. He had fought with them all the way through Greece during the big retreat. When the day came, he said to himself, they would give a good account of themselves.

Suddenly his attention was drawn from the men by the drone of aircraft engines. He looked up to the sky. It had to be a German. There had not been any British planes over the island for days now. He saw the dark outline high in the sky and told himself it was a recce plane. Soon it would be followed by the bombers.

He had just finished shaving when the Me 109 came roaring down the main street at 400 miles an hour, its engine drowning the screams of the Greek civilians and the curses of the troops scrambling for cover.

Kippenberger poked his head out of the window. Blue and red flames crackled along the wings of the fighter and dust spurted up along the pitted narrow street. Kippenberger was a veteran. He had seen it all before and he knew it would soon pass. He finished his dressing accordingly and went down to breakfast. The cooks pushed the porridge under the staff's nose. Obediently, as if they were participating in some age-old ritual, the officers bent their heads over the miserable meal and began spooning it up.

And then it happened. As Kippenberger recalls: 'I was grumbling about this (the meal) when someone gave an exclamation that might have been an oath or a prayer or both. Almost above our heads were four gliders, the first we had ever seen, in their silence inexpressibly menacing and frightening.'

Kippenberger sprang up, sending his plate spinning: 'Stand to your arms!' he shouted and without waiting for a reaction, ran to his room for his binoculars and rifle. (He was old enough a soldier to know that a revolver identified him to the enemy as an officer and a preferential target.) He noticed his diary lying open on the table; it would be four years before he was to see it again.[1]

He grabbed his rifle and ran down to the courtyard. When he reached it 'the thunder had become deafening . . . the troop carriers were passing low overhead in every direction one looked, not more than four hunded feet up, in scores.' As Kippenberger ran down Prison Road towards his CP 'the parachutists were dropping out over the valley, hundreds of them and floating quietly down'.

Von der Heydte had been awakened by his adjutant as they crossed the coast of Crete. He got up and walked sleepily to the open door where the dispatcher was already seated. 'Our plane,' he recalled later, 'was poised steady in the air, almost motionless. Looking out, beyond the silver-grey wing with its black cross marking, I could see our target—still small, like a cliff rising out of the glittering sea to meet us—the island of Crete! Slowly, infinitely slowly, like the last drops wrung from a drying well, the minutes passed. Again and again I glanced stealthily at my wristwatch. There is nothing so awful, so exhausting as this waiting for the moment of a jump. In vain I tried to compel myself to be calm and patient. A strange unrest gripped most of those who were flying with me.'

Now they were flying over the beaches. 'The thin strip of surf which looked from above like a glinting white ribbon, separated the blue waters from the yellow-green of the shore. The mountains reared up before us and the planes approaching

[1] A Cretan girl hid it for him and returned it to him after the war.

them looked like giant birds trying to reach their eyries in the rocks.'

Now they were flying inland. Suddenly their left wing dipped and the plane swung away from a mountain, beginning to circle. The pilot ordered: 'Prepare to jump!'

The paras rose and fastened their static lines, which ran down the centre of the Junkers. They were losing height rapidly.

'Ready to jump!' the dispatcher shouted.

In a couple of strides von der Heydte, making his first combat jump, crossed to the door. He grasped the supports on either side. 'The slipstream clutched at my cheeks, and I felt as though they were fluttering like small flags in the wind. Suddenly a lot of little white clouds appeared from nowhere and stood poised in the air about us. They looked harmless enough like puffs of cottonwool, for the roar of the plane's engines had drowned the sound of the ack-ack detonation.'

Below him appeared the stark outline of the village of Alikianou. He could see the peasants in the dusty street staring up at the Junkers, then running away and disappearing into doorways. The shadows of the planes 'swept like ghostly hands over the sun-drenched white houses while behind the village there gleamed a large mirror—the reservoir—with single-coloured parachutes like autumn leaves drifting down towards it.'

The transport slowed down. The moment of his first combat jump had come. The dispatcher shouted '*Go!*'

Von de Heydte went. 'I pushed with hands and feet, throwing my arms forward as if trying to clutch the black cross on the wing. And then the slipstream caught me and I was swirling through space with the air roaring in my ears. A sudden jerk on the webbing, a pressure on the chest which knocked the breath out of my lungs, and then—I looked upwards and saw, spread above me, the wide-open, motley hood of my parachute. In relation to this giant umbrella, I felt small and insignificant.'

The transports came on 'like the sound of a swarm of enormous hornets, rising to a crescendo of drumming, throbbing sound', one New Zealander remembered. The sky was so full of enormous planes that it seemed they would crash into each other. Below them the air was full of parachutes dropping from the planes and 'flowering like bubbles from a child's pipe, but infinitely more sinister'.

At Maleme, the vital airfield, the gliders came sliding in too. They braked in a great cloud of dust and the paras came tumbling out. The 22nd Battalion of the New Zealand Division took them under fire. Still they formed up swiftly enough and rushed for their objectives. Lieutenant Plessen's squad overwhelmed the anti-aircraft gunners at the river mouth, but the infantry at the eastern perimeter of the field were a tougher nut to crack.

Plessen fell dead. His men were pinned down. Behind them Major Koch's detachment landed in an exposed spot. The hero of Eben-Emael fell wounded. The survivors of his detachment scurried for what little cover there was, heading for the Tavronitis Bridge where their comrades under Major Braun, who had also been killed, had done a little better.

Meanwhile to the west of Maleme Airfield, General Meindl's brigade, which had been widely scattered, but which had landed away from the New Zealanders, started to form up. Baron von der Heydte recalled: 'More like a tramp than a soldier at war, I walked along the road towards the white wall before me. And now, as the last of the aircraft turned north towards base, the sound of engines grew fainter and fainter, more and more distant. Somewhere on the high ground ahead of me, to the left of the road, where the village of Galatos was situated, a machine-gun started stuttering. Another answered, followed by rifle shots. Part of the 2nd Battalion must have contacted the enemy.

'I registered this fact appreciatively, yet practically without concern, for I was not responsible for what happened over there.'

Then suddenly, from the mountains behind him, came the screech of engines, not the ponderous roar of a transport plane, but a sound more like a siren, followed by the fierce crackle of machine-gun fire.

'Automatically I hurled myself into the ditch—a deep concrete ditch bordering a large field of corn—and at that moment a German fighter with all guns blazing swept over within a few feet of where I lay. A stream of bullets threw up fountains of dust on the road and the ricochets sang away into the distance. Then as suddenly as it had appeared, the apparition passed. The fighter pulled up high and disappeared over the olive groves in the direction of what I took to be Canea. So the first shots aimed at me during this attack had been fired by one of my fellow-countrymen!'

The baron's experience was typical of the confused state of the German attackers at Maleme. The junior officers were full of vigour but they were jumpy and ill-trained. They wasted their men in abortive actions and were not helped by the fact that, as in Holland the year before, their weapons were dropped separately in containers. It did not take the New Zealanders long to realize that as the paras were only armed with pistols and grenades, they had to get to the containers for their heavier weapons and ammunition; as a result all they needed to do was to stake out the containers and wait for the Germans to come and be slaughtered. They did so dutifully.

Colonel Leckie's 23rd New Zealand Infantry Battalion found the German III Para Battalion landing right in its lap. In the first frantic, chaotic minutes the Colonel shot five paras himself without moving from his headquarters. His South Islanders, who were mostly old hands with a rifle, did just as well. Later one of them thought it was 'just like duck-shooting'. They killed German after German from their position in an olive grove, with the paras at their mercy, tied to their riggings.

It was sheer slaughter and when it was over the III Para Battalion was virtually wiped out. As one eye-witness recalls: 'The sloping fields of the vineyards where the paratroopers had come down in the open were littered with bodies, many of them still in their harnesses with the parachutes tugging gently at them in every mild puff of breeze and getting no response. Among the olives corpses hung from branches or lay at the foot of the gnarled trees, motionless on the trampled young barley. Only here and there a discarded overall like the discarded shell of some strange insect showed that its owner had got away and might be lurking in ambush in some gully or by a stone wall, ready to sell his life dearly if discovered and if not, to seek out his comrades when darkness came.'

On the whole it seemed to Brigadier Hargest, commanding the New Zealanders in the Maleme area, that his men had the situation well under control. Admittedly he had not heard any-thing from Colonel Andrew, CO of the 22nd Infantry Battalion, but otherwise all reports indicated that the invaders from the sky were suffering heavy losses; even the dubious characters in the Field Punishment Centre had proved themselves good soldiers, sallying out to tackle paras after being hastily armed by their guards.

His close neighbour, Kippenberger, in charge of the New Zealand 10th Brigade, with three Greek regiments attached, had also coped well. Once the poorly armed Greeks had broken, but Captain Forrester of the Queens had 'begun tooting a tin whistle like the Pied Piper and the whole motley crowd of them,' as an eye witness recalled, 'surged down against the Huns yelling and shouting in a mad bayonet charge which made the Jerries break and run.' Now Kippenberger consolidated his front, having inflicted heavy casualties on the attackers, and waited for the second wave of paras, which surely must come.

*   *   *

It came at one o'clock that same afternoon. And it ran into the same opposition that had met the dawn wave. Major Schulz, veteran of Holland and now recovered from his wound, came down not far from Heraklion itself. Like von der Heydte he found himself alone and cut off from the rest of the battalion by enemy snipers. He scurried for cover in a field of maize. But every time he tried to move out, the snipers would crack into action and slugs whiz above his head.

Then he realized why and tried a new tactic. He worked his way through the field, carefully avoiding the thick stalks which had given him away before, and emerged into a vineyard. Suddenly he froze. Someone was moving through the vines. He clicked the safety off his machine pistol and fired. The Tommy was flung to the ground, as if propelled by some gigantic fist. Behind him other figures in worn khaki appeared. He had dropped in the middle of an enemy concentration. Swiftly he pulled out a hand grenade, waited two seconds and then flung it. Even before it had exploded, he had squirmed to his right in the bushes. The explosion of the grenade was followed by an angry volley of shots directed at the spot where he had just been.

He began to crawl deeper into the bushes, but the bullets followed him. He stopped and loosed off a volley from his machine pistol. The enemy hesitated and came on. He flung away the empty magazine and clipped on another, his last. The soldiers were getting closer. What would he do when his magazine ran out.

When he was almost down to his last slug and the soldiers were less than thirty yards away, a heavy machine-gun started hammering close by and a voice shouted '*Herr Major!*'

Under the cover of the machine-gun, he slipped back to where First Lieutenant Count von der Schulenberg was crouched in the bushes and together the two men hurried back about 400 metres to where the Battalion was assembling. Schulz at once ordered his company commanders and platoon leaders to report to him under the cover of a grove of olives.

Their reports were depressing. The Battalion had taken very heavy losses indeed. Not only that, but they had lost their radio, their only link with Colonel Bräuer, whose objective was Heraklion Airfield.

Major Schulz decided to improvise an attack on Heraklion itself, dropping his original objective, which had been to seal it off from the west. Hastily he gave his orders: 'As soon as it's dark we'll move up to our start line. At zero two hundred hours, you,' he looked at von der Schulenburg and Becker, 'will take your men and attack the town from the beach. We'll follow forty-five minutes later through the west gate.'

It was a hasty plan, but it was typical of the events of that terrible, confused first day, which was even worse than battalion commanders like Schulz and von der Heydte suspected. For by now both the senior German ground commanders had been put out of action—Meindl had been severely wounded to be replaced by Colonel Ramcke[2] (of whom we will hear more later) and General Suessmann, now commander of the 7th Parachute Division in succession to Student, had been killed when his glider crashed off the island of Aegina.

Back on the Greek mainland Student was as yet unaware that he had lost both his ground commanders and that his forces had

[2] In the First World War Ramcke, then a sergeant, had used his leave to go into action with other units. Twenty-odd years later, in Poland, he had done virtually the same thing. Now he had rounded up a few scattered paras on the Greek mainland and asked Student if he could drop on the island with them. Student had agreed. When Ramcke landed he found the assault brigade was without a CO. Naturally he had taken over. It was, however, a 'pushiness' and type of career-seeking which made him unpopular with his fellow officers.

suffered severe losses. He did know, however, that none of the paras had as yet secured their objectives and that he himself could not fly across until they had taken an airfield. It was an anxious night for him. All the same he decided to go ahead with sea-borne landings of elements of the 7th Para and the 5th Mountain Divisions, which were scheduled for the morning (during the hours of darkness the Royal Navy ruled the sea between the mainland and the island, but as soon as dawn broke it had to withdraw for fear of a German air attack). Then Student decided to follow his intuition and gamble all on a military hunch. He radioed Meindl (in fact it was Ramcke, but Student did not yet know this) to concentrate on capturing Maleme and its airfield and forget his other objectives. Student reasoned that if he could get just one airfield he could start air-landing the 5th Mountain and turn disaster into success. He therefore ordered all parachute reinforcements to be dropped in the Maleme sector. If the decision paid off and they helped Meindl to capture the vital field he knew that he would be a hero and that the press would hail him as loudly as it had done the year before. If, however, their concentration at Maleme meant the failure of potentially successful operations elsewhere, thus endangering the success of the whole operation, he knew that Hitler would not hesitate to remove him; his military career would end in disgrace.

Three

At dawn on 21 May General Wavell in Cairo received Freyberg's message sent the night before. It read: 'Today has been a hard one. We have been hard pressed. So far, I believe we hold aerodromes at Retimo, Heraklion and Maleme and the two harbours. Margin by which we hold them is a bare one, and it would be wrong of me to paint an optimistic picture. Fighting has been heavy and we have killed large numbers of Germans. Communications are most difficult. Scale of air attacks upon Canea has been severe. Everybody here realizes vital issue and we will fight it out.'

In spite of Freyberg's attempt not 'to paint an optimistic picture' so as not to mislead his commander, Wavell interpreted the communication as indicating that the Germans had not got a firm lodgment on the island, and that the enemy might well be thrown off it in the next few hours.

But like Student and Wavell, General Freyberg lacked one vital piece of information, namely that Colonel Andrew, commander of the 22nd New Zealand Infantry Battalion and a VC like his chief, had withdrawn his men from the vital height 107 which covered the Maleme operation!

Today it is easy to condemn Colonel Andrew, a brave and experienced soldier, for making the withdrawal which was decisive to the whole course of the Crete landing; but in the chaos and bitter fighting of the first day, when the 22nd had been carved up by the para attack (or so it appeared), it had seemed the right thing to do.[1]

The Germans did not wait to discuss the matter. During the

[1] In essence Colonel Andrew withdrew his A and B companies after he thought his HQ, C and D companies had been wiped out by the Germans. When the latter fought their way back to the positions supposedly held by the former, they found they had gone. Their commanders, bewildered and confused, decided to withdraw, thus giving the feature to the Germans.

early hours of 21 May the 2nd Assault Regiment rushed the feature and captured it. Swiftly Major Stentzler ordered panel markers put out to indicate that it was now in German hands. The way was now open to bring the airfield at Maleme under the paras' control. Shortly thereafter Colonel Ramcke took over the exploitation of the unexpected windfall.

Before the First World War Ramcke had joined the German Imperial Navy as a ship's boy. During the course of the fighting he had won the highest award available to other ranks for bravery and had been commissioned. After the war he remained in the Reichswehr, transferring to the *Luftwaffe* because, as one German officer who knew him at that time pointed out, 'He could not get on in the traditional infantry regiment. The transfer was his only way of obtaining promotion'.[2] But if Ramcke was not particularly well liked by his fellow regular officers, he was adored by many of his men, who were prepared to follow their 'Papa Ramcke' to hell and back if he wished, which some of them did, although they never came back.

The Colonel threw the whole weight of his aggressive nature into the paras' push towards Maleme Field. He saw that it was the only hope of saving the operation. If Student, whom he did not particularly respect, was going to land the reinforcements which were so vitally needed, he would capture the airfield for him—and soon!

Roughly at the same time that Ramcke started reorganizing the paras' attack, Colonel Andrew reached Brigadier Hargest's HQ. Hargest was still as optimistic as he had been the day before. He listened attentively to Andrew's story of his misfortune at Height 107 and then ordered him to fit himself and his survivors into the line with the Brigade's remaining two battalions.

That dealt with, Hargest contacted his neighbour, Brigadier Puttick. The latter who like himself had had a successful previous day did not seem to be aware of the urgency of the situation at Maleme. As an eye-witness of the events in the New Zealand Division recalls, 'they were seemingly unconscious of the desperate need for haste.'

When dawn broke and the sky flooded with German aircraft once more, Hargest and Puttick agreed that no effective blow

[2] General Fahrmbacher to the author.

could be struck till nightfall. In spite of the fact that fresh
German paras—the result of Student's decision—were dropping
everywhere in the Maleme area, they decided that two battalions
would be enough to do the job. As soon as the sun went down,
the 20th Battalion, plus the Maori Battalion and three light
British tanks would counter-attack. Until that time the New
Zealanders would concentrate on fighting off German probing
attacks and preparing for zero hour. Again it was a fateful
decision.

While Brigadier Hargest waited and Colonel Ramcke pushed
his men increasingly closer to the airfield, Major Schulz had
fought his way into the streets of Heraklion. It had been a hard
fight and now, with his men slowly but surely running out of
ammunition, Schulz, who had not closed his eyes for forty-eight
hours, allowed himself a few minutes break. He sat down beside
Lieutenant Kerfin in the shelter of an old wooden house. 'If
something doesn't happen soon,' he said, referring to their lack
of ammunition, 'we'll have to evacuate the town again.'

'You can't mean that!' Kerfin protested.

'If we don't evacuate, then we'll be "sitting" somewhere else.'

Kerfin knew what his CO meant by 'sitting'—sitting behind
bars in a British POW cage.

Just then their conversation was interrupted by a sweating
sergeant who was followed by a strange procession of Greek
civilians, and one Greek officer. *'Was ist los?'* Schulz snapped,
surprised by the civilians' appearance in the middle of a battle.

The NCO then told him that the civilians wanted to offer the
Germans the surrender of the capital.

Schulz could not believe his ears. He turned to the dark-haired
girl who was acting as the group's interpreter, and asked if the
Greeks were empowered to surrender the capital. She nodded
and pointed to the officer: 'This officer is the Greek Commandant of Heraklion. He has come to offer you its surrender.'

Major Schulz did not waste time. Swiftly he dictated the
surrender terms to Kerfin. These were then translated into
Greek by the girl while the Commandant nodded continually as
if he approved of every comma and full stop. Finally, Schulz,
the Greek and the burgomaster signed the pencilled document—
in fact a scrap of paper torn from a field notebook.

Schulz dismissed the Greeks and called an officers' group to pass on the good news and orders for the occupation of the rest of the town. Von der Schulenburg, Becker, Kerfin and the rest doubled away to find their men and take over the positions allotted to them.

They had not gone far when the silence was broken by the hammering of a heavy machine-gun. It was so slow that Schulz knew it could only be British, and came from the direction of the citadel, which Becker had been assigned to take.

Schulz cursed and ran after Becker. 'What's the matter?' he panted, as he caught up with him.

'The English attacked us,' Becker cried. 'They don't recognize the agreement. They are going on fighting!'

The New Zealanders and a large group of British infantry which made up the town's garrison did more—they counter-attacked. Relentlessly they drove Schulz back the way he had come. Dogged by a growing number of casualties and a rapidly dwindling supply of ammunition, Schulz made the only decision left to him. Ordering a few volunteers to man barricades at the edge of the town, he withdrew the bulk of his battalion, telling the burgomaster as he left: 'German Stukas will come soon to attack the citadel and all the places where the enemy has dug himself in. Tell all civilians to evacuate those areas. Tell them to come to the walls. We'll hang panel markers up there so the Stukas won't bomb that area.'

The burgomaster hurried away to carry out the order—or was it a threat? Schulz turned and ran after his men. His attack on Heraklion had failed. Soon the enemy would be asking for his surrender.[3]

This was not the only defeat the Germans were to suffer that day. During the night of 20/21 May Student's seaborne reinforcements had assembled, ready to run the risky passage from the island of Milos to Crete. In all there were sixty-three small *caiques*, Greek fishing boats, carrying 6,300 men, divided into two convoys. As the heavily-laden boats sailed out, German bluejackets on the quays called after the unhappy mountain troops, who were mostly from the Bavarian and Austrian

[3] When, some time later, the British asked Schulz to surrender, he sent his answer on paper. It read: 'The German Army has been ordered to take the island. It will carry out this order.'

mountains and had never even seen the sea before: 'How does it feel in your nut shells?' (*Nussschalen*)

They received few replies and those they did were not very complimentary. Then when the 'midge flotilla' (as the convoy was also called) was well on its way to Maleme, it was recalled for some reason or other. For several hours the nervous mountain troops, packed like animals in the evil-smelling boats, sweated it out until the fleet was ordered to sail once more. This time, however they sailed not in daylight, when the *Luftwaffe* could protect them, but at night when they were at the mercy of the Royal Naval squadron known to be in the area.

The slaughter began at eleven-thirty that night. Admiral Glennie with the light cruisers *Dido*, *Orion* and *Ajax*, aptly named in view of the area in which they were fighting, covered by four destroyers, struck the 'midge flotilla'.

In the German ships the alarm sounded. The mountain troops in their jaunty caps, decorated with the *Edelweiss* of their native mountains, scrambled frantically on deck. As they did so, the British searchlights clicked on. A dozen white beams swept the water and pinned them down.

The first salvoes struck and a caique loaded with ammunition blew up. Others started to burn. One of the British destroyers sped forward, the white bone of foam in its teeth, and struck a caique squarely amid-ships. There was a great crunch. The destroyer shuddered. Then it was speeding on, leaving the two halves of the stricken caique to sink.

Within minutes the dark waters were full of struggling, screaming German soldiers, their faces bathed a sweaty red by the light of the burning caiques.

The *Lupo*, their only escort, a small Italian torpedo boat, did not flee as many of the Germans, contemptuous of the 'macaroni's' fighting ability, had predicted it would if they ran into trouble. Instead it headed for the British destroyers, tackling them with its pathetically small cannon and machine-guns, trying to divert their fire to itself. The destroyers, perhaps sickened by the slaughter they were having to inflict upon the defenceless soldiers, turned their attention to her. The first 4.5 inch shell struck the *Lupo* and she heeled over alarmingly, her superstructure seeming to touch the water. But then she righted herself and swung round in a rapid curve, showing the destroyers her wake.

They kept after her and hit her again and again. But still the skipper came in time after time, trying to prevent the slaughter all around him, his ship taking hit after hit until the super-structure was reduced to a confused mess of shattered metal and wood, in which lay the dead and dying, and her deck literally ran with blood.

Thus the killing went on for two and a half hours. Finally the British ships broke off the action, swinging south in search of fresh victims, leaving the survivors to limp back to port, still escorted by the brave little *Lupo*. Soon the *Luftwaffe* would take a terrible revenge on the Royal Navy for its slaughter of the 5th Mountain Division[4], but for the time being Student's attempt to reinforce his men by sea was off.

But in the midst of what appeared to be disaster there was one faint ray of hope. At exactly the same time as a confident Winston Churchill was telling the House of Commons that 'the greater part' of the airborne invaders had been wiped out, Student's gamble, aided by Ramcke's energy, paid off.

At five o'clock that same afternoon the little village of Maleme and its airfield finally fell into the hands of Ramcke's paras. Swiftly they rushed to clear the obstacles barring the 600-yard-long runway, seemingly oblivious to the shells of the New Zealanders' gun which came down at frighteningly regular intervals.

There was no time to be lost. For already the Junkers, carry-ing men of the 100th Mountain Regiment, were appearing on the horizon and the landing control officer signalled that the big transports should come in.

In the surrounding hills, the enemy guns started to roar. A New Zealand machine-gunner who had not been put out of action started to fire somewhere close to the perimeter. An officer bellowed an order and a group of paras jumped into one of the captured RAF trucks and roared away in a cloud of dust to silence the lone machine-gunner. Now the first Junkers was a mere fifty feet from the pitted surface of the field. Then came

[4] The next morning the Germans attacked in force, succeeding in sinking two cruisers, two destroyers and damaging a battleship and the only British aircraft carrier in the Mediterranean.

the squeal of brakes and the smell of burning rubber as the great three-engined plane struck the concrete, its engines shaking with the strain as the pilot throttled back.

With a jerk, the pilot brought the heavily-laden transport to a stop twenty yards from the end of the runway. The door was flung open and the troops began dropping out.

Throughout the next hour, plane after plane landed on the airfield and although only individual landings were permitted, there were crashes enough. But Student, who was soon to arrive at Maleme himself, was prepared to accept those losses. Ground crews using captured British armoured vehicles swiftly pushed the wrecks to one side and the landings went on. More and more infantry swarmed out of the Junkers to make their way to the perimeter, ready for orders and the battle of the morrow.

Provisionally, if precariously, setting up his command post at the edge of a chalk cliff, Student got down to planning the operation with his Chief-of-Staff, General Schlemm, who one day would command the final destiny of a whole parachute army, and General Ringel, commander of the 5th Mountain Division. Although he realized that things could still go wrong, 'somehow or other, I knew in my heart—though I wouldn't have told anyone on my staff it at that moment—that we had virtually won.'

Four

At three-thirty on the morning of 22 May, Brigadier Hargest at last launched his counter-attack—and even now it was three hours late. Together the Maoris and their friends of the white New Zealand infantry battalion moved along the main road which led to the German positions around Maleme.

They ran into trouble almost at once. During the day the 'hunters from the sky' had had time to entrench themselves in the little white Cretan houses or behind the thick prickly hedges, which were typical of the country and as effective as extensive barbed wire entanglements. The night sky was split by the red flashes of rifles and the yellow light of the German machine pistols.

Captain Upham of the 20th Battalion recalls: 'We went on meeting resistance in depth—in ditches, behind hedges, in the top and bottom storeys of village buildings, in fields and gardens beside the aerodrome. The wire of 5 Brigade hindered our advance. There were also mines and booby traps which got a few of us.

'There was TG (tommy gun) and pistol fire and plenty of grenades. We had a lot of bayonet work which you don't often get in war. The amount of MG was never equalled. Fortunately a lot of it was high and the tracer bullets enabled us to pick our way up and throw in grenades. We had heavy casualties but the Germans had much heavier. They were unprepared. Some were without trousers, some had no boots on. The Germans were helpless in the dark. With another hour we could have reached the far side of the drome. We captured as it was a lot of MGs, two Bofors pits were overrun and the guns destroyed. The POWs went back to 5 Brigade.'

But in spite of the bravery of men like Captain Upham and his own confidence in the success of the attack, as night gave way to day it became clear that Hargest's plan was riddled with weaknesses. He had given no consideration to the possibility of delays in the start of the attack; nor had he reckoned with German resistance so close to his own positions. He had calculated that he would be able to attack the field itself under the cover of darkness. As it was when dawn came with that spectacular suddenness typical of the Mediterranean, he found his attack had bogged down in the open, exposed to any attack the *Luftwaffe* cared to launch at it.

Still Hargest was a persistent commander and ordered the attack to continue. But now the impact of the reinforcements began to make itself felt. The German opposition stiffened. With no artillery support to speak of, it was now a 'corporal's war'—a battle of small sections, in which weight of numbers counted and there were more Germans than there were New Zealanders.

Visibly the *élan* started to go out of the New Zealanders' attack, as if a tap had been opened and their spirit had begun to drip out at ever-increasing speed. By noon the advance had degenerated into a slogging match and by early afternoon—as one British eye-witness recalled—'the British commanders knew the worst: without air support and much stronger infantry and artillery support, the counter-attack for that day had failed and there was nothing for it but to try to hold their positions'.

The front settled down into an uneasy truce. Baron von der Heydte described the position of his men on 22 May as follows: 'Nothing had changed during the past twenty-four hours. The ammunition and food situation had not improved. What little ammunition we had received during the previous day had already been used up and food was virtually unobtainable. According to plan each company had started to explore the backward areas for supplies. In abandoned British and Greek positions one would find a tin here, a packet of cigarettes there, and in some deserted farmhouse there might be bread and cheese, but there was nothing like enough to go round. The soldiers got hungry and in the awful monotony of waiting their morale sank.'

It was not much different on the other side of the line. A British infantry officer recalls: 'After breakfast there was nothing to do except to go to sleep or try to, all except one who acted as sentry. I visited the posts and talked with the soldiers; it was always the same question they asked me: how was the battle going and what was the news? Their high spirits had been replaced by a grim determination; for they were now playing the hardest of all games—namely, sitting tight, under orders to defend their positions to the last man, and with no prospect of relief.'

Their mood was reflected by that of their commander, General Freyberg. Only three weeks before he had remarked, 'Cannot understand nervousness; am not in the least anxious about airborne attack'.[1] Now as the sun went down on that third day of the attack, he began to grow very uneasy. Sitting in the poorly lit HQ, he took stock of his situation. He had seen the flashes of the Royal Navy's guns out to sea and assumed—correctly—that they had beaten off a sea-borne invasion. In addition, the news from Heraklion was also encouraging. The defenders had thrown out Schulz's paras completely and captured most of the urgently needed supplies which the *Luftwaffe* had tried to drop them.

But the failure of Brigadier Hargest's counter-attack was a bad blow; as was the fact that Brigadier Kippenberger's scratch force—the 10th Brigade—would not be able to counter-attack; their usefulness was limited to a defensive role.

As the hours passed and he brooded on what he would report to Wavell, the dust-covered dispatch riders and the panting runners came and went, bringing nothing but bad news. A failure here, a lack of initiative there—confusion, indecision, war-weariness everywhere. His uneasiness grew. His forces were too widely scattered. Now that they were no longer capable of offensive action and the Germans were obviously building up their strength as quickly as they could, should he not concentrate?

But he knew what that meant. In these last few months, his men had 'concentrated' more than once and concentration always meant withdrawal. Now after the series of withdrawals which had seen them flung off the Greek mainland a few weeks before, how would they take the order to 'concentrate'?

It was a terribly hard decision—one that Freyberg had to take all alone, but it was a sign of his toughness and self-reliance that he did not try to 'pass the buck' by asking Wavell in Cairo

[1] According to Churchill in *The Second World War*, Vol. III.

for his opinion. He made the decision himself and then told his Commander-in-Chief. *The big retreat had begun!*

*   *   *

Captain Dawson of Brigadier Hargest's staff brought the bad news to 23rd Battalion HQ. He was exhausted when he arrived at the infantry positions on the morning of the 23rd, but he tried to maintain that stiff-lipped flippancy which the British like to assume in moments of great emotion or great danger.

'I've got some very surprising news for you,' he told Colonel Leckie, the battalion commander.

Leckie kept up the pretext: 'What! Have they tossed it in?'

'No, we are to retire to the Platanias River Line. Will you get in touch with all battalions?'

As best he could he explained that the withdrawal was planned to start within thirty minutes.

The infantry commanders did not like the order, but they hurried to carry it out, spiking what guns they had left and retreating to a position east of Platanias, covered by a rearguard of Maoris.

But Ramcke's mountain troops and paras conveyed by RAF trucks moved faster. A battalion of the *Gebirgsjaeger*—the mountaineers—succeeded in outflanking the New Zealanders. They pulled back a little further. Now they were in poor shape and their casualties were mounting steadily. In the end it was decided to withdraw them from the fighting into the New Zealand Division's reserve. On the night of the 24th, they moved from their positions, 'carrying our wounded on improvised stretchers down the steep cliff face', as one of them recalls, 'and then along a difficult clay creek bed to the road. Mile after mile we trudged. Everyone was tired. All were vaguely resentful, although none of us could have put a finger on the reason.'

Later the same eye-witness would learn why they were resentful; the move of the 5th Brigade from its position that night marked the end of any Allied hope of throwing the Germans off the island. Now they were no longer in a position to counter-attack and push the paras into the sea. Now they themselves would be pushed, together with the rest of the Allied troops, further and further towards the south coast until all that was left for them was surrender or evacuation.

The Germans now put steadily increasing pressure on the retreating enemy, sensing that they had the upper hand. All along the front, the para units which—because of orders or because of necessity—had remained static and inactive on 22–23 May, went into action, aided by the 5,000 men of the 5th Mountain Division.

For a day the men under Freyberg's command managed to held their new line, but here and there were indications that small squads of paras and mountaineers had slipped through it in the hilly countryside. Soon it, too, would crumble.

Student threw in all the *Luftwaffe* planes that General von Richthofen could give him. Ceaselessly they hit the new line, especially that stretch of it around Galatos, which they had failed to take on the 24th.

Brigadier Kippenberger recalls that day: 'About four o'clock a dozen Stukas dive-bombed Galatos. We had no anti-aircraft defences and they must have enjoyed it. My headquarters had one or two near misses. At this stage I was standing on a table looking through a window that gave a view over the line from the village to the sea and every few minutes I had to stand aside to avoid being seen by one of the planes continuously cruising over the treetops shooting at everything in sight.'

But the Brigadier realized that his defences were slowly crumbling under the relentless aerial bombardment. And whenever the planes let up the German artillery and mortar shelling started again, followed by an infantry attack.

'The main infantry attack started against the 18th and the crackle of musketry swelled to a roar, heavily punctuated by mortar bursts. Inglis (one of Kippenberger's senior officers) rang and asked what all the noise was about and I could only say that things were getting warm. I estimated the mortar bursts at six a minute on one company sector alone. "Overs" from the German machine-guns were crackling all around our building in the most alarming manner.'

When his telephone system failed Kippenberger went forward a few hundred yards to get a better view of the fighting. Fascinated by 'the rain of mortar bursts', he stumbled over a hollow, nearly covered by undergrowth. In it 'I came on a party of women and children huddled together like little birds. They looked at me silently, with black, terrified eyes.'

Towards evening the pressure mounted alarmingly on Kippenberger's front. The Germans were now attacking with six
battalions, supported by an artillery regiment. On the 18th
Battalion's sector mortar bombs were howling in at twenty a
minute and the Battalion, which was down to 400 men, whose
sole supply of mortar ammunition was ten bombs, was about
at the end of its tether. Colonel Grey, the Commanding Officer,
led a counter-attack armed with a rifle and bayonet. It failed.
D company was overwhelmed.

'Suddenly the trickle of stragglers turned into a stream,'
Kippenberger wrote later, 'many of them on the verge of panic.
I walked in among them shouting: "*Stand for New Zealand!*"
and everything else I could think of.' He succeeded in calming
them, at least, for a few minutes.

At that moment his attention was caught by RSM Andrews,
coming towards him in a strange manner. Quietly Andrews said
he could do no more. Kippenberger asked why and Andrews
pulled up his khaki shirt and showed the Brigadier a neat bullet
hole in his stomach. Kippenberger gave him a cigarette, never
expecting to see him again.[2]

Shortly thereafter Colonel Grey, fixed bayonet in his hands,
returned from the fighting up the ridge, 'almost the last of his
battalion and looking twenty years older than three hours before'.
The Brigadier told him to reorganize with what he could find on
the right of the 10th's line. Now, however, the Germans had
switched the main direction of their attack to the left flank.

The volume of firing increased. Soon it would be dark and
this was obviously their last attack to try to break the New
Zealand line before the lack of light affected the movement of
their troops. Hurriedly Kippenberger tried to bolster up his
sagging line. But the sheer weight of German numbers carried
them through and into his HQ at Galatos.

But Kippenberger was not prepared to give up. He rallied
two companies of infantry and prepared to counter-attack. Just
at that moment two light tanks under the command of Lieutenant Farran of the 3rd Hussars also came rumbling up. To
Kippenberger they must have appeared as a gift from the gods.
As he wrote later: 'The men looked tired, but fit to fight and

[2] He did, three years later, in Italy. An empty stomach had saved
his life.

resolute. It was no use trying to patch the line any more; obviously we must hit or everything would crumble away.'

He told the two infantry company commanders from the 23rd Battalion that they would have to retake Galatos with the aid of Farran's two tanks. Hastily Farran unloaded two of his men who had been wounded, gave two volunteers from the New Zealanders a rapid course on their duties in the tanks, and set off at the head of the infantry.

Kippenberger stood in the twilight and watched them go as he had watched many brave men go into battle already in this war. 'The infantry followed up at a walk, then broke into a run, started shouting—and, running and shouting, disappeared into the village. Instantly there was the most startling clamour, audible all over the field. Scores of automatics and rifles were being fired at once, the crunch of grenades, screams and yells—the uproar swelled and sank, swelled again to a horrifying crescendo. Some women and children came scurrying down the road; one old woman frantic with fear clung desperately to me. The firing slackened, became a brisk clatter, steadily becoming more distant, and stopped. The counterattack had succeeded; it was nearly dark and the battle-field suddenly became silent.'

But the successful counter-attack at Galatos only gave the hard-pressed New Zealanders a breathing space. Inexorably they were pushed back ever closer to the sea and Suda Bay. On 26 May, Freyberg wrote to Wavell: 'I regret to have to report that in my opinion the limit of endurance has been reached by the troops under my command here at Suda Bay. No matter what decision is taken by the Commanders-in-Chief from a military point of view, our position here is hopeless.

'A small, ill-equipped and immobile force such as ours cannot stand up against the concentrated bombing that we have been faced with during the last seven days. I feel I should tell you that from an administrative point of view the difficulties of extricating this force in full are insuperable. Provided a decision is reached at once, a certain proportion of the force might be embarked.'

The unemotional military prose hid Freyberg's conviction that his force was finished. The Germans had won; all that was left for him was to get as many of his men away from the island as he could.

In the last three days in May, the survivors of the New
Zealand Divisions and what was left of the British and Australian battalions involved, fought their way to the evacuation
beaches, pursued by the mountain troops and the surviving
paras who, weary as their prey, were flagging badly now in spite
of Student's exhortations as he sped about their lines in his
motorbike sidecar.

Time and again, rearguard units sallied out and inflicted
heavy casualties on inexperienced or over-confident German
commanders who pressed them too hard. But there was no doubt
in Student's mind that the enemy was finished. Now the question
—at least for Freyberg and his subordinate commanders—was
how the retreating troops would survive the inevitable end. On
the 30th, men of 5th Mountain Division tried to cut off Kippenberger's men but the Brigadier was still not prepared to give up
without a fight. He sent a couple of his weary companies to
counter-attack up the ridge which the skilled German mountain
troops had taken with such apparent ease. As he records in his
own account of the action with such obvious pride: 'Upham's
platoon was slowly climbing up the steep 600-foot hill west of
the ravine. The men were weak and very weary but they kept
slowly going and we could see that Upham was working round
above the Germans still in the bottom of the ravine and pinned
down by Washbourn's company and by fire from the eastern
bank. Two hours after they had started the climb there was
another sharp outburst of firing. It lasted about a minute, there
were then some single shots, and then silence. A little later
Upham's platoon started to come back and then a message
came that all twenty-two of the enemy party had been killed,
completely helpless under his plunging fire.'

As the intelligence officer of the 23rd New Zealand Infantry
Battalion commented: 'The men who had worked dogs and
sheep in the Southern Alps of New Zealand had proved a match
for the men of V Mountain Division, trained in the Alps of
Austria.'

Thus it came to its sad, inevitable end. A cordon was thrown
round the evacuation beach while Freyberg pleaded with Wavell
and the New Zealand Prime Minister, Mr Frazer himself, for
more ships. But the Royal Navy, which would lose over 2,000

men in the withdrawal, could not afford to lose any more precious vessels.

Lots were drawn who should go and Freyberg himself had to detail the officers who would be evacuted and those who would stay. Hargst was told he could not be taken off and 'obeyed with a light heart'. Kippenberger's attempts to do the same were 'sharply overruled'. So he and the men who were to go with him tramped to the beach, 'the last part lined with men who had lost their units and were hoping for a place with us. Some begged and implored, most simply watched stonily, so that we felt bitterly ashamed.'

The Battle for Crete was over.

Five

But there was little rejoicing in the German paras' camp at the victory. Now came the reckoning—and it was hard. Baron von der Heydte recalls Student visiting his battalion after the fighting: 'Had fourteen days really elapsed since I had last seen him issuing orders in Athens? He had visibly altered. He seemed much graver, more reserved and older. There was no evidence in his features that he was joyful over the victory—his victory—and proud at the success of his daring scheme. The cost of victory had evidently proved too much for him. Some of the battalions had lost all their officers and in several companies there were only a few men left alive.'

Von der Heydte reported his experiences during the course of the battle. When he had finished, Student grasped his hand and held it for a long time. 'I thank you,' was all he could say to von der Heydte. But 'the grasp of his hand and those three short words were quite sufficient for me.'

Like the surviving battalion commanders he set about burying his dead. He ordered that a common cemetery should be erected near Canea in which he buried both his own and the Allied dead, erecting a pedestal on which was inscribed: 'In these olive groves and on the heights of Perivolia these men of the 1st Battalion of the 3rd Parachute Regiment fought and won and died.'

But in his grief at the loss of those young men who had left Germany with him only one month before, he did not forget the beaten enemy. On the reverse side of the pedestal, he ordered the following statement to be inscribed: 'In valiant combat against the Battalion one hundred and fifty-six members of the following British regiments died for their King and Country.'

The paras began to return to Germany, leaving Colonel Bräuer behind as Commandant of Crete. In Brunswick, Stendhal and half a dozen smaller stations they were welcomed and feted like conquering heroes as they returned to their home bases. But the goose-stepping, the garlands of flowers, the speeches and the cheering crowds could not hide the losses they had suffered. Out of the 22,000 German soldiers engaged in the battle 7,000 had been killed and every fourth para dropped on the island had been killed; another 3,400 had been wounded.

Student at once tried to fill the gaps. There were volunteers enough, eager, idealistic young men, inspired by the tremendous if pyrrhic victory on the island. They flooded to the training schools in their hundreds. Student was confident that he could bring the old 7th Parachute Division up to strength within six weeks, well aware that a new task soon lay before them—*Russia!*

Major Schulz and the survivors of his battalion had heard the surprising announcement of the German attack on Soviet Russia as they crossed the Danube in a long troop train, decorated with chalk parachutes and the magic word '*Kreta*', which brought cheers at every station they passed through. It caught Schulz and Kerfin by surprise. Their joy at returning home to what they thought would be a well-earned rest vanished immediately. For the rest of the hour-long journey their faces, bronzed by the Mediterranean sun, were set and worried. But as yet, Student was confident that if his division had to be sent to the new front, his paras would surely be used in the air-borne role—in some short, sharp surprise action for which their experience and training had prepared them. He was to be proved wrong.

On 19 August, 1941, Hitler invited Student and a select group of officers to his new HQ. Student knew that there would be some criticism of the Crete operation, in spite of its final success. But he had already prepared his justification of the heavy losses —the speed of the prevailing wind, the inexperience of the transport pilots, the appearance of the British tanks, the fact that there were more troops on the ground than he had anticipated.

Surprisingly enough Hitler was friendliness itself. He chatted aimably, handed out decorations and made no reference whatsoever to the losses. Student felt his confidence begin to mount again. Perhaps it was time to mention the continuation of the Crete operation which he had already planned—the attack on Cyprus or Malta.

Hitler did not give him a chance. Instead he invited Student to tea and then almost casually over the herbal tea which he preferred, the Führer remarked: 'General Student, I believe that the days of the paratroopers are over. They have no surprise value any more.'

Student looked at him amazed. 'Why, *mein Führer*?'

'Because the surprise effect is no longer there. Crete has shown that the days of the paratrooper are finished. The parachute force is purely and simply a weapon of surprise. The factor of surprise has now been used up.'

And there the conversation ended. Adolf Hitler, the man who would soon rule all of Europe from the Channel to the Urals, had passed sentence on the 'Hunters from the Sky'.

Crete, their greatest victory, was to prove, as Student told British military historian Sir Basil Liddell Hart in captivity after the war, 'the graveyard of the paratroops'.

Now the role of the paras would change. The days of the bold offensive actions, when they had come winging down from the heavens to fight some sharp surprise operation, were over. From now to the end, they would fight bitter rearguards on every German front, in the north, south, east and west, until they could fight no longer. From now on they were to be the 'Führer's Fire-Brigade'—the desperate men hurried to any and every front where a new fire had broken out. From now on they were expendable.[1]

---

[1] It is interesting to note in this context that at the same time that the Battle of Crete was coming to an end (27 May, 1941) Winston Churchill ordered the British parachute troops to be enlarged from 500 to 5,000 men. Within two years there were four times that number, organized in two divisions.

Section Two

The Middle Years

'When Germany is in danger there is only one thing for us:
To fight, to conquer, to assume we shall die,
From our aircraft, my friend, there is no return!'
                                    The Song of the Paras

1942-43—Mission for Mussolini

'*I have picked you and your paratroopers for a very special task.*'

Hitler to General Student, 25 July, 1943

One

The peace at Student's headquarters on the hill overlooking the French port of Nimes on the Mediterranean coast was broken in the morning hours of 10 July, 1943, by a message, which came top priority from Berlin. It had long been expected. All the same it came as a shock to the paratroopers, toasting in the sun or enjoying the delights of the little bistros and other less reputable establishments in the cobbled streets of the old port. 'ENEMY TROOPS LANDED DURING THE NIGHT ON THE SOUTHERN COAST OF SICILY.' The invasion of Europe had started!

1942 had been a bad year for the 'Hunters from the Sky'. In the winter of 1941–42 the 7th Para Division had been sent to Russia to bleed to death in the line as ordinary infantry. At one spot they repulsed 146 attacks in forty-one days and lost 3,000 men.

Once, in the autumn of that year, Student had tried to insist that his paras should be used in the air-borne role for the capture of important passes in the Caucasus, but Hitler's Chief-of-Staff, Jodl, no friend of parachute operations, had insisted that the suggestion be turned down. The slaughter in the Russian wastes went on with many of the veterans of Holland and Crete leaving their bones under Russian soil.

In the spring of 1942, however, Student received permission to withdraw his formations to refill their ranks before they were thrown into the Russian holocaust once more. Generously Hitler even allowed him to form two para divisions, the old 7th Para now being renamed the 1st Parachute Division with General Heidrich in command, and a new unit, the 2nd Parachute Division, under the command of the victor of Maleme, Colonel—now General—Ramcke.

But Ramcke had little time to build up the strength of his new command. In April, 1942, he was ordered to Italy to organize the fledgling Italian paratroop divisions. He did not stay there long. On 26 May Rommel burst loose in North Africa, and Ramcke and Student were ordered to Hitler's HQ to brief the Führer on 'Operation Hercules', the capture of Malta, which was to support Rommel's final thrust for the Egyptian capital. However, when Student had explained his plan, which was to be carried out with the aid of the Italian Navy, Hitler burst into a furious rage: 'I guarantee you when the attack begins, the British Alexandria Task Force will set sail immediately and from Gibraltar, the British Fleet will head for Malta. You'll see then what the Italians will do. As soon as the first radio message comes they'll all head back to port, the warships and the transports. *And you'll sit there on the island alone with your paratroopers!'*

And with that, Student was dismissed and the operation was called off. His 1st Para was sent to Russia once more while the nucleus of Ramcke's 2nd Division, classed as *Brigade Ramcke* and made up of four battalions, was hurriedly flown to North Africa to help Rommel out of a sudden emergency.

The emergency became a retreat, with the battered paras covering the rear of the fleeing panzers. Once Ramcke was given up for lost by Rommel. For days nothing was heard of him but then he turned up at the head of a column of captured British vehicles after an amazing journey of 220 miles through the desert. It earned him the 'Oak Leaves' to his Knight's Cross.

Meanwhile, those veterans of Eben-Emael, Major Koch, commanding the 5th Parachute Regiment, and Major Witzig, CO of the 21st Engineer Battalion, had been thrown into the fighting in Tunisia. There they stood, retreated, fought, stood and retreated again until, on 12 May, 1943, they laid down their arms with the rest of the *Afrika Korps*.

In the weeks that followed the North African tragedy which cost him some of his best men, Student had time to replenish the ranks of the battered 1st Para, now returned from Russia, and complete the training and arming of the 2nd Para. Thus on the morning of 10 July, 1943, when the long expected order to meet the Allies' first attack in continental Europe since 1940, General Student had two fully armed parachute divisions available—the 1st at Avignon and the 2nd at Nimes, and, by an ironic quirk of history, Student's old 1st Para was soon to go into action against the 1st Airborne Division, which his pyrrhic victory in Crete had caused Churchill to call to life two years before.

*   *   *

The planners in Africa had decided that Sicily would be a bolder operation than any ever undertaken by the 8th Army before. Now under General Montgomery it was a well-trained and confident formation which had finally thrown Rommel out of Africa. As a result Alexander, Montgomery's chief, and Eisenhower, the Supreme Commander, decided that the 8th would conduct its campaign on the Italian island in a fast and furious manner, unlike the pedestrian, plodding operations which had characterized it up to now.

The 8th would hurry up the major coastal road, with its right flank on the sea and its left on the impressive bulk of Mount Etna, heading for Messina, at the head of the straits that separated Sicily from Italy. But in order to ensure that rapid progress was made through the 'stepping-stone between Africa and Europe', three vital bridges would have to be captured—Ponte Grande, the bridge guarding the entrance to the town of Syracuse, the Ponte dei Malati, north-east of Lentini and, the third and furthest, the girder bridge crossing the Primosole on the southern outskirts of Catania.

Operation 'Marston', as the attack on the Primosole Bridge was called, was handed to the 1st Parachute Brigade of the 1st Airborne Division, and planned to the last detail, including the type of food the British parachutists should eat before the drop (plenty of sugar, but little fat). It envisaged two platoons of Colonel Alastair's 1st Battalion, with the 1st Field Squadron Royal Engineers, led by Major Murray, landing right on the bridge or as close as possible to it and capturing it by a *coup de main*.

The rest of the 1st Battalion under Alastair, who had already won four DSOs and an MC in the last eighteen months, would then organize the defence of the bridge, while the 3rd Battalion would establish themselves in a loop of the River Simeto roughly 1,000 yards to the north of Primosole, with Colonel Frost's 3rd Battalion seizing and holding the high ground to the south of the bridge.

In short it was the type of bold operation which Student had originated but which he had no longer the resource or the authority to carry out. Yet the old fox and his men were the best prepared of all the German troops available in Southern Europe to meet the kind of threat which the 1st British Airborne was soon to pose.

At sunset on the 29th, the British paras took off from their airfields in North Africa for the long haul to Sicily, being towed to their objectives by Dakotas of the US Air Force.

The flight was uneventful until the air-borne armada reached the coast of Sicily. Then, as the Dakotas were passing their own invasion fleet, the anti-aircraft gunners, below, inexperienced and nervous, opened fire at them. Several of the American planes were hit and went down in flames. Others turned back, while the rest hastily altered course. Thereafter everything went wrong.

The men of the 3rd Battalion who had been sent sprawling on to the metal floors of the carriers by the nervous pilots' evasive action were ordered to jump while they were still over the sea. And they did. Others dropped to their deaths in the inhospitable hills of the interior where their skeletons were found years later. And in the case of the 1st Battalion, the pilots ordered the men to jump when they were far too low, so that the casualty rate from broken bones and twisted limbs shot up alarmingly.

But in spite of the absolute confusion, which the paras were to learn in the course of the years was standard-operating-procedure in landings of this kind, some fifty men of the 1st Battalion managed to drop in the right area. Soon they were joined by a small group of air-borne men under Colonel Pearson, who took over the defence of the bridge.

Swiftly he mustered his forces to face the inevitable counter-attack. In spite of the confusion and the darkness, Pearson managed to assemble three anti-tank guns, two mortars, a machine-gun and 250 men of the 1st and 3rd Battalions. These he disposed on the northern edge of the bridge, facing Catania airfield, a short distance away. He had just finished his dispositions, when a panting paratrooper came hurrying up from the direction of the Italian-held field, where he had been dropped by mistake. Hastily he explained to his CO what had happened and then said that, during the confusion, he had bumped into another paratrooper, who had come down close beside him. 'But he spoke in German—he asked where his Schmeisser was!'

The first men of Colonel Heilmann's 3rd Parachute Regiment of the 1st German Para Division had landed, ready to engage their British opponents of the 1st Airborne Division in battle. The fight for the Primosole Bridge had begun![1]

The Messerschmitts came in first at treetop level. Hastily the 200-odd men guarding the bridge buried their heads in their holes and waited for the attack to pass, as it always did. They knew what it was—the softener up.

But even though the 'Red Berets', as their German opponents called them, realized that the air attack was only a prelude to the ground attack, they were still caught off guard. The British had anticipated that the Germans would come from the north, but they didn't. They came from the south.

By mistake the leading troops of the 3rd Para Regiment had been dropped on the wrong side of the river, but the experienced Colonel Heilmann used the mistake to his own advantage. Under cover of heavy mortar fire, the thin wave of paras rushed their British counterparts. But by now the men of the 1st Airborne were no longer the amateurs who had gone to Africa the year before. They waited till the mortar barrage had stopped and then popped up from their hastily dug holes and let the enemy have the full weight of their fire power. The paras simply melted away, leaving the rocky earth littered with their dead and dying.

Two hours after their attack, one of the few wireless sets which had managed to survive the British drop came suddenly to life. Its short resurrection lasted exactly four minutes, but in that brief space of time the British learned that the 4th Armoured Brigade of the 8th Army was battling along the road to link up with them at all possible speed. But it was meeting very stiff opposition. Then the set went dead and stayed dead. The hours passed but the promised tanks did not come. The Germans, however, did time and again. And as the morning passed into a burning hot afternoon, with the thirsty, hungry British para-troops panting like dogs in the bottoms of their slit trenches, the attacks steadily grew in strength.

Now it was only a question of time before Heilmann's men recaptured the bridge. Already the men defending the northern

---

[1] The two parachute forces had had occasional brushes in North Africa, but this was their first real engagement on equal terms, i.e. two brigade-sized forces landing simultaneously from the air.

end had been withdrawn to give additional strength to those on the southern extremity who were under continuous and increasing artillery and small arms fire, the signal for yet another counter-attack.

The Germans started to wade across the river lower down in an attempt to turn the British flank, and even managed to get an 88mm cannon close to the bridge and started to pound away at the powerless defenders at the southern end. In a crump of yellow-red flame, the first British pillbox was hit and disappeared in a cloud of smoke and rubble. Moments later the second one followed it.

Captain Gammon of the 1st Parachute Battalion, taking cover in a third pillbox, watched the gun work them over anxiously. 'At any moment,' he recorded his emotions at that time, 'the 8th Army must come. At any moment their armoured cars would sweep down the road and up to the bridge, but time wore on and no 8th Army came . . . the pillbox on my left, fortunately empty, was taking a bashing. To this day I swear as each round of solid shot struck it, it heeled over and bounced up again. Perhaps it was the heat haze or the dust or my fevered imagination or perhaps it really did—it was made of reinforced concrete. I realized that each pillbox in turn was to take its punishment and that mine was next . . . I watched the dusty white bridge, keeping my head well to the side of the embrasure . . . Suddenly there was a crash, fumes, dust, and something hit me in the chest. I could hardly see. Where's the door? Had it collapsed? A shaft of light and I groped my way out into the blinding sunshine.'

Captain Gammon escaped with his life if 'rather light-headed'. But he had little time to consider his luck. Brigadier Lathbury, commander of the 1st Parachute Brigade of the 1st Airborne, had ordered what was left of his men on the bridge to withdraw to some high ground close behind it in order to make a last stand. Then German tanks were arriving and his paratroopers were rapidly running out of ammunition.

The Germans pressed home their advantage. Corporal Stanton of the 1st Battalion, who had been hit in the neck and knocked out, recalls waking up and finding a 'couple of German machine-gunners in the ditch where our troops should have been. A shell burst in front of me and under cover of this I ran back to the bridge. The battalion had gone.'

A little later Stanton, one of the few survivors of the men on the northern side of the bridge, was captured again. 'I sat there for an hour or two while they argued among themselves as to who was to take me back. Then apparently our chaps started firing into the reeds. Two Jerries got hit on the head straight away. The others ran back and I crawled along through the reeds, which were smouldering in parts.'

There Stanton hid himself, scared to identify himself for he was in full view of the advancing Germans and the retreating British. 'It was then about four-thirty in the afternoon. I lay there waiting for darkness to come.'

He was one of the lucky ones. Of the defenders twenty-seven were killed, seventy-eight wounded and over fifty were missing out of the original 200. Now as darkness fell the German paras took possession of the most important bridge in Sicily and waited for the British to try again.

In their first action in continental Europe against the men they then called the 'Red Berets' but would soon name the 'Red Devils', they had won. It appeared that, in spite of their terrible losses during the last two years in Russia and Africa, the 'Hunters from the Sky' were a match for the best that the Allies could send against them.

Two

After a forced march of twenty-five miles that morning, the weary infantrymen of the Durham Light Infantry reached the bridge at two in the afternoon. They were tough men, products of the depression and two years of continuous fighting in Africa with the 8th Army, but now they were whacked. Utterly exhausted, they flung themselves down on the ground and fell asleep at once.

But the officers, weary as they were, had no time for sleep. A group of them approached the bridge, littered with shot-up vehicles and German and British dead in their camouflaged coveralls, and surveyed it in silence. It did not look good. Although the bridge itself was clearly visible, nothing could be seen of the paras' position north of the river where the tree-lined countryside offered good cover. For all the DLI officers knew a whole division of German paratroopers could be hidden out there. By contrast the land on the south side was perfectly flat and devoid of any cover whatsover.

They turned their binoculars on the bridge itself. Primosole Bridge was 400 feet long; built of girders, it was about eight feet above the sluggish, brown river, whose banks were bordered by thick, green reeds. North of the bridge, on either side of the exit road which ran straight to the town of Catania, the DLI officers saw two farms. They were typical Italian buildings— dirty white walls of immense thickness, narrow windows, barred with thick oak shutters, and red-tiled roofs. At present there was no movement at the farms, but even the most inexperienced subaltern among them knew that they would make ideal strong-points for the Germans. They crept back the way they had come and started to plan their assault on the bridge.

Colonel Lidwell, the CO of the 8th Battalion, did not like the situation one bit. As the Durham Light Infantry's regimental history records: 'The prospects looked gloomy indeed for the

8th Battalion.' But Lidwell did not show his unease to his officers, as he explained their plan of action for the morrow.

Ninety minutes before the attack the gunners would put down an artillery concentration on the bridge area moving it slowly to about 500 yards to the left of the bridge. Then for the last ten minutes of the barrage, the gunners, swinging their fire back, would plaster the bridge itself. As soon as the barrage had ended, the 8th DLI would ford the river—it would be full moon by then—and go for the bridge from the far bank.

It was a bad plan and Lidwell knew it. Already that afternoon their running mate, the 9th DLI, had attacked the river further up and been thrown back with heavy casualties. Another frontal attack looked 'suicidal'.[1] But Monty wanted the bridge and he wanted it quickly—it was holding up the advance of the whole 8th Army.

It was about then that a stranger appeared at the entrance to the small cave in which Lidwell had set up his HQ. As an eyewitness recalls: 'He was unshaven, his khaki shirt and trousers were covered in stains and grime and he looked dog-tired.' All that the surprised Durhams could see was that he was British. Who he was and what rank he bore were not at once apparent.

Wearily the stranger walked over and sat down next to the CO. 'My name's Pearson,' he said. 'I commanded the paratroops down at the bridge. I understand you are attacking again this afternoon. I think I can help you.'

Pearson's information was invaluable. He pointed out that a direct attack on the bridge was out of the question. The German paras had concentrated all their firepower on its approaches. However, he did know of a spot about 300 yards upstream where it was possible to wade across. 'In fact,' he said, 'I'll show your assault companies the way over to the other side.'

At 12.50 am the barrage opened up. The gunners concentrated on a narrow front and the crash and crump of the twenty-five-pounders, combined with the chatter of the heavy Vickers machine-guns, was deafening. For ninety minutes the bombardment continued, then stopped as suddenly as it had started. In the silence that followed A and D companies of the DLI forded

[1] Regimental history *8th Battalion, the Durham Light Infantry* (1939–1945).

the river, guided by Colonel Pearson and his handful of surviving paratroopers.

The operation was a complete success (apart from a few men who were submerged in the deep holes caused by shells). The unexpected direction of the attack caught Heilmann's paras off guard. Under light automatic fire the infantrymen doubled for the bridge. A few paras were encountered but 'to the accompaniment of shouts and cheers (as the regimental history has it) these were speedily disposed of with bayonets, grenades or Tommy guns'.

With the first phase of the battle successfully carried out, the remainder of the 8th Battalion could now cross the bridge. But Colonel Lidwell, who had lost his radio sets during the river crossing, was at a loss as to how to contact his rear HQ. Then in the midst of the battle an observer from the War Office suddenly made his appearance, riding up on—of all things—a bicycle! He was at once told of the problem and sent back, pedalling for all he was worth, to bring up the rest of the Battalion.

It was already daylight when B and C Companies appeared, marching in single file. As they passed one of the blazing farmhouses, a wag popped up his head and shouted, 'Push on B Company! There's only a few Eyties up in front!'

The burst of spandau fire that met them a few moments later told them that the wag was wrong. They had hit the first line of the German paras! The DLIs scattered hastily, scrambling into the fields and the ditches. Lieutenant Jackson, with a handful of men, rushed the machine-gun. They were cut down, but others followed and a grim game of hide and seek began in the thick undergrowth of the vineyards on both sides of the road. As the regimental history says: 'It was very difficult to distinguish friend from foe in the shadows, and it meant every man for himself with no quarter asked or given on either side.'

Some of the DLI were shot down at point-blank range as they blundered into the paras' positions. Others stalked the Germans and shot them in the back where they lay. To the advancing infantry, it seemed as if there was a German para behind every bush. Men on both sides fired at trees, thinking they were enemy. Both groups flung grenades, though they caused more casualties to their own side than to the enemy. Most were afraid to use their automatic weapons at a range of more than a yard for fear of hitting their comrades.

Within twenty minutes—the hardest twenty minutes of the whole war for the 8th DLI—both sides fought themselves to a standstill. The front half of B Company and the Germans facing them suffered nearly 100 per cent casualties. As if by some strange form of mental telepathy, both sides broke off the action and withdrew, leaving their dead and dying behind them.

But soon the German paras fixed bayonets and rushed the withdrawing British. They overran the rear platoon under Sergeant Mitchson. The sergeant went down and shammed dead. A para kicked him in the side and, satisfied that he was dead, ran on. Mitchson counted ten, then sprang to his feet, grabbed his Tommy gun and blasted the Germans in the back.

At that moment Sergeant-Major Brannigan seized a Bren and, standing up in full view of the paras, shot at them from the hip. He fell dead, still clutching the automatic. But his and Sergeant Mitchson's efforts allowed what was left of B Company to withdraw to the cover of a nearby embankment.

By now the DLI were under heavy attack and their losses were mounting hourly (B Company was already down to thirty men). Colonel Lidwell, who had set up his HQ in the shattered farm, knew that his hold on the bridgehead was tenuous, and the urgency with which he tried to obtain artillery and armoured support from brigade headquarters revealed to his officers that their CO was well aware of the seriousness of their position.

All that day Colonel Heilmann's paras kept up the attack, with Lidwell's mortar section breaking up their rushes time and again with their well-aimed 'stonks'. (That day the section fired 600 bombs.) Then late in the afternoon they heard to their relief that the bridgehead was to be enlarged after dark by both the 6th and 9th Battalions of the DLI.

Anxiously Lidwell waited for darkness, knowing that any large-scale German attack would throw him off the bridge before the other two battalions arrived. Just before dusk a Sherman came clattering up the road, raising a huge cloud of dust. The dust made the details hard to see, but the watching infantry could just discern the figure of a man in the turret waving his arms excitedly, and held their fire as the tank rumbled nearer. Suddenly, when it was about 200 yards from the English line, it stopped, the man in the turret disappeared and the next moment the Sherman opened fire with all its guns. Then, as suddenly as it had appeared, it swung round and raced back the way it had come. The Sherman had been captured a few hours before and been pressed into German service. As the DLI history records: 'The paratroops did not miss a single opportunity of inflicting casualties. They were first-class fighting troops and fanatics to a man.'

The fresh battalions started their attack at one-thirty the following morning, but the Germans were not caught off their guard and fought back savagely. In the tangled chaos of the vineyards they stood and fought it out until—as an eye-witness records—'they either shot down their enemies or were shot down themselves.' The DLI pushed in their six-pounder anti-tank guns and started to winkle out the paras individually at point-blank range; but still the Germans held on, so the British commanders asked for tanks, and at seven o'clock the first Shermans started to rumble over the bridge. At the far end the Brigadier himself met them and ordered the tankers to deploy to left and right of the road to Catania, showing them the enemy positions.

The Shermans plunged into the vines, firing their big guns at everything in sight. It was too much even for the paras and they began to surrender. A captured 8th Battalion man rose with a dirty handkerchief in his hand. Behind him a few rimless para-troop helmets peeped over the vines. The DLI men thought that this was yet another German trick, and kept up their fire and it was with some difficulty that their commander got them to stop firing. Now white handkerchiefs appeared all along the line held by the paras. Forty—fifty—sixty—they came streaming in, hands raised above their heads, urged on by the bayonets of the sturdy little men from the north. It was all over. The DLI had captured the road to Catania.

And what a fantastic sight the road made as the infantry-men viewed it in peace. It was a shambles of broken rifles and machine-guns; littered with blood-stained clothing, overturned ammunition boxes, a shattered anti-tank gun—and the dead! Along its whole length lay the bodies of German and British paratroopers and those of the DLI. Now the DLI started to tidy up. As their history states: 'Men who had experienced the fiercest fighting of the North African campaign at Alamein and

Mareth said they had never seen so much slaughter in such a small area.' The three battalions had lost 500 men, killed wounded or missing, 300 German dead were found and another 160 were taken prisoner.

That afternoon, just before the battalion commander of the paras was led away, Colonel Clarke of the 9th DLI stopped his escort for a moment. The British commander stretched out his hand towards the puzzled German, as he stood there in the blazing sun. Colonel Clarke wanted to shake hands with him!

Thus Student's paras fought and lost their first battle against the Allies in Europe. One day later the paras slipped away. As British tanks rolled over the Malati Bridge towards Catania, the 'Hunters from the Sky' crept in single-file under the bridge, jumping from spar to spar, the rattle of the tank tracks drowning the noise they made. Thus they broke out of the trap. For another day they slipped between the various British forces heading north until finally on the night of 16 July they made contact with the German troops holding the newly established line.

Student was overjoyed when he heard the news that Colonel Heilmann, of whom nothing had been heard for nearly three days, had escaped the Sicily *débâcle*. In the coming weeks he knew he would have need of him on the Italian mainland where events were shaping up for a strange three-sided confrontation of a kind which made his simple soldier's brain reel in confusion.

Three

The news of Mussolini's overthrow had been received at Hitler's HQ at Rastenburg three weeks before the Sicily landing. Goebbels, who telephoned Hitler to tell him the alarming news, realized at once that parallels might be drawn with their own régime. His first thought recorded in his private diary for that day was: 'What are we going to tell them anyway?'

Surprisingly enough, Hitler, although the news came as a complete shock to him, reacted to the events in Italy with ice-cold judgement—perhaps for the last time in his career. He called a conference of his top military and civilian aides for 9.30 on the evening of 25 June, 1943. Hitler knew full well that the allies would take advantage of the situation. The King of Italy and Marshal Badoglio would, he guessed, surrender to the enemy now that Mussolini was out of the way. The country would be left wide-open for a swift thrust to the Brenner Pass, something which Hitler was going to prevent at all costs.

That evening his manner was clear and calculating. 'The Duce has resigned,' he announced. 'Badoglio has taken over the government.' Then he sketched in the meagre details of the events in Italy at the time available: the Duce had disappeared, Badoglio had taken over, the military situation was fluid.

Jodl was the first to react. He urged that they should wait for further details from von Mackensen, the German ambassador in Rome, or from Field-Marshal Kesselring, the military commander, before deciding on any kind of military action against the Italians.

'Certainly,' Hitler agreed, 'but we still have to plan ahead. Undoubtedly in their treachery they will say that they will remain loyal to us, but of course they won't remain loyal ... Although that bastard [Badoglio] stated at once that the war would continue, that won't make any difference! They have to say that, but it remains treason. We'll play the same game while preparing to take over the whole crew with one stroke. Tomorrow I'll send a man down there with orders for the commander of the Third Panzer Division to the effect that he must drive into Rome with a special detail and arrest the whole government, King and all, right away.'

He turned to Jodl. 'Work out the orders, telling them to drive into Rome with their assault guns and arrest the government, the King and the whole crew. I want the Crown Prince above all.'

Hurriedly the details of the operation were worked out. The Alpine passes must be secured. Rommel would take care of that. Student's 2nd Air Corps must be alerted, ready to move from France if the situation warranted. Hitler himself would attend to the problem of Benito Mussolini.

The six officers snapped to attention when he entered. Five of them—all of field grade officers—saluted. The sixth man *bowed!*

Hitler looked at him in astonishment. The man was worth looking at. He was at least six feet six and broad with it. The side of his face was slashed with duelling scars and looked as if a clumsy butcher's apprentice had done a bad job of work on it. In spite of his absurd bow he looked a very tough man indeed.

The first officer stepped forward and gave a brief outline of his military career, and, one after another, the others followed suit. The big man was last. He stepped forward and clicked his heels:

'Skorzeny, detached from the "Adolf Hitler Bodyguard Division" after service in Russia. Now in charge of the Friedenthal organization.'[1] Hitler nodded. The SS man took a pace backwards.

'Which of you know Italy?' Hitler asked.

Captain Skorzeny was the only one to reply. 'I have travelled through Italy twice by motorcycle, *mein Führer.* As far as Naples.'

'What do you think of the Italians?'

Skorzeny shrugged. 'I am an Austrian,' he said. No more, no less. Hitler knew what Skorzeny was hinting at—that he resented

[1] The SS equivalent of the commandos, trained for special operations behind enemy lines.

the loss of Austrian territory in South Tyrol to the Italians after the First World War. 'The other gentlemen can go,' he said. 'I want to speak with *Hauptsturmführer* Skorzeny.'

When the others had gone, Hitler relaxed and asked his fellow Austrian to sit down. 'I have a mission of the highest importance for you,' he explained. 'Mussolini, my friend and our loyal ally, has been arrested by his own people. I cannot and *will* not abandon Italy's greatest son. Under the new government, Italy will leave the alliance. But I will maintain my loyalty to my ally. He has to be rescued! Otherwise they'll surrender him to the Allies. This is an all-important mission which will affect the whole course of the war. You must do your utmost to carry out this mission—*and you will succeed!*'

Immediately after his interview with Hitler, Skorzeny was informed that General Student was waiting to see him in the next room. The two men were to end the war as bitter enemies, but now on first sight Skorzeny was impressed by the appearance of the general: 'A jovial-looking, somewhat rotund gentleman with a deep scar from his severe wound in 1941 at Rotterdam.' Skorzeny started to explain the mission the Führer had given him, but was interrupted by a little tap on the door which opened to reveal one of the 'great' men of the Nazi régime, Heinrich Himmler, the most feared man in Occupied Europe.

Himmler greeted Skorzeny coldly, then chatted a few moments with Student, whom he obviously knew well. After that he turned to the SS captain and explained that nobody in Germany —or in Rome—knew where the Duce was being kept hidden. However, his own SS secret service, under General Schellenberg, suspected that the 'renegades' (as he called the new Italian régime) were preparing to hand him over to the Allies as part of a package deal. Mussolini would serve as a scapegoat to cleanse their own consciences and smooth over the transition from ex-German ally to whatever their new status would be.

Himmler then turned his attention to people who might help Skorzeny in his search for Mussolini and rattled off a dozen names, while Skorzeny fumbled in his breast pocket for a piece of paper and a pencil to jot them down.

Himmler stopped in the middle of a word. 'Are you crazy!' he shouted. 'You can't write these things down! They're top secret. You must memorize them, man!'

Skorzeny's face flushed with embarrassment.

But his troubles with Himmler were not over. As Himmler was leaving the room, he took out a cigarette to steady his nerves. At once Himmler spun round. 'Those eternal cigarettes!' he sniffed disdainfully. *'I can see that you're not the right man for the job!'*

*   *   *

In the nerve-wracking weeks that followed, Skorzeny more than once was tempted to believe that Himmler had been right. He, Student and Kappler, the German Embassy's police attaché,[2] who was also involved in the secret search, followed one red herring after another. Just when Skorzeny thought he had found the missing Duce, the latter vanished again. Once in the course of the hunt, which was unknown even to Kesselring, the German Commander-in-Chief in Italy, Skorzeny's plane had been shot out of the sky and he had broken three ribs; but he had no time for hospital—both Hitler and Himmler were breathing down his neck for results. The latter had even gone as far as to release eighty clairvoyants from German concentration camps to help him in the search.

Then Student had a stroke of luck. In the first week of September he had called on the commander of a *Luftwaffe* squadron, based at Lake Bracciano, thirty-two miles north of Rome. He had gone there with the intention of enlisting the man's aid in an air search of the many small islands off the Italian coast. But even before he could bring up the subject, the CO said casually: 'We've just had an interesting visit. We had an air raid and during it a white seaplane landed here. I think the Duce got out and was taken away by ambulance.'[3]

Student knew that the Italians guarding Mussolini had pulled the air raid trick once before when moving him; it cleared people off the streets. Perhaps they had done the same at Lake Bracciano. He drove back to his HQ and passed on the news to Kappler, who could add a little bit of information of his own to it. One of his informants had told him; 'Security precautions round Gran Sasso d'Italia have been completed.' Could the

[2] The last remaining German 'war criminal' in Italian captivity; today a forgotten man after over a quarter of a century in Italian jails.
[3] General Student in conversation with the author.

landing on Lake Bracciano mean that Mussolini had been transferred from there to the Gran Sasso, the highest peak in the Italian Apennines? Student thought so and decided to do a little snooping himself. He detailed Lieutenant Leo Krutoff, a doctor he kept on his personal staff because of the ulcer which troubled him, to find a convalescent home for the paras' malaria cases, telling him: 'There's a hotel on the Gran Sasso. Whatever the circumstances, you must inspect it yourself. Don't let them turn you back.' Then he hinted that 'a person of high standing' was being kept there. The young doctor realized that there was more to his mission than finding a hospital for the paras.

Arriving at the base of the mountain, which could only be ascended by funicular, he found the *carabinieri* guards unfriendly and suspicious. He persisted that he must see the hotel. The guards, equally insistent, maintained it was '*impossibile*'. In the end the young doctor asked to be connected with the officer in charge of the hotel at the top of the mountain—the Campo Imperatore. The officer's reply was negative and threatening. 'If you don't leave at once,' he was told, 'I'll have to arrest you.'

The doctor's story of his adventure on the mountain convinced Student that Mussolini was being held in the hotel and he made up his mind to go ahead and plan a daring rescue operation. 'I didn't tell Hitler, but decided to do it under my own steam.'[4] He did, of course, tell Skorzeny, who sprang to attention and bellowed, in true Prussian fashion: 'Reporting with twenty-five men ready to jump over the mountain!'

Student smiled and said, 'No, we'll do it more elegantly, Skorzeny.' Nevertheless, he decided to let him be in charge of the operation. As he recalled later: 'I thought my main task was to concentrate on the situation in Rome and after all Skorzeny had rescued a couple of my men when his Heinkel had been shot down.'[5]

Thus Student and Skorzeny began the operation which would startle the world and make the latter famous or infamous, depending on which side one was on, throughout the world.

[4] Student to author.

[5] After the operation Student felt that Skorzeny had carried off the kudos unfairly, neglecting both Student's part and that of his men. As a result, in his conversation with the author, he soft-pedalled Skorzeny's part in the mission. Skorzeny, for his part, does the same respecting Student's role.

The great rescue was fixed for dawn on Sunday, 12 September, 1943. But dawn came and Student's gliders which were to be flown in from Southern France had still not made their appearance. Skorzeny consoled himself with the thought that if they landed around noon, as was now predicted, he could drop on the mountain at a time when the Italians would be resting after a heavy Latin lunch.

In the meantime his adjutant, Radl, had used the enforced delay to rush to Rome and pick up the pro-German Italian General Soletti, whom he bustled into a staff car, telling him he was needed for an 'important enterprise'. The Italian had no idea what he was in for, but Skorzeny felt that his presence would be useful to prevent 'any unnecessary bloodshed'.

At eleven the gliders finally arrived and Student began his final briefing at the field just outside Rome. He explained to the newly arrived glider pilots, who thought they were going to be used in operations against the Americans, what they were really about to do, ending his introduction to the situation on the Gran Sasso with the words: 'Then once again I must point out that we must risk this operation on the basis of incomplete data. The latest information we have about the Gran Sasso is already some days old.'

One of Student's most skilled young glider pilots, Lieutenant Meyer-Wehner, who had arrived late at the briefing, heard Student say, 'Whether Mussolini is still there is rather uncertain.' *'Mussolini,'* he thought. *'How the hell did he get into this?'*

His fellow glider pilots gave him a whispered briefing while Student continued. At just past noon twelve gliders, each containing the pilot and ten men, under the command of a man named Skorzeny would leave the airfield, heading for the Gran Sasso. One hour later they would be cast off from their towing Heinkels to crash-land on top of the snow-covered mountain peak itself. One hundred and eight men to tackle whatever the Italians had waiting for them up there!

Student did not seem to notice the pilots' agitation at the prospect of a crash-landing on the top of a mountain they had never seen before. He continued the briefing: 'There'll be no dive-landing like at Eben-Emael. You'll circle and then make a pin-point landing. Keep your nerve. This mission will be carried out like a peacetime manoeuvre. There won't be a shot fired. It will be a total surprise. You have only to concentrate where you land and keep to your landing places.'

Student's intelligence officer, Captain Gerhard Languth, now took over the briefing. There were no aerial recce pictures of the Gran Sasso. However, he and Skorzeny had carried out a couple of hasty flights over the hotel and taken some pictures. They were exceedingly poor, but when Languth asked them to come closer to have a look at them, they could see that around the white mass of the hotel, the ground looked like a moon landscape, with only one spot that looked as if it might make a landing area.

After the Captain had finished, Skorzeny explained his part in the operation. Gliders 1 and 2 would be filled with Student's paras; gliders 3 and 4, under his command, would contain his own Friedenthal commando, dressed as *Luftwaffe* officers. This group would disarm Mussolini's guards, free him and then hold the hotel against any possible counter-attack, while down below a battalion of the paras under Major Mors would seize the valley station of the funicular railway. Once Skorzeny was sure everything was under control, Student's personal pilot, thirty-year-old Captain Gerlach, would take off with Mussolini from the minute landing area in his Fieseler-Storch—the only plane in 1943 that had a chance of succeeding in such conditions.

At noon the twelve gliders were drawn up ready to go. Above them the sky was a beautiful bright blue, a perfect day for their mission. Skorzeny, at the head of his men, left the briefing room and started to walk to the planes. Suddenly the calm was shattered by the thin wail of the airfield siren. It was taken up by others scattered all over the hangars. As Skorzeny swung round, twin-engined Mitchells came winging in low across the field. Skorzeny flung himself down, hands pressed over his helmet. The others needed no urging to do the same, as the bombs came hurtling down towards the gliders. His last recollection was Radl, his adjutant, grinning across at him with a deathly white face and saying: 'Take it easy.'

Four

The raid lasted half an hour, but when it was over Skorzeny saw to his astonishment that, although the field had been badly damaged, his gliders were unharmed. His mission—albeit a little late—could start after all.

Just after one o'clock the little armada finally took off. Skorzeny went with the second flight, with General Soletti between his legs. Almost immediately, the leading gliders were lost in a cloud bank—they never made it. But Skorzeny had no time to concern himself with their fate. 'I suddenly noticed,' he recalled later, 'that the corporal behind me was being sick and the general in front had turned as green as his uniform. Flying obviously did not suit him.'

Skorzeny also realized that the pilot was flying blind and relying on Skorzeny's knowledge of the target area to get them there, now that their glider was the lead plane. A few moments later it was confirmed that the first wave of gliders had disappeared altogether. The towing plane's pilot came over the telephone to report: 'Regret flight one and two no longer ahead of us. Who's to take the lead now?'

'This was bad news,' Skorzeny recollected later. 'What had happened to them? At that time I did not know that I had only seven machines left instead of nine behind me. Two had fallen foul of bomb craters right at the start.'

'We'll take over the lead ourselves,' he told the pilot. Seizing his knife he hacked away at the glider's canvas wall until he had carved a hole. The General's colour changed back to normal and Skorzeny could see where they were going, which had been virtually impossible through the scratched perspex window at the side of his head.

While all this was going on, Gerlach had finally spotted the gliders. But there were only two of them! What had happened to the others? How could they pull it off with only eighteen paras? Alarming thoughts flashed through his mind. But if the eighteen paras were still prepared to go in, he'd go in with them.

Skorzeny saw the valley of Aquila far below. He bellowed, 'Helmets on!' and the paras snapped into action. Grabbing their helmets they seized the crossbar inside the glider. Up front Meyer-Wehner felt the lurch as the pilot of the towing plane slipped the towrope. They were on their own now. All the tense men within the plane could hear was the rush of the wind. Slowly the glider pilot swung round in a lazy circle while Skorzeny searched for the land strip. Then he saw it—the triangular patch of grass which he had spotted on his flight over the hotel. He swallowed hard. Now, for the first time, he saw to his horror that the patch was terribly steep—*and littered with boulders!* It would be madness to attempt to land there, but there was nowhere else. The glider started to dive. *'Crash-landing!'* Skorzeny bellowed.

Up in front a desperate Meyer-Wehner saw the ground— scrub, parched yellow grass, boulders—racing up to meet him at a speed of fifty miles an hour. Beyond it was the squat horseshoe shape of the hotel. Suddenly he jerked the glider upwards and flung out the brake-flaps, hoping that the nose in that position would act as an additional brake. Over 2,000 pounds of glider and men hit the ground. There was a grinding crash. The barbed wire, wrapped round the skids to shorten the braking distance, snapped like string as it hit the boulders. Wood splintered and tore. One last mighty heave and they slithered to a stop. Bright sunshine came pouring in through the holes in the tattered canvas. Through them they could see the hotel, its terrace a bare twenty yards away. They had made it—*with the hotel's main ski-run as their landing field!*

But Skorzeny had no time to consider his luck. He burst out of the wrecked glider after the first man. Above him on the terrace a lone Italian soldier was standing staring open-mouthed at the arrivals from the sky. The Austrian did not give him a chance to sound the alarm. He dashed forward, followed by Sergeant Otto Schwerdt. *'Mani in alto!'* he roared in Italian. The soldier's hand shot up. He charged through the door. In a little room close to the entrance, a soldier was crouched over a radio set. Skorenzy's heavy boot sent the man's stool flying from under him. With his whole weight he brought the butt of his machine pistol down on the radio. It splintered and went dead. Skorzeny and Schwerdt ran on. Up to now not a single shot had been fired.

Outside there was pandemonium. The roaring of the German towing planes echoed like thunder from the surrounding mountains. Gliders were smashing to a halt all over the rocky plateau outside the hotel. Inside the guard dogs in their kennels were howling hysterically. The alarm had been sounded.

Skorzeny, determined to be the first to rescue Mussolini, raced ahead with a half-dozen men. Before them a ten-foot wall barred their progress, but one man sprang forward, without being told, as if they had practised the operation a dozen times, and offered his back as a ladder. In an instant Skorzeny was on it and over the wall. The rest followed.

On the other side he paused, wondering which way to go next. Suddenly the decision was made for him. Above his head at a second-floor window he saw a heavy-jawed old man with a completely bald head. It was the Duce!

'Away from the window!' he bellowed, knowing that the Italian guards had been ordered to kill him if it looked as if he might escape or be rescued. The Duce disappeared at once.

The men raced through the lobby and collided with a mass of cursing Italians, struggling into their helmets and clothes. Skorzeny cut right through them and clattered up the stairs, where he bumped into two young Italian officers, behind whom he saw Mussolini's pale face. Schwerdt came panting up. Suddenly two grinning faces, surmounted by the rimless helmets of the paras, appeared behind the Italians at the window. The 'Hunters from the Sky' had shinned up the hotel's lightning conductor. The Italians raised their hands. Resistance was useless. Now it was all over and Mussolini was in German hands. In exactly four minutes, Skorzeny had rescued the man who was being sought by two German intelligence services as well as those of the United States and Britain!

Skorzeny, with that Viennese talent for finding the right words to suit the occasion, stepped across to the pale, unshaven dictator, dressed in a crumpled blue suit, and clicking his heels together announced: 'Duce, I have been sent by the Leader to set you free!' It was an historic moment and Skorzeny, a man well aware of such things, felt he had said the right thing.

The Duce did not fail him: 'I knew my friend Adolf Hitler would not leave me in the lurch,' he said in German and embraced Skorzeny warmly.

*   *   *

Now a strange lull came over the victors on the mountain. While Skorzeny drank a glass of wine given him by the Italian commandant—'for the victor,' the Colonel said courteously—Captain Radl talked to Mussolini. 'What are my Romans doing?' the Duce asked in his best fascist manner.

'*Looting*, my Duce,' Radl answered.

Mussolini waved his plump hand irritably. 'I don't mean the looters. I mean the true fascists.'

'We didn't find any, my Duce,' Radl answered.

Mussolini bowed his head.

Suddenly Skorzeny made a decision. He turned to Gerlach and announced that he would also fly off with the Duce in the Storch. Gerlach turned down the suggestion at once. He would fly Mussolini out by himself. The Storch was a two-seater and he could not risk endangering the flight by the addition of Skorzeny's 200-pound bulk.

Skorzeny took him to one side. 'You are going alone by air,' he said. 'Suppose something happens to you on the way and you have to make a forced landing and are killed? If so, he's alone in a desert. And if he's lost and I fail in my duty to the Führer, there's only one way out for me. I'll have to put a pistol to my head.'

Gerlach continued to argue. The primitive runway which the paras had now cleared was about 200 yards long. With only the Duce as a passenger, he might get airborne before it ran out. With Skorzeny, it would be impossible to clear it in time.

Skorzeny persisted and in the end Gerlach gave in, snapping angrily: 'Well, for God's sake come, but if something happens on take-off, it's not my responsibility!'

Thus they clambered aboard the Storch, with Skorzeny crouched behind the passenger seat. Gerlach, his motor running at top speed, gave the signal to the paras to release their hold on the fuselage. The machine lurched forward. Outside there were a few dim '*Heils*' and '*Evvivas*'. Peering over Mussolini's shoulder, Skorzeny could see that the plane was eating up the runway at an alarming rate. A hundred—120—150. Still they were not air-borne. A ditch loomed up in front of them. 'God, if we go into that!' Skorzeny thought.

The next instant the Storch hit it and took off—*downwards*, plummeting towards the valley far below. Gerlach pushed the stick forward, increasing the Storch's speed, and hoped the slipstream would raise the wings. Suddenly the Storch responded and Gerlach wrestled it back to an even keel. Slowly Skorzeny opened his eyes. On the ground Radl, who was in charge of Mussolini's personal luggage, fainted.

Skorzeny had not yet arrived at his destination when Student called Goering in Berlin and told him the exciting news— Mussolini had been rescued.

Goering was astonished: 'Is that really true?'

Student assured him it was and that Mussolini was flying to Vienna.

When they arrived the first person to congratulate Skorzeny was Himmler himself—by phone. Thereafter a whole series of Nazi notables called on him at his hotel. He was awarded the Knight's Cross on the spot and ordered to bring the Duce to Munich personally for a reception by Hitler.

But while Skorzeny enjoyed his triumph, which was to make him Hitler's favourite junior commander, Student, back in Rome, was overcome by a growing sense of bitterness. 'The hero against his will', as Student called Skorzeny, was harvesting the fruits of an operation which he had planned and which his paras had executed. The 'Hunters from the Sky' were being completely forgotten, as Himmler made sure that his indirect subordinate hogged the limelight in the orgy of celebrations in Berlin.

But as he recalled later, 'I had too much to do to worry over much about Skorzeny. The Italian withdrawal from the war gave me headaches enough.' Individual battalions of his 1st and 2nd Divisions were hurried into action all along the peninsula, capturing an Italian staff here, disarming a division there, forcing the British to evacuate a newly captured island, taking a vital port. Overnight his paras had become the fire brigade of the Italian front and were to continue to be throughout the coming year. Disgruntled as he was by the Mussolini episode, Student, empowered by Hitler to raise four more divisions after the Gran Sasso (the 4th, 6th, 7th and 9th), realised that his paras were going to play the most important fighting role in Italy in 1944.

1944—The Führer's Fire-brigade

'During my whole combat service in two wars I never met better fighting troops than the Germans had in Brest, especially the men of the 2nd Parachute Division.'
US Corps Commander Troy Middleton, 1945

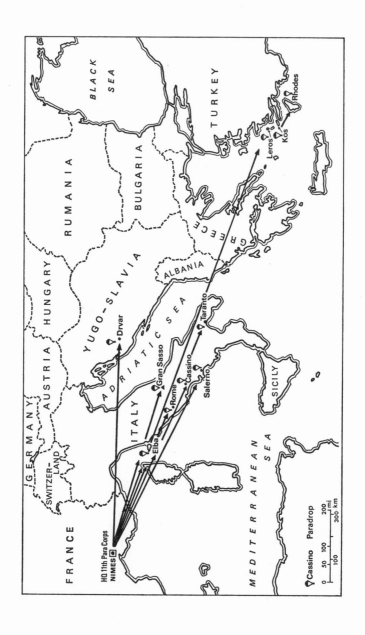

1. German paradrop over the Corinth canal, 1941. The Troop Transports are the standard Junkers 52, affectionately known as 'Auntie Ju' by paratroopers

2 and 3. Hitler's secret weapon—back and side views. Most of this equipment was later copied by Anglo-American paratroop forces

4. The secret weapon goes into action over the low countries, May 1940. Note kneepads disdained by allied airborne forces

5. The victors of the amazing attack on Fort Eben Emael, Belgium, in which 80 paratroopers forced the surrender of 1,500 Belgian soldiers, being interviewed by a war correspondent

6. German glider-borne troops go into action; the cream of pre-war German glider pilots including several world champions flew gliders and then went into action as infantry soldiers

7. This Junkers 52 containing German paratroopers whose task it was to capture Queen Wilhelmina and the Dutch government was forced by Dutch ack-ack fire to make an emergency landing on the Hague-Rotterdam highway

8. Paratroopers go into action behind the feared Spandau M.G. somewhere in Holland

9. Paratroopers take over in Rome after the Italian capitulation in 1943. Note the Schmeisser machine pistol now standard paratroop equipment

10. Monte Cassino—1944. A handful of survivors from the 2nd Paratroop Division view the ruins in which they held out until the bitter end

11. Baron Fredrich von der Heydte with men from his 6th Parachute Regiment

12. Paratroopers of the 3rd Parachute Division with SS Colonel Joachim Peiper

13. and 14. Hard-pressed GIs of Patton's 26th Division

15. Bastogne today—a Sherman tank sits near the Flame of Liberty

16. Hunters from the sky

17. Mass grave of German paratroopers in Crete, the operation which marked the end of the employment of paratroopers in an airborne role

One

'The Mussolini business and the subsequent defection of Italy to the Allies,' Student recalls, 'was the start of the busiest period of my whole military career. Hitler and the High Command became aware of the value of parachute formations once again after virtually wasting my highly trained, valuable men in an infantry role in Russia and Africa.'

Throughout the summer, autumn and winter of 1943, the men of the Parachute Corps were thrown into action after action in an attempt to stop the rot which had started in Italy and the Balkans after Mussolini's downfall. The 2nd Battalion, the 3rd Parachute Regiment, executed a daring drop over the Italian Army HQ at Monte Rotondo near Rome and succeeded in occupying the top Italian command, although General Roatta, the Chief of Staff of the Italian Army, had already fled.

Some time later another para battalion dropped on the island of Elba, where the Italian coastal artillery, loyal to Marshal Badoglio, whom Hitler hated so vehemently, had been harassing German supply operations along the Tyrrhenian coast with their heavy guns. The Italians fought hard, as had their comrades at Rotondo, but the 'Führer's Fire Brigade', as the paras were now being called, overcame them. Elba was denied to the Allies and 10,000 Italian prisoners went off to the POW cages.

While this was going on, the Allies had done a little island hopping themselves and had seized the islands of Kos, Leros and Samos in the Aegean. Again the Hunters from the Sky went into action at Student's command. Together with the mountain troops, who had been their comrades in Crete two years before, the 1st Battalion, 2nd Parachute Regiment, commanded by Major Kuehne, dropped on Kos in October. For the next six week, the mountain troops and the paras battled against the British occupiers, finally forcing the survivors to surrender on 16 November, 1943. It was the last time that British troops would surrender to the paras in the Second World War, but the damage had been done and apart from the strategic value of the islands their capture effectively kept Turkey from joining the Allied side; it was clear to the generally pro-British Turks that the German eagle still had very sharp claws indeed.[1]

In September, 1943, the *Fallschirmjaeger* were sent to repel the Anglo-American landing at Salerno and nearly succeeded in throwing them back into the sea. All in all it was 'a damn close run thing' and the British and American survivors of those first terrifying days on the narrow beaches were more than glad when Student was ordered to pull his paratroops out for a well-earned rest in the mountains of the Abruzzi.

In January, 1944, the German High Command in the Balkans, alarmed by the ever increasing power of the Jugoslavian partisan leader, 'Marshal' Tito, decided that he would never be put out of action by conventional methods. A year earlier it had looked as if Tito would agree to some sort of unwritten peace agreement with the Germans if they would allow him to deal with his greatest rivals for power in a post-war Jugoslavia, the monarchist Chetniks and the pro-German Utaschi, the feared militia recruited in the pro-German 'independent' state of Croatia. All that had changed immediately the Italians had surrendered. The Italian forces in Jugoslavia, which made up the largest component of the Axis occupiers, had willingly surrendered their arsenals to the Tito partisans, eager to take advantage of the new situation. The former blacksmith, who had received his military training as a sergeant in the old Austrian Imperial Army, had not only received thousands of rifles and machine-guns from the Italians, but also heavy equipment, such as artillery and tanks. Now safely ensconced in his mountain fastness, Tito had established a provisional government and the 'National Committee for the Liberation of Jugoslavia' in November, 1943.

It was clear to the Germans that Tito had ambitious plans for getting rid of them and that he could no longer be put out of action by conventional means, so they turned to Admiral

[1] One interesting aspect of the battle for the island was that General Mueller, the overall German commander, actually agreed with the British HQ at Cairo to let the British evacuate their forces without attack: a completely unprecedented action and indicative that some high-ranking German officers had realized that they were losing the war.

Canaris' *Abwehr*, the German Secret Service. The mysterious Admiral, whose real role in the war still remains an enigma to historians,[2] had previously turned down any unconventional action against enemy military leaders, rejecting a plan to assassinate the Soviet High Command. Seemingly, however, he did not have the same scruples about Tito. Accordingly he made his agents in Jugoslavia plan two attempts to get rid of the 'Marshal'. Plan One was to have his own special 'Branden-burger' formation, working with the Chetniks, assassinate Tito by a *coup de main*. Plan Two was to drop two bodies in British uniform close to Tito's HQ. As there was already a British mission with the partisan leader, his followers would undoubtedly bring them to the HQ. There they'd find two letters, addressed to Tito from Churchill. Tito would open the first and that would be his last action in this world, since it contained high explosive! However, both plans failed and thus it was that the German Command in Jugoslavia planned a military operation against the elusive Marshal, based on the surprise element of a para-glider attack.

By February, 1944, Canaris's agents had pin-pointed Tito's newest headquarters to the Bosnian town of Drvar and now the German planners got to work with a will. An SS para battalion under the command of *Hauptsturmführer* Rybka, plus a section of Student's best glider pilots and a select group of the Hunters from the Sky, were alerted to drop right on Tito's HQ itself, while the tough, multi-national troops of the SS *Prinz Eugen* Division were to seal off the partisan area and then fight their way to the aid of the paras. The date for the operation was 25 May, 1944, Tito's fifty-second birthday.

It was a bold operation, but it went wrong from the start. Tito had agents everywhere and suspected that the Germans were planning an attack on Drvar. As a result his men were on the alert, although they did not expect the attack to come from the sky. Tito's suspicions were also aroused by the fact that, three

[2] There are those in Germany and elsewhere who maintain that Canaris was really in the employ of the Allies. In fact, it does seem that he did warn the West of the intended attack on France and Holland in 1940; and in 1943–44 some of the conspirators against Hitler were located in his organization. Sir Kenneth Strong, Eisenhower's Chief-of-Intelligence feels that 'he was playing both sides of the game, aware of Germany's final defeat'.

days before his birthday, a German plane appeared over his HQ. Instead of dropping bombs, however, it spent its time flying round at about 2,000 feet. It was obviously a reconnaissance plane.

The representative of the British Military Mission saw the plane too, but he misinterpreted its function. He went to see Tito in his cave headquarters and warned him that the recce plane heralded a heavy German bombing attack, adding that the mission was going to move out of its present location into the hills. Tito agreed with the British officer's interpretation of the plane's appearance and went on preparing for his birthday which was going to be celebrated by the partisans and peasants in high style. He had even ordered a special 'Marshal's' uniform to be made for the event.

Two days passed and nothing happened, but with the dawn of 25 May came the Germans. The scruffy partisans in their odd mixture of German, British and Jugoslav uniforms, sounded the alarm as six Junkers 52 came flying in at low level straight out of the rising sun. The Junkers flew straight ahead, and then the paras started dropping. As one of the Mission recalls: 'Something fell from the leading plane and, falling, billowed out into a great canopy with a man dangling from it. Then more and more, from one plane after another. The air seemed full of them. More planes followed, and gliders, bringing guns and reinforcements to the parachutists, who by now were shooting their way into the village. A glider seemed to be landing almost on top of the little house which the Mission had left three days before.'

Although Tito had been forewarned about the operation, the manner of its execution had come as a surprise, but the partisans reacted quickly and Student's men, most of whom had been on the Crete operation, were in for a series of unpleasant shocks as their gliders came sailing down. Just before they had set off they had been told by the boastful bomber crews of the *Luftwaffe*, 'It's a moon landscape down there. There's not a living thing left.' The first glider, which landed just outside Tito's cave, was met by savage fire. The occupants were killed instantly, their bodies sprawled over the rocks, and the paras who followed them fared little better. Although the startled partisans had never seen a parachutist in their lives before, they reacted quickly as more and more gliders came crashing down in the cave area.

One group of paras was fortunate, however. Their plane had crashed, landing among a pile of boulders, the impact of which had momentarily knocked out the occupants. Now the partisans came rushing out of their positions, crying joyfully and waving their weapons, obviously wild with excitement at having killed this great bird which had arrived so unexpectedly in their midst. They overlooked the paras inside, who had by now come to. It was a fatal oversight. Next moment, ten automatics opened up and bodies were soon scattered all around the glider. This unexpected piece of luck, which cost the partisans some forty casualties, gave the German attackers the chance they had been waiting for. Now they pushed forward towards the mouth of the cave which, they suspected, housed the man who had been such a thorn in the Germans' flesh for these last months.

Inside the cave, Tito's Chief-of-Staff, Jovanovic, who had always sworn that a German air-borne attack was impossible, reacted quickly to the danger. He organized a rough-and-ready defence force out of his staff and the one hundred men of the defence battalion, telling them in the melodramatic idiom of the partisans: 'If you fail and the Germans capture Tito, then it will mean the end of our battle for freedom. Are you clear what this means? Tito and the Party must continue to live. We can deal with a defeat, but *Tito must live!*'

'*Tito must live!*' came back the chorus.

The speech had its effect. The teenage partisans, mostly potential officers, tackled the paras with a will. In a wild rush they tried to break through the German ring around the mouth of the cave. They failed but their sudden attack stopped the Germans from attacking—at least for a while.

Tito took advantage of the momentary lull to send for assistance and change out of his fine new uniform, ready for the fierce battle he anticipated would begin at any moment. Meanwhile *SS Hauptsturmführer* Rybka had been informed of the resistance at the mouth of the cave and immediately radioed the commander of the Second German Panzer Army in charge of the whole operation: 'Either there is vital documentary material in the cave—or Tito himself. I shall try my utmost to take the cave.'

He was as good as his word, but his paras could not penetrate the screen of fire put up by the partisans. Rybka ordered his artillery to zero in on the cave. This time he would soften it up before he attacked again. It was the chance Jovanovic had been waiting for. He ordered the immediate evacuation of important personnel, including the most important one of all. But how? If they used the ordinary way out of the cave they would undoubtedly be mown down by the tremendous weight of the German fire. Tito solved that problem himself. With the aid of a rope he hoisted himself up a cleft in the rock to the high ground above the cave, where he was met by the main body of the partisans.

While Tito entrained in the 'Partisan Express', the Germans pressed home their attack. But the ancient locomotive successfully negotiated five miles of track through the Bosnian forest, in spite of the German bullets whizzing from the firs on either side of the track. Then Tito, a handful of his chief advisers and his dog, aptly named Trigger, dodged into the trees and were gone.

Finally the paras and the men of the SS parachute battalion achieved their objective, but by now the bird had flown. All they captured was the brand new uniform which Tito had worn so proudly. (Later it was publicly exhibited in Vienna.) But their casualties had been prohibitive. The SS para battalion was virtually wiped out and it was months before it was ready for combat again. Captain Bentrup's paras of the 1st Para Division had been reduced to seventy men, so worn and exhausted that they were of little use in the further fighting that took place in the Balkans.

Operation 'Roesselsprung' (as the Germans called it) was a total failure. Tito got away and when the weary paras finally linked up with the SS tankmen of the *Prinz Eugen* Division, he was already on board the British destroyer HMS *Blackmore*, heading for the port of Komisa, with the British and partisan survivors of the raid, all in high spirits thanks to the liberal spirits allowance broken out by the skipper, Lieutenant Carson RN.

Far away at his headquarters a worried General Kurt Student was no longer concerned with the failure of the Jugoslavian operation which had been so much after his own heart. Now his whole attention—like that of most of the Axis and Allied military world—was directed on the fighting in Italy. In that country, during the same week which had seen the preparations for the surprise air-drop on Tito's HQ, there had been the third and final battle for a fortified position which would immortalize the Hunters from the Sky long after General Student was dead— the Third Battle of Monte Cassino.

Two

A British officer who was there just before the third and final attack on Cassino remembers the two commanding hills which dominated the Liri valley like this:

'If the morning was clear we could see the Garigliano in the moonlight as it bent in and out, appearing as a series of tiny dots. Often the valley was hidden completely by drifting smoke from the generators at the station so that I looked out over the billowing clouds to the Monastery which stood gleaming in the early sunshine. Behind soared Monte Cairo, six thousand feet high, its gullies streaked with snow, which ran down from its white pyramid. Gradually the mist thinned out as the wind veered and in a few minutes the whole valley was clear.

'At this time of day visibility was at its best. I looked down on the near part of the valley so vertically that it seemed to be spread out like a map; the river curved, each bend easily identifiable, the railway, the roads and paths stretched like tapes, the farm buildings dotted among the trees and tracks in chessboard fashion.'

To Captain R. L. Banks it was somehow an idyllic picture in the midst of war. But then he was not alone in his assessment of Monte Cassino. Before him over these long months, other sensitive men of many nations had come to the same conclusion. New Zealanders, Britons, Poles, Frenchmen, Americans—the whole vast multi-national Allied force in Italy—had viewed that seemingly peaceful prospect for the first time and felt it was impossible that death could be lying in wait for them among the hills and fields, which seemed so close, so easy to take.

But they had been mistaken. For hidden in the olive groves, behind the loose stone walls, the innocent folds in the ground, the roofless wattle-and-stone barns, the paras were waiting intently, ready to deny this key to Rome yet one more time.

They had arrived there in time to check the Allied attempt to force the River Rapido with two divisions in January, 1944. General Clark, the immensely tall and immensely publicity-conscious American commander of the ground forces, had ordered the 36th Division, a Texan National Guard unit, across the river that month; and from their heights they had watched the 36th shot to ribbons. In the bitter history of that Division, the Rapido became 'blood river' and after the war the survivors forced a public enquiry into Clark's conduct of the operation which cost them 1,700 men in dead and wounded.

But the Americans were only the first. The French came next—Free French of General Juin's Expeditionary Force. Juin was highly regarded by his German opponents and he attacked skilfully and with *élan*. His colonial infantry captured height after height until a desperate German counter-attack brought them to a halt.

On 25 January, the Americans had another go with the 34th Infantry and the German position became critical. The Americans allowed them no rest as more and more German reinforcements were thrown into the battle. January gave way to February and then on 5 February, the 34th Infantry gave up; they had had enough. Colonel Schulz had stopped them with his 3rd Para Regiment.

Now it was the turn of the British. The 'New Zealand' Corps, made up of the 4th Indian Division, the 2nd New Zealand Infantry Division and the British 78th, moved into the line; and they had an old score to settle, for the Corps Commander was no other than General Freyberg, whom the paras had chased from Crete so ignominiously three years before!

Freyberg assumed responsibility for the Monte Cassino sector on 12 February and at once made a decision which was to shake the Allied camp and become a great propaganda victory for the Germans. He decided that if he were ever going to turf the paras off the mountain, he would have to remove their eyrie, the monastery, one of the world's greatest art treasures, which dominated the whole area. He ordered the bombing of the monastery, for as he wrote to the New Zealand government: 'From the vantage point of the Monastery, the enemy can watch and bring down fire on every movement on the roads or open country in the plain below.'

It was a fatal decision, which Clark, Freyberg's superior,

attacked in his post-war account of the campaign *Calculated Risk,* passing the buck in an unprecedented manner (after all he had to approve the course of action taken by Freyberg) and writing: 'I say that the bombing of the abbey... was a mistake and I say it with full knowledge of the controversy that has raged around this episode... Not only was the bombing of the abbey an unnecessary psychological mistake in the propaganda field, but it was a tactical military mistake of the first magnitude. It only made the job more difficult, more costly in terms of men, machines and time.' But that was *after* the war. At the time Clark did not object.

British war correspondent Christopher Buckley, watching from five miles away, recalls the scene vividly: 'As the sun brightened and climbed up the sky I could detect little modification in the monastery's outline as each successive smoke cloud cleared away. Here and there one noted an ugly fissure in the walls, here and there a window seemed unnaturally enlarged. The roof was beginning to look curiously jagged and uneven... but essentially the building was still standing after four hours of pounding. Just before two o'clock in the afternoon a formation of Mitchells passed over. They dipped slightly. A moment later a bright flame such as a giant might have produced by striking titanic matches on the mountainside, spurted upwards at half a dozen points. Then a pillar of smoke five hundred feet high broke upwards into the blue. For nearly five minutes it hung around the building, thinning gradually upwards into strange, evil-looking arabesques such as Aubrey Beardsley at his most decadent might have designed.

'Then the column paled and melted. The Abbey became visible again. Its whole outline had changed. The west wall had totally collapsed.'

Surprisingly enough, Freyberg did not immediately take advantage of the chaos he had created on the mountain and the blinding of the German forces, but waited for two days before he finally launched his main attack at the enemy—his Fourth Indian Division.

On the morning of 17 February, five infantry battalions of the division attacked simultaneously, their objectives Calvary Hill and Monte Cassino. At the point of the whole attack was the Royal Sussex Regiment, whose positions on the littered hillside were only seventy yards away from those of Schulz's paras. They got within fifty yards of the enemy when the Germans met them with withering machine-gun fire and a hail of grenades and they went to ground. Time and time again individual groups tried to work round the paras' flanks, but the steep ground, reminiscent to the older hands in the battalion of the great killing grounds of Flanders, defeated them. Their own ammunition and grenades began to run out. Down below other companies not in contact with the enemy passed up their own grenades from hand to hand. By the time the attack had petered out, the Royal Sussex had lost 10 officers and 130 men killed out of the 12 and 250 who had set off so optimistically that morning.

And the casualties were not much less in the 4th's other battalions. The two Gurkha battalions involved, on whom Freyberg had set high hopes because of the little men's skill in mountain fighting, were pinned down after they had gone a few hundred yards and their running mates, the Rajputana Rifles, fared little better. By the end of the morning only one of the four company commanders was still on his feet—the other three had been killed or wounded.

There was nothing left for Freyberg to do but to order the withdrawal of the survivors. One day after it had started the First Battle for Monte Cassino had ended and General Freyberg found himself defeated yet again by the Hunters from the Sky.

*   *   *

The Second Battle of Cassino began with a massive air attack. On 15 March, 1944, the city was transformed suddenly and brutally into a heap of rubble and ash by a massive bombing raid by the US Air Force, with a large number of Allied generals, including the overall commander, Field-Marshal Alexander, watching the operation from nearby Monte Trocchio. Then as soon as the last of the bombers had disappeared over the horizon, the artillery crashed into action—nearly 2,000 guns. Hundreds of shells started to fall on the German defences.

Undoubtedly the Allied officers watching the operation through their field glasses must have thought that no one could live through such a bombardment; and indeed Major Foltin's Battalion of the 3rd Parachute Regiment had suffered severe casualties; 220 of his 300 paras lay buried in the smoking rubble when the gunners finally ceased their barrage. But Foltin's reserve company, which had been sheltering in some rocky caves, were still alive and full of fight. They were waiting for the New Zealanders when they came.

The New Zealanders made fair progress into the centre of the shattered town. But once the rubble and boulders prevented their tanks from giving them any further support, their advance bogged down. It was the same with the 4th Indian Division, which had been assigned the mission of capturing the monastery itself. After absorbing an estimated 3,000 casualties, the Indians gave up. It was a blood-letting from which the division would never recover. Thus the Second Battle of Monte Cassino[1] came to an end, with bitter recriminations being heaped on Field-Marshal Alexander by Churchill[2] regarding the conduct of the battle.

But the victory had been an expensive one for the Germans. General Heidrich's six understrength battalions, supported by the 1st Para Division's artillery and other ancilliary units, had indeed fought off the attack of two *élite* divisions, but at tremendous cost. One company returned from the line with exactly one officer, one sergeant and one private left; and it was not an exception. The time had come to withdraw Colonel Schulz's 3rd Para Regiment and replace it by Colonel Heilmann's 4th which, though it had taken part in the 2nd Battle of Monte Cassino, had not suffered such great casualties. Now the man who had launched the first blow against the Allied invaders of Europe a year earlier in Sicily was ordered to defend the vital fortification which barred the way to Rome and from thence to the Reich itself—with exactly 700 men!

[1] I am using the German division of the Cassino campaign into three separate battles.

[2] Lord Alanbrooke noted in his *Diary* that 'He (Churchill) had torn Alexander to pieces for lack of imagination and leadership in continually attacking at Cassino'.

Three

Punctually at eleven o'clock on the night of 11 May, 1944, a call broadcast by the BBC in London gave the signal for the start of the last battle. All along the Cassino front from Aquafondata on the upper Rapido to the Tyrrhenian Sea, the guns fired their opening salvoes—2,000 guns manned by Britons, Americans, New Zealanders, South Africans, Frenchmen, Poles—even Brazilians newly arrived at the front. 'Only numbers count,' Alexander had told his staff, echoing Nelson's famous words, and now, grimly determined to wipe out the mountain and its para garrison which had stood in the path of his advance for so long, he threw in every division available.

Almost immediately after the first shells landed on the German positions, the 85th and 88th US Infantry Divisions on the coast jumped off. Forty minutes later two French divisions—the 2nd Moroccan and the 4th Alpine—launched their attack on Monte Faito. Five minutes after that, the British 4th and 8th Divisions began their own push, forcing the River Rapido by storm. And finally, when the artillery bombardment came to a stop, the exile Polish Corps of General Anders went into action, heading for the mountain itself.

The Polish Corps contained two divisions, composed of men who had suffered unbelievable hardships since they had been taken prisoner by the Russians in 1939. After the miseries of the Soviet POW camps, many had been released in 1941 and shipped to East Africa where they had been nursed back to health before being sent to join the new Polish divisions then being formed in England, Italy and North Africa. Now they went into action with an *élan* that scared even the veterans of the 1st Para Division.

The 5th Polish Division attacked Colle Sant' Angelo, defended by the 2nd Battalion of the paras, but the main Polish attack, made by the Carpathian Division, supported by the 2nd Polish

Armoured Brigade, was directed at the peak of the Calvary Mountain, which had to be taken before they could make the final advance on the monastery hill itself.

The Polish attack was a complete success. Before the paras knew what had happened the 15th Carpathian Brigade had over-run the company holding the Calvary Mountain peak and the survivors were streaming down the other side to the safety of what was left of the German line.

As always the Germans reacted more swiftly than the Allies did to such surprise moves and Heilmann ordered his 2nd Battalion to counter-attack immediately. But the Poles were waiting and as the leading paras came close to the top of the peak, they ran into hastily scattered mines and intense fire from the Polish machine-guns. Desperately their officers tried to rally them, but the Poles were too tough and these paras who remained fled the way they had come.

The 1st Para Division did not, however, give up quite that easily. Half an hour later they came again, this time more cautiously, aware that they were facing a more skilled opponent than most of those they had encountered in these last five months on the mountain. But the Poles had not been lulled into a false sense of security by their earlier victory. They were alert and waiting, the same terrible slaughter began once again and once again paras fled the way they had come.

The aptly-named peak was turning into a miniature Verdun, but Heilmann was determined to recapture it. He scraped the barrel of his remaining man-power, assembled an attacking force of company strength, made up of the reserves of the 1st and 2nd Battalions and, as dawn broke, the paras went in for the third time. Again the Poles, now weakened a little by casualties and lack of reinforcements, were expecting them. This time, how-ever, it was not a clear-cut victory. They broke up the German attack, but they did not succeed in pushing the paras back down the mountain side. The surviving *Fallschirmjaeger* succeeded in going to earth in craters or behind boulders and began to snipe at the Carpathians' positions, only some seventy yards away. Now it was the Poles' turn to feel pinned down.

When darkness came there was still no peace for either attacker or defender, for Heilmann ordered yet another attack. Under the command of Sergeant-Major Karl Schmidt an assault

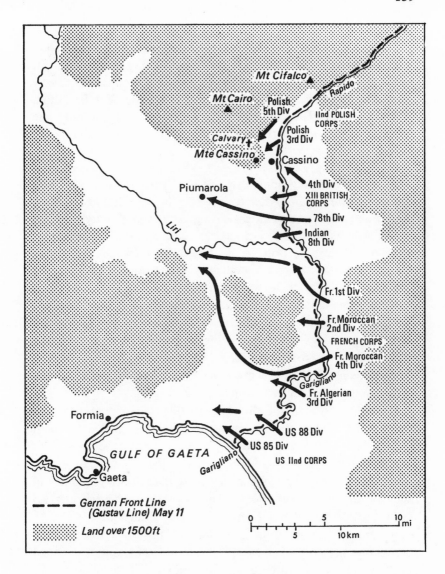

squad was selected for the job. Under the cover of mortar fire
which kept the Poles' heads down to the last moment, they crept
closer and closer to the enemy positions until they were so close
that they could hear the Poles talking to each other in the darkness between each salvo of mortar fire. Then the 'stonk' stopped
and the paras rushed forward. Desperate little battles broke out

everywhere. Here and there men struggled back and forth on the edge of the holes, momentarily outlined with every shell burst. Then the shooting and the shouting began to peter out until it ended altogether. The Paras had won and Calvary Mountain was back in German hands. Of the 2nd Battalion, 15th Carpathian Brigade which had occupied the peak only one officer and seven men remained alive.

*   *   *

That night General Anders ordered his Corps to withdraw to its departure point again. After twenty-four hours of savage fighting and equally savage casualties, he had achieved exactly nothing.

But Anders was as determined as the man who opposed him and on 13 May, he ordered his Carpathian Division to attack the mountain once again. Obediently a new brigade took up the challenge and started its weary progress up the hill. This time, however, the Germans were waiting for them, having the advantage of their observers on the 3,000-foot high Monte Cifalco. From this vantage point the artillery observers could cover the entire offensive area of the 2nd Polish Corps. Anders ordered smokescreens to hide the approach of his attack force but the screen was only effective from time to time.

Heilmann ordered the divisional artillery into operation and shells rained down on the advancing Poles, weighed down with half a hundredweight of equipment. (Long experience had taught the Allied commanders to make their men take everything possible with them since supplying the attacking infantry in such terrain often cost more casualties than the initial attack.) Grimly the Poles plodded on, taking casualties all the way. As they came within sight of the German positions the artillery bombardment stopped. Now it was the turn of the paras, armed for the most part with automatic weapons. They mowed the Poles down mercilessly, and the Slavs reeled back. Thus it went on all that day and the day that followed until, in despair, Anders called off the attack. In the last three days his two under-strength divisions, plus the armoured brigade, had lost 281 officers and 3,503 other ranks and it was with bitter pride that his men would soon erect their memorial on the mountain with the following inscription:

We Polish soldiers
For our freedom and yours
Have given our souls to God
Our bodies to the soil of Italy
And our hearts to Poland.

Elsewhere, meanwhile, the Allies had been more successful. The French broke through in the hills at Monti Aurunci on the same day that the Poles suffered their last defeat on Calvary Mountain. On the coast the green US 2nd Corps was also steadily pushing back the Germans trying to link up with their comrades of the 6th Corps at the Anzio salient. But it was the British 13th Corps which was making the running and presenting the German High Command under Kesselring with his major problem. On 17 May the British 78th Infantry Division took Piumarola while further north the 4th pushed on west of Cassino up to the Via Casilina, so that the paras of the 1st Para Division found their rear communications severed. Their position was now extremely grave.

Kesselring decided that, if he was going to keep his line intact, he would have to order the paras to withdraw from their positions and so maintain contact with the 14th Panzer Corps. Unfortunately the 1st Para 'did not dream of surrendering *its* Monte Cassino' (as Kesselring wrote after the war). To him the paras 'were an example of the drawback of having strong personalities as subordinate commanders'. On 17 May, 1944, as bad news poured into his HQ, it looked to Kesselring as if he would have to order the 1st Paras to withdraw personally, if he wanted to save what was left of his line.

On that same day, General Anders ordered the Poles to attack again and this time he was determined that his men would capture Monte Cassino. The day, Wednesday, dawned chilly and grey and the leading companies were subjected to a brisk shower of rain as they moved up to their start-line. There their commanders briefed them, leaning over the bonnets of their jeeps with outstretched maps, unsuccessfully illuminated by the yellow light of torches. All the familiar phrases. 'Barrage . . . four hundred guns . . . tie up with tanks at forming up place. 'Officers scribbled their instructions and marked positions on maps which were already sodden in the drizzle.

By now it was just after seven. The infantrymen slung their equipment on their backs: weapons, extra ammunition, picks. The mass of anonymous khaki, distinguished only by the stiff overlarge epaulettes, which made the Poles look so squat and broad-shouldered, sorted itself into sections, platoons, companies. The COs checked and received the same old answers. 'A company ready to move, sir—B, ready to move, sir—C—D.'

They moved off down that same path that had seen so many of their fellows go to their deaths a few days before. Faraway in England the headlines in the popular papers were already announcing that the Gustav Line was smashed save for Monte Cassino and the Monastery Hill. Now it was their job to ensure that that qualification, a matter of half a dozen words of newsprint, was removed.

The artillery opened up. The infantry waited for the barrage to end. Then the guns stopped and their moment had come.

What was left of Heilmann's paras reacted quickly. As the sun burned away the early morning mist the German guns began to pound the Polish infantry. The German artillery stopped. The *Nebelwerfer*, the six-barrel electric mortars took over, tearing the air apart with their stomach-churning howl.[1] There were several regiments of them and they concentrated on both the advancing infantry and the farms and woods below them, crowded with reinforcements, supplies and trucks. They could hardly fail to hit.

Smoke shells were now poured on to Monastery Hill by the Polish gunners in a frantic effort to replace the mist, but they had little success; they could not blot out the advancing infantry from the prying eyes on Monte Cifalco. The Poles struck the first German trenches. Here and there a para surrendered, but most of them fought to the bitter end. The Poles pushed on, but the steam was going out of their advance. Already they had lost most of their NCOs and officers. They hit some of the new

[1] British writer Fred Majdalany, who was present, described their sound as being 'like someone sitting violently on the bass notes of a piano, accompanied by the grating squeak of a diamond on glass'. All those who have been subjected to their fire agree that their sound was frighteningly unlike that of any other weapon employed by the Germans.

German pillboxes, an all-steel prefabricated affair—an 'underground three-roomed flatlet' as a British correspondent described it.

Heilmann poured in more artillery, for, as he wrote after the war, 'I demanded from my artillery that they use up their ammunition without any consideration of the morrow ... I did not tolerate any complaints.' As a 'poor infantry soldier' (as he called himself), 'I wanted to show my boys that I was right behind them'. In addition Heilmann had gathered together all the Division's machine-guns and mortars, using them at any point seriously threatened by the Poles.

In the end the Poles were fought to a standstill; the bravery of the paras and Heilmann's concentrated artillery and mortar fire had paid off. As night fell over the battlefield, Monte Cassino was still in the hands of a few bearded, begrimed German paras.

But if the paras were not yet beaten, their commander Marshal Kesselring was. The flanking movement executed by the French and the bold push made by the British 13th Corps had finally made it imperative that he evacuate Monte Cassino if he did not want it to be cut off altogether. The mountain had already lost its tactical significance and now it was time to get out. But the paras still did not want to leave and in the end Kesselring personally ordered them to evacuate the heap of rubble; as he writes in his *Memoirs*, 'I had personally to order these last, recalcitrant as they were, to retire.'

So on the evening of 17 May, Colonel Heilmann, whose lead company was down to one officer, one corporal and a private soldier, finally pulled out.

At a quarter to six on the morning of Thursday, 18 May, the Poles attacked again. The earth trembled for one last time as the barrage descended on the heights and once more the weary Polish infantry disappeared into the smoke. But this time (as a British officer recalled) 'We were going in for the kill. The Poles were sweeping round from the right; we, two and a half miles away in the valley, were on our way to seal it off from the left. It shouldn't be long now. And once we had cut the Highway the very qualities that had made the Monastery an impregnable bastion for so long would turn it into an equally formidable death-trap. For so long the guardian and protector of its garrison,

it would round on them in its death-throes and destroy them.'
This time the advance was easy compared with the days before.
The Poles of the 12th Podolski Regiment moved up the heights
with unusual speed, their progress halted solely by rearguard
parties and the occasional para who had volunteered to stay
behind and protect the withdrawal. The action involved no more
than a series of light individual actions against sniper and
machine-gun teams.

Down below the 8th Army were finding the advance equally
easy. One British battalion, accustomed to the habits of the
paras and not wishing to incur any further casualties at this
stage of the attack, sent out a special patrol of three corporals,
all veterans and holders of the Military Medal, to reconnoitre
the German positions. They searched the silent gullies and ruins,
only to find them filled with dead paras. But as the chronicle
records: 'Their time was not wasted however. Each returned
with a Schmeisser gun, a camera, a watch and a pair of binoculars of impeccable German manufacture.'

Finally the Poles achieved their objective; but as is so often
the case, the entry into Monte Cassino was an anti-climax. The
Germans had flown and all that remained were dead paras staring blind-eyed into nothingness. As the correspondent of the
American military paper *Stars & Stripes* wrote, 'Today there is
nothing left of Cassino. It stinks with the dead bodies of horses,
dogs, mules, cattle, civilians and soldiers still there in the rubble.
Its water mains are wide open; its fabulous tunnels are cleared
of Nazis ... Cassino now belongs to the engineers and the grave
diggers!'

At his headquarters, Field-Marshal Alexander proudly pro-
claimed 'Cassino has fallen'. The news flashed around the world,
and in spite of the shock occasioned by the details of the casualties incurred by the 8th and 5th US Armies,[2] Allied correspondents at the front could not hide their admiration for the fighting
qualities of the German *Fallschirmjaeger*.

[2] General Clark put the total of US Army losses for January–June,
1944, at 107,144 killed, wounded or missing. The British 8th Army
(including the Poles) lost 7,835 men during the Third Battle for Cassino.
German losses were never estimated. But at the German Cassino
Cemetery, where many of the defenders were buried, there are 20,000
graves.

Sergeant Len Smith, soldier-correspondent of the Oran *Stars & Stripes*, wrote in the paper's 20 May issue, three days after Cassino had fallen:

'There is another undeniable truth—the fighting of Cassino's defenders was magnificent even after taking into consideration the tremendous advantage they had in defensive positions and observational posts. They survived the terrific air and artillery bombardments that levelled all of Cassino except the schoolhouse, the jail and the Continental Hotel and came back to fight like demons. They turned every inch of Allied destruction into a strongpoint for themselves: they fought off the best the Allies had to offer, yielding only to death. To them must be accredited a great defensive victory, for, at least, they delayed by many months the liberation of Rome.'

The correspondent of *The Times*, well aware of the fighting qualities of the paras and the fact that the 1st Para Division—or what was left of it—had escaped to fight again, avoided any panegyric to either attacker or defender. The capture of Monte Cassino was not a great victory for him for, as he cabled dourly, 'In the Battle for Cassino, the 1st Parachute Division, Germany's best fighting troops, escaped with half its strength.' His unspoken conclusion was obvious. The paras had escaped to fight in more desperate ventures. As the Allied landing in France drew near, the 1st Para and their like would be waiting to battle for other Cassinos. In this year of victory the Hunters from the Sky would still make the Allies pay very dearly for their triumphs.

Four

On 15 June, 1944, General Ramcke, the man who had turned the scales in Crete, was driving with a small convoy of camouflaged staff cars on the road which led from the little, medieval French town of Auray towards Pontivy. He had eaten a good lunch at the officers' club at Auray and now he was relaxing on the back seat of the open tourer beside his chief-of-staff, Major Schmidt. It was a lovely day and there was no Allied air activity over that part of France. Idly he took in the sights—the villages where his 2nd Para Division had been stationed the previous year, the pretty Gothic churches, the apparently friendly peasants who raised their berets as the car passed.

The apparent friendliness pleased Ramcke. Four days before, when he had been ordered to Student's headquarters at Nancy, he had not been pleased at being taken away from training his reformed division near Cologne. But Student had told Ramcke: 'Move your division at once to Brittany for further training. There you will also have the task of defending the port of Brest against any enemy air-borne attack.'

Ramcke knew that, although his division still contained some men who had fought in Crete, Africa, Italy and Russia, there were far too many new recruits in the division who needed further training. But Student did not give him time to protest. 'Your advance party has already been warned by telephone to set off for Vannes under the command of your chief-of-staff. You can meet him there. The first troop transport trains will start leaving tomorrow, early. I emphasize that I should like you to set off yourself at the latest tomorrow morning. You've got the afternoon to discuss the move with the quartermaster.'

Although Ramcke was overjoyed at the thought of fresh action, especially against the Anglo-Americans who were landing in ever increasing numbers in Normandy, he told Student that, under existing transport conditions, it would take his division at least three weeks to be ready for combat. Student shrugged. He had tried every possible excuse to get the High Command to postpone the move, but 'all my objections were overruled.'

That was four days ago. Now lulled by the sun, the food, the beauty of the countryside and the friendly populace, so different from the sullen Russian peasants or the bitter Italians, he told himself that the move of the 2nd Para Division to Brittany might well be for the best after all. Still he was not entirely at ease. There had been some talk at the officers' club of partisans in the area—the FFI and FTP—called by the locals the '*Diables bleus*'. Apparently these 'blue devils,' armed by the British SOE, and assisted by British and American officers, were already beginning to attack lonely and unwary Germans, following the order, published in their secret newspaper *La Defense*, 'to beat the Germans dead like dogs'.

He glanced behind at the second car which carried an aide and his two faithful runners, Sergeants Engler and Seeberger, who had been with him since Crete. Both of them had machine pistols on their knees and their eyes swept the fields and ditches on either side of the dusty road.

Now they were only twelve kilometres from Pontivy. Ramcke yawned. He was finding it hard to keep awake. Before them a farmer, dressed in the typical Breton peasant smock, started to cross the road. Sergeant Dietinger took his foot off the accelerator. Major Paul, seated in front beside the driver, turned to Ramcke: 'That fellow looks a bit suspicious,' he began but he never finished the sentence.

Bursts of machine-gun fire came from the ditches on both sides of the road. Major Schmidt cried out in pain and fell forward across Ramcke's lap, bleeding heavily from the side. Seconds later he was dead.

Dietinger, whose peaked cap had been pierced by a bullet, hit the brakes and the car squealed to a stop. Ramcke and Paul sprang out grabbing for their pistols. Behind them Engler and Seeberger did the same, running for the bushes from whence the firing had come, machine pistols held at the ready. But they were too late. The operation had been a typical Maquis hit-and-run affair and the gunmen had flown. Saddened and shocked, the little group returned to Ramcke's car, where a white-faced Dietinger was staring down at the dead officer.

Ramcke nodded and they got back in their vehicles and, with the dead man propped up beside the General, made their way to Pontivy where Ramcke handed over the body to the local military hospital. He realized that the murder was significant of how much things had changed in Occupied France since the previous year. Now he knew that he must expect ambushes and sabotage all along his division's line of march before they were finally assigned to their real fighting objective—whatever that may be.

His forebodings proved correct. Several times his car was fired on from the tall hedges which bordered the narrow Breton lanes as June gave way to July and he sped about on his various inspections. Each time he was lucky to escape with his life.

Not so, many of his men, of whom 130 were killed or taken prisoner by the Maquis. But in spite of the danger that lurked close by every time the paras were not present in strong force, Ramcke kept up the training of the new recruits in his formation. He was confident that, once the Allies broke out of their present containment in Normandy and charged into Brittany, his division, the best that Corps Commander Fahrmbacher had, would be at the forefront of the defence. Ramcke knew the call for action would come soon but it was to come even sooner than he or the German High Command had thought.

*   *   *

The GIs plodded heavily down the road while the tanks of the 6th US Armored Division clattered past them towards the point of breakout. On this first day of August the soldiers were grey with dust and the backs of their combat jackets were streaked with sweat as they ploughed doggedly onwards to the sound of the guns and the ruined town of Avranches.

In front of them the 6th's vehicles began to pile up as they reached the centre of the town. Staff cars, laden with officers, honked their way through the press. Tanks rumbled to a halt. Tankers, their faces grimed with dirt and oil, poked up their heads to stare at the confusion all around them. The centre of Avranches on that hot afternoon was one massive traffic jam with sweating red-faced MPs, urged on by angry staff officers, trying to keep the traffic, made up of most of the vehicles of the 80,000-strong US VIII Corps, rolling.

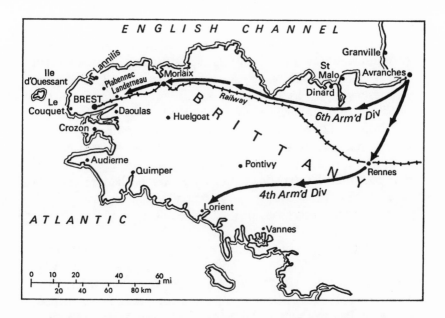

Finally General Grow, the commander of the 6th Armored, took charge himself, standing under a French policeman's sun umbrella, directing the tanks towards the sound of the guns. While he was thus engaged a jeep, driven by an immaculate sergeant, followed by an armoured car, forced its way through the press and halted near the rostrum. A tall imperious, figure sprang out. On his head he wore a gleaming, lacquered helmet, bearing three over-large gold stars. General George S. Patton, Commander of the US 3rd Army, had arrived.

Patton wasted no time in chit-chat. He had been waiting for this opportunity for offensive action ever since he had arrived secretly in Normandy the month before. At fifty-nine, one of the oldest of active US generals overseas, he had 'a horrible feeling that the fighting will be over before I get in'. Now the man who had written in his diary the previous month that 'I am destined to achieve some great thing—what I don't know' had been given his chance to conduct the breakout into Brittany in his own way and he had no time to waste. Seizing Grow by the arm and leading him away from his staff officers, he said, 'Listen, Bob, I've bet Monty five pounds that we will be in Brest by Saturday night.'

Grow did some quick thinking. Today was Tuesday and 200

miles of enemy territory lay between him and Brest. It was a
tall order, especially with his whole division still bogged down
in Avranches. But Grow was of the same school as Patton himself
and he had come to know the latter's tactics well during the
year he had spent as Patton's G-3.

'What are my objectives, sir?' he asked.

Patton explained that he wanted him to capture the Brest–
Rennes railway, 'And I want you to by-pass all resistance'.

Grow hurried away to start planning the operation with his
staff to whom he explained jubilantly that he had received 'a
cavalry mission from a real cavalryman'.

The race for Brest was on!

But Patton had not reckoned with his one-time subordinate,
now his superior, General Bradley. When Bradley visited VIII
Corps HQ the day after Patton had given Grow his order, Troy
Middleton, the Corps Commander, had complained to him that,
owing to Patton's action, his flanks were now wide open. 'I'm
left with nothing,' he said despondently. 'I hate to race on towards Rennes and Brest with so much of the enemy at my rear.
If the Germans were to break through here at Avranches, to the
coast, I'd be cut off way into Brittany with maybe as many as
eighty thousand of my men marooned.'

Bradley grew angry. 'Damn it!' he exploded. 'George seems
more interested in making the headlines than in using his head.
I don't care if we get to Brest now or in ten days' time.'

Bradley then empowered Middleton to overrule Patton, his
own army commander. Middleton did so, ordering Grow not
'to bypass Dinant and St Malo'. Grow did as he was told—but
not for long.

On the evening of the 3rd, Patton drove into his HQ in a
towering rage. Springing out of his jeep with his white and very
ugly bulldog Willie snapping at his heels, he strode through the
wheatfield in which Grow's CP was located in a tent. Grow
came out with a big grin on his face but when he saw Patton, it
vanished immediately.

'What the hell are you doing sitting there?' Patton shouted at
him. 'I thought I told you to go to Brest!'

Grow paled. 'My advance was halted, sir,' he stuttered.

'On what authority?'

'Corps orders, sir.'

Patton was handed Middleton's message. He read it, then said to Grow, 'I'll see Middleton about this. Don't take any notice of the order or any other order telling you to halt unless it comes from me. Get going and *keep* going till you get to Brest!'

The race for Brest was on again.

By 5 August it looked as if Patton might win his bet with Monty. By that morning the two lead columns of the 6th drove into Huelgoat, less than forty air miles from Brest. In the light of the opposition he expected to encounter that day, Grow was confident that he would reach the port by nightfall.

But then the 6th ran into trouble. Just outside Huelgoat 500 paras, well dug in and supported by heavy artillery and a few tanks, were waiting for them. This time Grow could not avoid action. There was no way of avoiding the German positions. It took all day, but when the Americans finally cleared the wooded height barring their way, they had time to glance at the corpses of the teenage Germans who had held their slit trenches to the last; they were wearing the camouflage smocks of the *Fallschirmjaeger*. Patton's tankers had hit Ramcke's Hunters from the Sky.

On 7 August a fighter-bomber appeared over one of Grow's tank columns and signalled Patton's request for information. 'What is the situation in Brest? Where are your forces? Does the 6th Armored Division need infantry assistance?'

Grow did but, before committing himself to a pitched battle with the Germans entrenched before Brest, he wanted to see if he could bluff the Germans into surrendering. He had done it before at Granville where several thousand of the enemy had surrendered to a single tank platoon. This time he sent an officer and a sergeant to ask for the garrison's surrender, but the trick did not work a second time. The Germans said bluntly, 'We will not surrender', and Grow knew that he would have to make good his threat to attack. But before it could be launched, remnants of a whole German division blundered into his rear echelons and the plan to attack was hurriedly called off.

For a whole day Grow turned and fought what was left of the 266th Division and when it was over the 6th had captured 1,000 prisoners and Grow could report to Middleton that he had destroyed what was left of the 266th German Infantry Division.

But the unexpected diversion had put him badly off stroke. When he attacked again on 11 August, the Germans were ready and waiting. The tankmen fought all that day and well into the next day, but when darkness fell on the 12th, Grow realized that the headlong rush to Brest was over. The Germans had dug in their toes and although Grow did not know it, General Ramcke's paras had slipped into Brest on the same day that he had tried to bluff the garrison into surrendering.

Patton, however, passed on to greater fame in Central and Northern France, and the dirty work was left to VIII Corps Commander Troy Middleton—and a heartbreaking job it was to be.

*   *   *

On the same day that Grow broke off the attack on Brest, leaving the job to Middleton's infantry, Ramcke took over command of the port and handed over the day-to-day running of the 2nd Para Division to Colonel Kroh. But he continued to play an active part in the Division's operations, as well as organizing the port's defences during the lull which now set in.

Ramcke had 35,000 men under his command, counting the German civilians working in the harbour installations. In addition he was responsible for the 40,000 French civilians, many of whom had fled to the outlying suburbs, refusing to take advantage of the bombproof submarine bunkers which were now being used to house most of the civilians and soldiers not actually engaged in front line duties. In essence then the non-combatant population of Brest, both French and German, went underground and stayed there until the city surrendered nearly two months later.

Ramcke was not particularly concerned with the non-combatants. His problem was the disposition of his fighting men— the 8,000 paras and the several thousand second-class troops and sailors whom he distributed among the port's many defensive works. The Bretons, a Celtic people, are small, hot-blooded and unmethodical. Now, in the summer of 1944, a forceful methodical people had descended on them and had taken over their fog-bound hills and transformed them into defensive positions, ranging from simple foxholes to intricate bunker lines. Behind this initial defensive line, manned by the paras, Ramcke rested his defence on the old French fortress line, built in part by the great seventeenth century military engineer, Vauban. Although some of these forts were nearly 300 years old, they were still very formidable with walls up to fifteen feet thick and thirty-five feet high, especially as Ramcke integrated high velocity 88s, minefields, extensive wire entanglements and cunningly sited machine-guns among them. Even his second-line troops could hold such positions.

To back up the forts, Ramcke ordered sunken ships, which had been sent to the bottom of the harbour by Allied bombing, to be stripped of their guns, which were emplaced with the heavy coastal artillery on the Daoulas promontory and the Querlern peninsula. Together with twelve batteries of field artillery and eighteen batteries of naval flak used in a ground role, they could offer Ramcke artillery support on virtually any part of his ten-mile long front.

Ramcke naturally had no illusions about the gravity of his position. After the war he wrote: 'There was no doubt that our position was hopeless, but all of us, from the oldest commandant to the youngest para, rifleman, sailor and dock worker were prepared to do our duty to the utmost.'

Five

Thus while Ramcke prepared, the victorious American infantry rested, enjoying their time out of war. They lazed in the August sunshine and rehashed the events of the past week, or they listened to Major Glenn Miller's Air Force Band, broadcast from London. Above all, they got drunk. As Lieutenant Paul Boesch, an infantry officer, who was soon to go into action for the first time with the 121st Regiment, recalls: 'A carnival spirit reigned. Some of the men were well supplied with "liberated" bottles of wine from Dinard and this, together with lots of good, hot food, warm tents and no enemy made us feel as though we were on manoeuvres back home.'

Meanwhile the build-up for the attack on Brest got underway. Day after day the trucks rolled down the lanes towards the port, filled with ammunition for the coming battle. The heavy equipment followed—great sixty-foot long bridging sections to cross the many stretches of water which surrounded Brest—ponderous self-propelled guns which shook the earth as they clattered towards the front—towed eight-inch cannon of a kind the infantrymen thought they would never see save on a battleship. As one infantry remarked to Boesch as he watched them roll by: 'Damn, look at the size of that pistol! This fight ought to be a lead pipe cinch, if we got all that stuff behind us!'

Another GI was not so confident. 'Son,' he said soberly, 'you ain't been in the Army long enough to know to lace yer leggings. Don't you know they wouldn't be sending us those things if they didn't think Brest was going to be the toughest nut to crack in the whole damned continent of Europe!'

By the third week of August the infantry divisions were in position. The 8th Infantry, a regular division nicknamed the 'Golden Arrows', commanded by General Stroh, took up its position at Plabennec. The 2nd Division, another regular outfit, whose divisional patch was a large Indian head, took up its position at Landerneau under the command of General Robertson. It was joined four days later by General Gerhardt's 29th Infantry Division, which moved into the line just south of Lannilis.

Thus they waited while the Army Group Commander, General Bradley, discussed the situation with General Patton. Both men wanted to avoid the heavy infantry losses they had suffered during the Army's attack on Dinard and St Malo the previous month. But both men wanted Brest captured, in spite of the fact that it was becoming steadily less important as a supply port for the US build-up. As Bradley told Patton in a moment of confidence: 'I would not say this to anyone but you, and have given different excuses to my staff and higher echelons, but we must take Brest in order to maintain the illusion that the US Army cannot be beaten!'

On 21 August, 1944, Task Force B, under the command of General James van Fleet,[1] assistant commander of the 2nd Division, set off on the first attack. The single instruction given to van Fleet was to capture Hill 154, a dominant feature on the approaches to Brest, south of the River Elorn. At first the attack went well, the first few miles were covered rapidly with few casualties and it looked as if it would succeed easily. Then the leading unit hit the first serious German line of defence and were stopped dead! A massive volume of fire descended on them and within a matter of minutes their attack had fizzled out with the survivors digging in frantically.

A hastily assembled group of staff officers crawled forward to study the enemy positions. The paras were well dug in on the hill at the base of which they had entrenched themselves in eight steel and concrete pillboxes. Between them and the crest, which was defended by a network of trenches, the officers could count some twenty-five machine-guns, plus several mortars and anti-tank guns. Hill 154 was obviously important to the Germans. Despondently the staff officers crawled back to their CP and started to plan a full-scale attack.

The morning of 23 August was misty. The rain had crept in from the sea during the night and everywhere there were pools

[1] Later commander of the 8th Army in Korea.

of mist so that the infantry walked like noiseless grey ghosts to their rendezvous with the tanks.

The Shermans began to rumble up and the guns crashed into operation. Unable to make themselves heard above the roar, the officers waved their arms to indicate 'forward' and the GIs formed up behind the tanks, slipping in the churned-up grass. The battle had begun.

The Germans reacted quickly. The paras, shooting along well sighted lines of fire, poured lead into the ranks of the advancing GIs. Then the first pillbox loomed up out of the mist. An infantry officer called for a Sherman and the tank lumbered up and pumped three rounds of armour-piercing shot at it. A young soldier, using the opportunity offered by the tank, dashed forward and lobbed a satchel charge through the pillbox's aperture. There was a muffled crump. A thick cloud of oily black smoke billowed out and the attack went on.

The barrage ended and the American artillery started to pick out individual targets. In spite of the steep slope, the progress of the advance quickened. Back at the advance CP, the radio messages flashed back and forth. 'Charlie Company here... Two machine-guns giving me trouble... Okay! Target—victor eighty-two north—one hundred. Five rounds HE... FIRE!' For a while the GIs halted and let the artillery have another go at softening the German positions. When it had finished, Staff Sergeant Alvin Casey rushed the pillbox which was holding up his company. He was badly hit, but rising to his feet again, he staggered forward and slipped his last grenade through the pillbox's side-slit. He died moments later,[2] but the advance went on. And in the end the weary infantry of van Fleet's task force took Hill 154.

The news encouraged Middleton to let Task Force B push on and clear the remainder of the promontory. Using a whole arsenal of weapons, including flame throwers, van Fleet's men pressed steadily forward to clear the entire peninsula, and to take 2,700 prisoners for a relatively small number of casualties.

The whole operation was, in Middleton's words, 'an outstanding success'. He decided to form a similar command, Task Force S, to do the same job as van Fleet's outfit—this time on

[2] He was later awarded the Congressional Medal of Honor.

the right flank. Commanded by Colonel Leroy Watson, assistant commander of the 29th Division, the job of the 3,000-man-strong task force was to clear the tip of Brittany between Brest and Le Conquet.

Watson's men jumped off on 27 August and advanced rapidly. That day they cut the Brest–Le Conquet highway and, aided by 200 Russian deserters from the German Army who knew the area well, the task force took and held the fort at Pointe de Corsen before surrounding the artillery batteries at nearby Lochrist. But here the advance came to a sudden halt and the Americans had to begin the same heartbreaking siege operations as before. They lasted one week until finally a young American infantry soldier decided that he had had enough of German obstinacy. The man, First Lieutenant Bob Edlin, set off with a four-man patrol on 9 September. Amazingly enough they managed to break through the main Lochrist positions and sneak into the fort. Once inside Edlin did not waste time. Running down the corridor with his men behind him, he found the Fort Commandant's office and burst through the door. The German officer looked up startled. Before he could call for help, Edlin had pulled the pin from the grenade he was carrying and, holding it above his head, shouted in English, 'It's surrender or death!'

The commandant half raised himself from his chair, '*Ja, ja,*' he stuttered, '*es ist gut.*' Then, in English, 'I surrender!' and within the hour, he had convinced the rest of the garrison Lochrist to surrender. Some time later the young American officer handed over the Fort, plus 1,000 men, to his amazed superiors.

With his flanks cleared, General Middleton set about the main attack on the city itself. Using his three infantry divisions—the 2nd, 8th and 29th—in a line abreast, with the 8th under General Stroh in the centre, he planned to attack the German defensive perimeter.

This formed a rough semi-circle around the mouth of the River Penfeld. Here there were two defensive lines—the outer of field fortifications in depth—the inner, four miles in length and some 3,000 yards in depth. But because of the shallowness of the defensive area, Middleton knew it was logical that Ramcke would make the first outer belt his main battleground. In essence, as he told his staff officers, 'the fate of Brest hangs on that line'.

* * *

The attack on the outer line began with a massive sea and air bombardment. Miles off shore the British battleship HMS *Warspite* steamed back and forth, unseen to the German defenders, pouring huge 15-inch shells at the port's two major strongholds—the Naval School, and the tunnel warehouses which were virtually immune from land-based artillery fire, but as the tunnels' entrances faced the sea, they were vulnerable from that direction.

Simultaneously seven groups of medium bombers, plus 150 four-engined Flying Fortresses from England, swept over Brest unloading their bombs with impunity. Fires broke out everywhere, and when they had gone, the night bombers of the RAF —Lancasters and Halifaxes—swept in at 7,000 feet to continue the destruction.

Ramcke ordered all non-combatants to take to the shelters and stay there. While the paras waited for the new American attack which he knew would come once the softening up had ceased, the many thousands of sailors, soldiers and German civilians in the port's enormous bunker system got drunk, and in many cases, were to stay drunk for the remainder of the battle. Signal Corporal Erich Kuby, who was present, recalled that on that day he noticed that his gums had begun to bleed, a sign that the garrison's diet of meat and potatoes, without any green vegetables, was beginning to have an effect. He noted also that two fellow corporals permanently employed in cleaning the overused latrines were awarded the Iron Cross, 'and I must say they earned them too!'

But Ramcke was unmoved by the bombing and its results. On the morning after the British raid, he visited one of the former U-boat pens, where an Allied bomb had penetrated the seven-yard-thick ferro-concrete roof. His staff were amazed that the enemy had bombs capable of penetrating the supposedly impregnable U-boat pens. Ramcke flicked his cane at the great hole and said, 'Well gentlemen, what do you say now? Did a good job, the *Amis*? Pretty nice hole, what!' and strode off, seemingly oblivious to the roar of the *Warspite*'s guns far out to sea.

Middleton now judged it was time to launch his final attack. Sixty thousand infantry followed up the bombardment of 2,000 guns. But instead of the US divisions advancing miles as Middleton had anticipated, they crawled forward by the yard. Fog, rain and Atlantic squalls set in and added to the GIs' misery as the paras fought them for every yard of mud. Ammunition started to get low. Two companies of the 29th were cut off by the paras and ignominiously marched into Brest as prisoners.

Lieutenant Paul Boesch, a one-time professional wrestler, now with the 8th Division, recalls pushing forward to positions abandoned by the captured men and being shocked by the shambles. 'Though we had become accustomed to seeing Jerry's belongings scattered all over the area, it came as a jolt to see US equipment spread about in the same manner. Not only was there issue equipment like belts, packs, raincoats and helmets, but also clothing and personal effects of every conceivable nature —well-worn letters from home, half-written letters, shaving kits, combs, tooth brushes, writing paper, pictures of sweethearts, wives and kids.'

Middleton sent in the bombers and fighter bombers once more. Up front, General Donald Stroh of the 8th watched the P-47s come in and then break off into dive-bomber formation. Time after time they dived at the German positions, appearing about to crash headlong into the ground until, at the last moment, the pilot pulled the plane up and the bombs began to fall. The General was pleased. This was the kind of support he expected from the Tactical Air Force. It was the best way to take the pressure off his hard-worked infantry companies who were taking a terrible beating.

Suddenly he lowered his field glasses. One of the P-47s had been hit on the wing by the flak. With smoke pouring from its fuselage, it roared down in a 500-mile-an-hour dive. The next moment the plane crashed into a nearby hill and exploded into a red ball of flame. General Stroh turned away. Two hours later he found out that the pilot of the plane was his son, Major Harry Stroh. He was dead.

The carnage went on. The infantry crawled forward against

fanatical resistance from the paras who had been told by Ramcke, 'I rely on my paratroopers that they will carry out their duty to the end with fanatical energy. The First Division was immortalized by its defence of Monte Cassino. The Second Division will become immortal by its defence of Brest.' And although the rank-and-file in the underground tunnels complained that Ramcke was holding out so long only in order to gain the coveted 'diamonds' to his Knight's Cross, his paras fought on.[3]

The price of the American advance was prohibitive. Lieutenant Boesch remembers stopping at the command post of a fellow officer 'and was shocked to find the company commander on the verge of a nervous breakdown. He babbled continuously and incoherently about the trials and tribulations his company had experienced in the advance. He never stopped talking or staring. I began to feel strange and got out as soon as possible and made excuses before his condition proved contagious.'

He was not the only officer fighting against the Brest paras who was beginning to despair. Middleton himself was well aware that Patton and Bradley had expected him to capture Brest by 1 September. The date had come and gone and he was still not within sight of his final objective. In addition his ammunition supplies were beginning to get low, air support 'left a lot to be desired' and, as he admitted in a frank letter to Bradley, his troops were 'none too good'; they had begun to show alarming signs of combat weariness and lack of aggression.[4] In the second week Patton and Bradley, alarmed by the situation at the beleaguered port, flew to Middleton's HQ to confer with him. They did not find him at his HQ. Instead he was just south-east of Brest, actually supervising a battalion strength attack there himself.

Middleton pulled no punches. He knew that it had taken him

[3] After the war Ramcke, who was the most decorated man in the paratroopers, sued author Erich Kuby for stating, in a radio documentary about Brest, that the only reason for his fanatical defence was Ramcke's desire for decorations. Ramcke lost the case.

[4] The doyen of US military historians, Colonel (later Brigadier) Marshall recalls being told by a company commander at Brest at that time: 'Don't you realize that the regiment which fought at Omaha (beach) no longer exists! I'm talking about the people. We've been replaced wholly. The June Sixth men are all either dead, in hospital or missing . . .'

nearly thirty years to get to his present position. Joining as a private in 1910, the fifty-five-year-old General had risen to the rank of Colonel by 1939 when he had retired. Recalled two years later, he had handled the inexperienced 45th Division well in Sicily, but a knee injury had cut his career short and he had been evacuated to the Walter Reed Hospital in the US. There he had languished, seemingly forgotten by the military world until Eisenhower found him and demanded that he should be sent back to Europe, commenting: 'I would rather have Troy Middleton commanding VIII Corps from a stretcher than anyone else I know in perfect health.' The new command had soon cured his knee, but he knew that Patton would have no hesitation in firing him on the spot if he did not produce results. He would not be the first corps commander Patton had fired and he would not be the last.

Middleton explained the situation at Brest while the two other generals listened attentively. In view of the many delays in the supply of heavy ammunition and the general lack of support for his operation, he felt it had become something of a side-show for Patton, fighting on the main front some 400 miles away. He went on to tell them about the fighting capacity of his infantry. As Patton recorded the discussion later, 'He was not sanguine about the capture of Brest, and was full of complaints about the lack of daring on the part of the infantry.'

Surprisingly, Patton took Middleton's complaints calmly. He had already decided to wash his hands of the situation at Brest and contented himself with remarking mildly that the infantry lacked daring because 'they are tired. They have fought too long.'

On the way back, Patton told Bradley that he could not fight on four fronts indefinitely and would like VIII Corps turned over to someone else. Bradley agreed and thus Middleton's corps changed hands, passing to the command of the US 9th Army. To Middleton it seemed as if Patton, ever concerned with his reputation, was stepping out of the whole sorry affair because he knew that the Americans would never be able to break the German paratroopers' resistance at Brest.

Six

It was in the same week that Ramcke decided to indulge in a little offensive action himself. He ordered *Leutnant* Erich Lepkowski, a twenty-seven-year-old East Prussian and a veteran of the 2nd Para Division who had worked himself up from the ranks after winning the German Cross in Gold twice and the Knight's Cross, to come to his headquarters. Together the two men went over to the large map of Brest which decorated one wall of the command post. Ramcke nodded to Lepowski's battalion commander, Major Ewald, who launched into a brief exposé of the situation.

'Near Huelgoat one hundred and thirty of our comrades are being held prisoner by the French partisans. Today the French sent us a demand to surrender the city. If we don't do so within forty-eight hours, they will be shot.'

Lepowski knew what Ramcke wanted of him. He had heard the rumours going round the Division that two escaped paras had reported that French partisans were treating their German captives with the utmost brutality. 'The Fifth Company is supposed to get them out?'

Ramcke nodded.

The briefing went on. 'The prisoners are in the village of Braspart, sixty kilometres behind the line. In all you will have to pass through six villages. How you get the men out is your business. You have complete freedom of action.'

'What weapons can I take?'

'You'll get an armoured car for your point and twin flak cannons mounted on a half track—that's all.'

Several hours later Lepkowski set off on his mission, with his forty-five volunteers from the 5th Company travelling in trucks driven by navy men. It was pitch dark, something for which Lepkowski was grateful. The Americans might well hear them, but undoubtedly they wouldn't take the vehicles for German ones. He was right. They hit the thinly held US line and broke through it before the alarmed GIs had time to collect their wits.

They raced up the road at top speed. They roared through the first village. If it contained the Maquis, they did not show themselves. On the other side Lepkowski ordered the armoured car to stop and detailed a couple of men to cut the nearest telephone wires. Then they were off again. They circled the next two villages. Again no resistance and on they went. Just as the sky started to turn white on the horizon, they reached the village of Braspart. They had reached their objective before dawn!

Hurriedly the paras clattered through the still-sleeping village. According to Lepkowski's information, the prisoners were supposed to be in the local school. Directing the search from the armoured car, he ordered the half-track to follow at a discreet distance, ready to fire at any sign of resistance.

Then came a shout followed by a rifle shot. The paras had hit the Maquis! The school was occupied all right, but not by German POWs. The partisans had been using it as a billet. A regular fire fight broke out. The paras flung their stick grenades. The school's only window flew out with a clatter of glass. Moments later the partisans started to come out, some half clad, their hands above their heads in surrender. One of them, who spoke some German, told the paras that their comrades were imprisoned in another school at the other end of the village. They pushed on. Lepkowski dropped from the turret of the armoured car and led the paras in their attack on the school. With a kick he thrust open the door and jumped back. He squeezed the trigger of his Schmeisser and could hear the slugs hitting the wooden partitions at the end of the corridor. He ran down the corridor followed by a handful of his men.

They found the prisoners in a large barnlike room which might once have been an assembly hall. They were a sorry sight. According to an eye-witness account 'many were without shoes, clad only in tattered civilian clothes. Others had been badly treated. All of them had had their personal effects stolen from them.'

Outside it was getting light and the Germans could see the locals peering at them from behind their shutters. Hastily the paras and their comrades scrambled into their vehicles, the former thrusting captured French weapons into the eager hands of the latter, and the convoy set off the way it had come. Now there was no time for skirting the villages on their road. Soon the *Amis* would be alarmed and would be after them with tanks and planes, so Lepkowski ordered his vehicles to race through the first village at top speed. According to an eye-witness account of the return journey, the paras were met with an ovation. The local civilians mistook them for their own troops heading for the front. 'They even threw flowers at us!' The same thing happened at the next village.

But then 'the warm greetings gave way to hot lead'. The partisans had finally woken up to what was going on and hastily threw up barricades all along the road. And there they waited for the paras to dismount and clear them away.

At the first obstacle, Lepkowski said, 'Dismount and work up both sides of the road!' The well-trained first platoon did as he ordered and under their protection the armoured car started pushing away the barrier, while the flak halftrack fired a steady stream of 20mm shells above it into the French positions. The Maquis fled, leaving fifteen prisoners to the not too tender mercies of the recently released paras.

The fantastic journey continued and it was not long before Lepkowski reached the safety of the German lines after an amazing journey of 120 kilometres behind the Allied front. Immediately he was ushered into the presence of General Ramcke. Silently, he tendered the young lieutenant two epaulettes with the star of a first lieutenant. Just as once he had been promoted from sergeant to lieutenant on the battlefield for a similar piece of heroism, he now honoured ex-corporal Lepkowski in the same way.

*   *   *

But Lepkowski's amazing luck, which had made him one of the most decorated men in the paras and had seen him safely through Crete and Russia, now ran out. Emboldened by the success of the rescue mission, Ramcke decided to use his battalion, under the command of Major Ewald, to break the ring around the fortress, now completely cut off from the nearest German troops, some 400 miles away.[1] He ordered a limited counter-attack, with Lepkowski's 5th Company having the point yet once again.

The attack started out well and the paras pushed forward with their *élan*. Erich Kuby, who saw them go, thought that 'for the first time in this war I saw men to whom one could safely apply the old lie "nothing is too good for the German soldier". They lived like princes and just like fat geese they were given excellent food to prepare them for an early death.' They took the complicated complex of ruins at the edge of the city and reached the northern boundary of St Pierre, pushing all before them. Then they struck the main US line. The Americans alerted their artillery, and the advance came to an abrupt halt.

Lepkowski dropped to the ground. 'We need reinforcements, if we're going to break through,' he panted and turned to one of his corporals. 'Heimann, let's have a go.' Heimann contented himself with a nod and in the next instant the two were racing madly across the pitted ground. Heimann was hit first—a gaping wound in the small of his back—and was dead before he struck the ground. Then it was Lepkowski's turn. A shell fragment hit him and he was sent flying. *Oberleutnant* Lepkowski's war was over for good.[2]

[1] There was some loose link with Germany via plane and fast motor boats and although French historians do not like to go into the subject, there were probably a number of Frenchmen working for the Germans behind the Allied lines who crossed back and forth with messages.

[2] His body was recovered and he was laid among a group of dead paras. A friend, Dr Marquard, spotted the corpse and established that Lepkowski was not dead after all. For five days he remained unconscious and was still a sick man when the Americans captured him. Finally, a year later, an American doctor in the USA opened up his chest and found that a piece of shrapnel had penetrated the left chamber of the heart. It was removed after a very complicated operation and Lepkowski was repatriated as a 60 per cent cripple. But he lived on to become an officer in the West German Army and the world record holder in parachute jumping. Today, at fifty-three, he is a Colonel and, as the author can testify, still a vigorous and bold soldier.

Seven

On 13 September, 1944, Middleton, who had a high regard for Ramcke's fighting ability by now (after the war he testified that 'of the twelve German generals that fell into the hands of my troops during the war, he was the most outstanding soldier'), decided to ask Ramcke to surrender, and wrote as follows to his opponent:

> As always in war the situation has reached a state where a commander cannot justify further bloodshed and the sacrifice of his soldiers' lives. We have discussed the situation of the German garrison with officers and men who fought bravely but who are now our prisoners. They are all convinced that the military situation is hopeless and that nothing can be gained by a continuation of the battle. We believe, therefore, that the German garrison of Brest has no justifiable ground for further action. Your soldiers have fought well. About 10,000 men are now our POWs. You know your own losses. In addition the supplies you need are gone and your troops are trapped in a narrow area. You have done your duty and served your country well.
>
> Accordingly, we ask you as one professional to another to end the unequal battle. We hope that you, as an old and experienced soldier, who has served honourably and has already done his duty will give this suggestion favourable consideration.
>
> Signed Troy H. Middleton[1]

Ramcke answered the very same day.

> To General Troy H. Middleton.
> I reject your suggestion.
> Ramcke.

[1] The original was in German. Author's translation.

The general meant to keep his promise to Hitler to defend the fort to the last. So Middleton published the letters so that his men would know that it was not *his* fault that the carnage still went on, adding the angry exhortation: *'Now take the Germans apart!'*

The men of VIII Corps needed no urging. The attack on Brest had taken far too long and they were sick of the whole bloody business. On the Crozon Peninsula, the Division launched a fierce attack against the German positions. At the village of St Eflez, they ran into heavy opposition and one by one the officers of the lead company were hit. By late afternoon the only senior man left was Tech Sergeant Charles Ballance, who took over what was left of his company and indeed what was left of the whole 3rd Battalion. But the Americans still pushed on. The 8th's running mate, the 29th Division, was throwing all its weight against the vital Fort Keranroux. It, too, suffered heavy losses in officers, but again a sergeant took over. Staff Sergeant Sherwood Hallman leaped over a hedgerow and ran towards the Germans. Firing from the hip, he burst in among the Germans, his men supporting him with grenades. The defenders reeled back as Hallman plunged on and his squad burst among them. The short battle was brutal and bloody. When it was over seventy-five of the surviving Germans surrendered.[2]

Now Middleton's men took on the Fort from both ground and air. While the dive-bombers roared in among the smoke, the great eight-inch guns pounded the place. Two infantry companies used the smoke as cover and raced for the Fort. For the loss of fifteen men, the GIs reached the main gate and ran inside into the battered courtyard. When it was all over they had rounded up a hundred Germans, some of whom did not even know that the Americans were within striking distance of the fortification. By dusk Fort Keranroux had fallen.

The next stronghold, Fort Montbarey, was a more difficult proposition. A typical old Vauban fortress, it had earth-filled masonry walls some twenty-five feet thick and was garrisoned by 150 German soldiers, armed with 20mm guns and protected by extensive minefields. A very tough nut to crack indeed, thought Colonel Winston, VIII Corps engineer. Then he had a

2 Sergeant Hallman was awarded the Medal of Honor.

brainwave. He requested British aid—the 'funnies'.[3] Thus the British made their first appearance in the battle, in the shape of the flame-throwing Crocodiles of the 141st Regiment of the Royal Armoured Corps.

In the second week of September, US engineers started to clear a path through the minefields for the first British tanks. Under the cover of an artillery bombardment, well laced with smoke shells, the first four Crocodiles waddled towards their objective, towing their fuel carts behind them. It was just after dawn and the four squat iron monsters stood out clearly against the sky, but the British were undaunted. They moved on in single file in spite of the fact that they were sitting ducks. In typically British fashion, the American observers thought, they were treating the whole thing in their usual nonchalant fashion.

Then came a violent explosion and the first tank lurched to a halt. It had run over a mine! The US engineers had not done their job too well. The crew baled out and doubled to the rear, leaving the smoking vehicle to be hauled away later. The other three rattled on at ten miles an hour. Then it happened again. Another Crocodile edged too far off the cleared path and ran into the minefield. In a flash of violent yellow flame, which erupted directly below it, it lurched to one side, flipping a severed track behind it. This time the crew did not get out. The remaining two rumbled on. The enemy spotted them and shells began tearing up the ground all around them. The British gunners, sweating in the interior of their vehicles, heavy with the smell of diesel, pressed their foreheads against the telescopes, watching their target grow ever larger.[4]

Now the two commanders prepared to fire. They rapped out their orders in a crisp fashion. 'Traverse left—anti-tank position —range one zero, fifty yards!' The gunners adjusted their range drums. And then, while the commander of the leading tank watched in horrified fascination, there was a spurt of flame

[3] Prior to D-Day the Americans had scorned the whole range of peculiar armoured vehicles which Montgomery's brother-in-law, General Hobart, had built at Churchill's command. They nicknamed the vehicles, designed specifically to deal with all sorts of obstacles, 'the funnies'. But as the campaign progressed, they were often only too glad to avail themselves of them.

[4] Unlike US tanks, British tanks were not fitted with air conditioning.

from the fort and coming towards him, curving slightly upwards, was the solid shot of an armour-piercing shell. Instants later came the clang of steel on the turret. 'Like the knell of doom', one of the survivors recalled later. A blast of flame swept into the tank, knocking the breath out of the crew. For a moment the men were too dazed to do anything. Then they reacted. 'Let's get out of here!' one cried and began to fight his way out of the blood-stained shambles of severed cables and smashed armour. They clambered out of the burning wreck and scrambled frantically for cover, German machine-gun bullets whizzing around them. The attack was called off.

But the tankmen were willing to 'have another go', as they told the Americans. The next day they moved forward once again, this time covered by thick clouds of white chemical smoke. Luck was with them. All four tanks reached the moat surrounding the walls of the Fort successfully and soon were in action with their terrible weapon. Long streams of blue-red flames shot from the nozzles of the 'cannon', as they clattered up and down the moat. Aperture after aperture was 'flamed' by their deadly fire.

Now, under British covering fire, the US engineers rushed forward. Working feverishly against time, they placed their charges —over 2,500 pounds of explosive—at the base of the wall. The job was done in a matter of minutes, but the engineers did not wait to admire their work. Supporting their wounded, they ran back the way they had come. Moments later the charges went off, showering the engineers squatting in the nearest ditches with dirt and chunks of concrete. The first breach in the wall had been opened.

While the British Crocodiles and the engineers had been busy, other US troops had not been idle. They had worked their way (again under the cover of Crocodiles) to within 200 yards of the Fort's main gate. Now they too joined in the action with their tank destroyers and 105mm cannon. At point-blank range, they could not miss. Every shot hit home and within a matter of minutes the main gate had been blasted away and a second breach had been opened.

The infantry swept forward. At the double they charged over the shattered wreckage of the gate and through the hole in the wall. A few German paras staggered out into the littered courtyard to meet them. Here and there a soldier tried to fight it out but was shot down mercilessly. They gave up in a matter of minutes and Fort Montbarey was American at the cost of eighty casualties. Colonel Winston's idea had paid dividends. As the weary GIs hauled up the Stars and Stripes flag, fresh troops started to push forward to the city of Brest itself.

*   *   *

The capture of Fort Montbarey was the beginning of the end, but there were still three days of hard fighting ahead of the American divisions. Now the German command was divided into two parts: the eastern sector commanded by Colonel Erich Pietzonka, a paratrooper; and the western one under the command of the former fortress commandant (before Ramcke had taken over that post himself), Colonel von der Mosel.

Captured documents had pinpointed the defences of Colonel Pietzonka's command and the 2nd Division's artillery was able to bombard them with deadly accuracy. But Pietzonka was of the same metal as his Divisional Commander and in spite of the terrible bombardment at close range, he stuck to his positions. Slowly the hospital bunkers began to fill with the dying bodies of the young paras who formed the core of his defence. Even Erich Kuby, who felt the whole defence of Brest was senseless, noted in his diary that day, 'They are indeed a different race than we are'. (He meant the other troops.) The 7th Parachute Regiment bled to death in the shattered streets of the old port.

The bunkers filled up at an ever-increasing rate. In the darkness, lit only by flickering emergency lighting, the 2nd's divisional surgeons operated against time, sawing, cutting, stitching and passing on to the next pitiful victim, stretched out stark naked and dirty on the bloodstained tables.

Now Pietzonka knew that the end was close. Leaving his CP he took Ramcke to one side so that no one could hear their whispered conversation. The curious observers noted that Ramcke's face hardened at first, then he nodded. Thereafter Ramcke disappeared.[5]

[5] With the surrender of Brest, Colonel W. Shambora, the US Army Surgeon, faced an unprecedented situation. A survey revealed that there were 5,902 wounded in Brest and 1,900 outside, all packed together in deplorable conditions in underground bunkers, lacking light, ventilation and medical aid.

Outside the American artillery was giving direct support to the attacking GIs, firing at the German-held houses and strongpoints at point-blank range over open sights. The GIs swept through the ancient eighteenth century sewers and an unguarded railway tunnel, somewhat fearfully following the patrol which had stumbled into this unexpected windfall. Thus they penetrated the inner city.

The fight for the road to the beaches began. Shortly after noon the leading patrols were pressing hard at the heels of the retreating paras when a German delegation appeared, carrying white flags. Cautiously the GIs approached them, weapons held at the ready. On the whole the paras were reputed to be fair fighters, but they had been known to use such tricks to lure unsuspecting or green American troops into the open. But this time the white flags were genuine.

Even then, as Erich Kuby recalls, there were those among the paras who were not ready to give up. He was present as a parachute major turned from the periscope through which he was observing the shattered battlefield and called down: 'They're coming back (the Germans attempting to negotiate the surrender). Let's hope the shooting's going to start again.'

But the blood-thirsty major was in for a disappointment. As the four para officers who had been dealing with the Americans crossed their lines and he asked: 'Are we going to fight on?', one of them shook his head and answered, 'No, old boy'.

Half an hour later US Colonel Chester Hirschfelder received Colonel Pietzonka's pistol as a token of surrender. The 7th Para Regiment had had enough.

That afternoon, the paratroopers surrendered the eastern sector of Brest, formally relinquishing control in a centrally located square called, appropriately enough, *Place du President Wilson*. There while the GIs, ragged and weary from the days of fighting in the rubble, watched in amazement, nearly 10,000 German prisoners, their uniforms clean and their faces freshly shaven, marched in formation into captivity.[6]

---

[6] As Kuby recalls, the officers even 'had their cases carried for them by common soldiers'. Obviously they were going to play their role of superior beings as long as they could get away with it. When, however, a German private stood stiffly to attention for a US officer, he was told to 'stop that business. *We* have no time for those Prussian inventions.'

But if General Middleton was overjoyed by the news of the mass surrender, he was still worried by one thing: the US 2nd Division had failed to capture Ramcke. Now the question was uppermost in his mind—where was he? And did he plan to surrender, when he was found, like his subordinate, Colonel Peitzonka?

He was soon to find out where Ramcke had gone. Intensive and rapid grilling of the POWs by 2nd Division intelligence men revealed that Ramcke had left the mainland, fleeing with a handful of paratroopers across to the Crozon peninsula. When he heard the news, Middleton sighed. Wearily he ordered that an attack should be launched on Crozon.

*   *   *

We do not know what went through the head of *General der Fallschirmtruppe* Ramcke's head on that last day of the battle for Brest. His book on his wartime experiences has little time for reflections. Did he think of suicide? Did he reflect on his promise to Hitler which committed him to fight to the end? Or did the hard-boiled soldier, who had seen so many battles and suffered so much for his Fatherland, weaken in the end and sense for the very first time the fear which had overcome so many of his men? We do not know.

But on that last day, when the Allies were already over the border of his Fatherland and he had fought the Americans in this sideshow for nearly three months, he sat a long time in the gloom of the bunker and thought about what he must do now.

In years to come he would join radical political parties, give bitter provocative speeches and eventually bring about the downfall of a well-known democratic politician;[7] but all the energetic activity, the venomous hatred of democracy in all shapes and forms, the dislike of the new 'soft' democratic Germany of the post-war years could not erase the shame of what he had to do.

He pulled himself out of his reverie and hurried to the weapon

[7] In 1963 Ramcke was the first to accuse Eugen Gerstenmaier, President of the German Parliament, of abusing funds. The charge didn't stick then but six months after the General's death it did and Gerstenmaier had to resign. Even in death, Ramcke was as aggressive and vindictive as he had always been.

pit where his last 75mm gun was located. It was his last remaining gun and it had one last shell. Surprised at the appearance of their commander, the layers sprang to attention and reported in German Army fashion: 'Reporting obediently—one shell left, *Herr General*!'

Ramcke raised his cane to his cap in acknowledgement and said, 'Let me get down there'.

He pushed aside the gun layer, knelt and peered through the telescope. Satisfied, he ordered, 'Load!'

The loader did as he was ordered and the shell clanged home into the breech. Ramcke turned to the sight, left knee raised, right knee bent. Carefully he took aim at the tiny khaki figures stumbling through the ruins outside. Then he pulled the firing lever. The empty shellcase clattered on to the concrete floor of the bunker. The last shell of the last cannon had been expended.

Ramcke shrugged slightly, then he rose, dusted his knees and issued a few last orders. They were the last he was ever to give. His military career, which had taken him from ship's boy to the most decorated man in the German paratroops, was over.

Squatting in a hole in the dunes outside the Ramcke bunker, young Lieutenant Durban of I Company, 13th Infantry was suddenly alerted by one of his men crouched in the next hole crying: 'Sir, have a look at that!' Durban followed the direction of the man's gaze.

A handful of German paras, their hands raised in the air, were advancing on them bearing a dirty piece of white cloth.

'Hell, they're surrendering!' someone said.

Quickly Durban wound up his discussions with the paras. Ramcke was willing to surrender if the Americans sent a high enough ranking officer. He passed the word back speedily. The CO of the 13th Infantry, Colonel Griffin, contacted General Canham, assistant commander of the 8th Division, and together the two officers arrived at the front to accept Ramcke's surrender.

Accompanied by a handful of GIs from I Company, they descended the seventy-five-foot shaft to the para's underground HQ. There Ramcke was waiting for them, dressed smartly in a hip-length coat with the Knight's Cross of the Iron Cross, complete with oak leaves and diamonds, dangling from his throat, a leather-bound stick in his hand.

Arrogantly he listened to the Americans' terms, then he snapped through the interpreter: 'Let me see your credentials?'

Canham flushed. For a moment he was at a loss for words. Then he saw the victors—the grubby, unshaven men of I Company—standing in the doorway. 'These,' he announced with a dramatic wave of his hand in their direction, 'are my credentials!'

Silence descended on the bloody heap of rubble that had once been the great port of Brest. The survivors of those GIs who had first approached the place in such drunken confidence nearly three months before squatted in their pup tents on the littered beach and tried to warm themselves in the thin rays of the autumn sun. A few went naked into the grey waters of the Atlantic, as if they wanted to wash away the memory of the 10,000 of their comrades who had been killed and wounded. But not many. The battle for Brest had been too long and they were numb.[8]

As for the surviving 'Hunters from the Sky'—some 5,000 of them—they marched into the cages, but they were fated to see their 'Papa' Ramcke one more time before he disappeared behind bars for seven years.

After meeting Middleton and being told that he was welcome to go hunting with him, if he, Ramcke, ever came to the States as a free man, Ramcke asked if he could speak to the surviving paras. Surprisingly enough his wish was granted and, defiant and obstinate to the last, he told them, 'The battle for Brest was hard. Many of you must have asked what's the use. But every bomb, every shell and every burst of machine-gun fire directed against us was one less for the homeland.

'We had to obey as soldiers. When you have to make the bitter trip into the prisoner of war camp, you can do so with raised head, proud in the knowledge that you have done your duty as soldiers. If in enemy territory you are faced—contrary to international law—with working for the enemy against the German People, you know what you must do... At this

---

[8] It was to take nearly three months before the formations used at Brest were ready for serious combat again.

moment we must think of our loved ones at home. God protect our people and country, *which we greet with our last Sieg Heil!'*

While the American guards looked on, the response rang out from 5,000 throats, 'SIEG HEIL . . . SIEG HEIL . . . SIEG HEIL . . .'

Hastily hustled into a jeep, Ramcke was followed by repeated cries of *VATER RAMCKE . . . VATER RAMCKE* and they continued till long after he had vanished from their midst for ever.[9]

[9] Ramcke proved a thorn in the flesh of both the American and French authorities. On New Year's Eve, 1945, he broke out of a US POW Camp at Clinton Camp, Mississippi and spent the day in Jackson until he returned to the camp of his own accord. A few years later he broke out of France, returning to his own country probably with the able assistance of ex-paras. The German government, fearful of trouble with the French, forced him to return to stand trial, at which his former enemies at Brest, Generals Middleton, Gerhardt and Stroh, gave testimony on his behalf. He returned to Germany in 1951.

Section Three

To the Bitter End

'You won't find any reserves, Student!'
General Jodl to Student, April 1945

1944-1945—The Last Drop

'The Führer has ordered a great offensive. Within the framework of this attack, there will be a para drop!'
General Student to Baron von der Heydte, 8 December 1944

One

1944 had seen General Student's parachute formations develop into an army of ten divisions, fighting on all the fronts of the shrinking Nazi Reich. In September, Hitler's HQ had called Student in Berlin and ordered him to form a parachute army— the 1st Para Army.

Two weeks later Student himself had seen active service again —after three years on non-combatant duties—at Arnhem. On the afternoon of 17 September, he was at his cottage HQ in Vught, Holland when, as he recalls himself, 'About noon I was disturbed at my desk by a roaring in the air of such mounting intensity that I left my study and went on the balcony. Wherever I looked I saw aircraft; troop carriers and large aircraft towing gliders. An immense stream passed low over the house. I was greatly impressed but during these minutes I did not think of the danger of the situation.' Turning to his Chief-of-Staff, he said enviously, 'Oh, I wish that I had ever had such a powerful means at my disposal!'

The wheel had come the full circle since the day when he had planned and carried out the great landing on Rotterdam four years earlier.

After helping to fight against the 101st Airborne Division, Student toyed with the idea of a great two division German surprise attack on the Allies which would send them reeling back the way they had come. But in the winter of 1944, that grey season of defeat after defeat, with the enemy on Germany's frontiers to both east and west, that idea seemed nothing but a vain dream.

Then overnight the whole situation changed radically. Student was informed of Hitler's 'last gamble'—the Führer's dramatic attempt to change the whole situation in the West by one last great offensive, which would split the Anglo-American armies and throw them back to the Channel. By this means, Hitler hoped to relieve the Allied pressure and prepare the ground for a negotiated peace with the West which would be far more favourable than the harsh 'unconditional surrender' terms which were presently all they had to offer. And within the framework of this offensive, Hitler wanted to include a parachute operation!

In the first week of December Student called one of his most experienced officers to his office to impart to him the great secret —Colonel Friedrich August, Baron von der Heydte. Von der Heydte had come a long way since his first combat drop in Crete. He had fought in Russia, Italy, North Africa and latterly in France, where he had escaped capture by the skin of his teeth. Now, with his arm strapped tightly to his chest, the result of an air crash in Italy, he was the Commandant of the Para Training School, where the 3,000 men—out of a total 130,000 paras—received real jump training.

But von der Heydte was not Student's favourite officer because of his proven military ability alone. Student knew that the Baron was an intellectual, who had begun his career as an assistant professor of law at Berlin University. Thereafter he had studied in Austria, France and Italy, being offered a $16,000 Carnegie scholarship for the study of international law at Columbia University in 1935. This scion of a long line of Catholic Bavarian aristocrats had turned it down to join the 15th Cavalry Regiment, a unit usually regarded as being dominated by aristocratic Catholic officers like himself. But in spite of his somewhat staid background, the Baron was a bold aggressive officer, ideal for the unusual mission which Hitler had allotted him.

Student, who had been inactive since Arnhem, greeted von der Heydte enthusiastically with the words, 'The Fuhrer has ordered a great offensive. Within the framework of this attack, there will be a para drop. You, my dear Heydte, will have the task of selecting and leading the para group.' Von der Heydte was naturally flattered that he had been selected for the job, more especially as he had felt himself under suspicion ever since the generals' plot to assassinate Hitler in July, 1944. His own cousin, Colonel von Stauffenberg, had been the man who had planted the bomb and in the spring of that year, Rommel when visiting his unit had asked: 'Are you sure of your regiment?'

'Absolutely,' von der Heydte had replied.

Rommel had nodded and remarked somewhat mysteriously: 'We want a lot of units like yours.'

Later, after the generals' plot had been uncovered, von der Heydte had realized who the 'we' were—the assassins. Now he realized that he must be off the list of suspects. All the same the magnitude of his new and mysterious task worried him. He asked for further details.

For once the usually outspoken General Student was devious. He was not even prepared to tell von der Heydte whether his select unit would be employed on the western or eastern front, though the Baron guessed it would probably be the latter. However, he did tell him that he would not be using his old regiment —the 6th. For reasons of secrecy the 6th would remain where it was, in case its move would tip off the Allies.

Von der Heydte's face revealed his disappointment but Student went on to assure him that he would be given the best—one hundred well trained parachutists, all select and experienced men, from every battalion of the 1st Parachute Army to form his own battle group. He would, however, be allowed to pick his own platoon and company commanders. And with that same consolation he had to be satisfied.

Von der Heydte went to work swiftly. That same evening, he sketched out his organizational plan and swearing his own officers to secrecy he initiated them into the vague details of the new *Kampfgruppe*.[1] Late that night he fell into his bunk and dropped off into an uneasy sleep, his mind full of confused details and half-formed plans.

He woke early and went out to meet the drafts sent to him by the various parachute battalions. As is the case with armies the world over, the COs requested by Student to send von der Heydte their best men had done the exact opposite—they had drafted him their dead-beats and trouble-makers. As the Baron commented later, 'Never during my entire career had I been in command of a unit with less fighting spirit.' Of the 1,200 men on parade, only 200-odd were veterans of Crete and had the requisite parachute experience. *Indeed the great majority of them had never even jumped before!*

But von der Heydte was not easily daunted. He set to work to knock his hybrid force into shape for the still somewhat

[1] Battle group.

confused mission. Four days later he had formed four para companies, a signal section, one company of heavy machine-guns, a section of heavy mortars and a pioneer company. Thereafter he moved his battlegroup to the North German training area of Sennelager close to the transport squadron which was going to drop them over their still unknown objective. But even here his problems did not end. The CO of the camp had no room in his barracks, which were bursting at the seams. In despair, von der Heydte telephoned the Chief-of-Staff of the Munster Air Region, the man responsible for all *Luftwaffe* personnel in the area. Again his request for accommodation for himself and his 1,200 men was turned down with the curt statement: 'If this sort of thing goes on, anybody could turn up.'

Thus at four o'clock on a freezing December morning, von der Heydte and his command were left, standing shivering in the cobbled, blacked-out street of the little Westphalian town of Oerlinghausen, no one apparently concerned with the welfare of the men who were designed to play such a vital role in Hitler's forthcoming offensive.[2]

But although the young para commander eventually found warm beds for his men that night, his problems were still not over. Major Erdmann, whom he had known since the drop on Crete, and who now commanded the so-called 'Stalingrad Squadron' of transport planes, was an experienced pilot, but his crews who were to drop von der Heydte's men from their 120 Junkers 52s were completely inexperienced. For the most part they had come directly from the training schools and had never dropped paratroopers—especially at night, as was to be the case with *Kampfgruppe von der Heydte*. Erdmann was horrified when the Baron told him what little he knew of the forthcoming operation. But both commanders knew they had to accept orders without question and, in spite of their grave doubts, continued with their planning.

On 13 December, 1944, both of them were summoned to the HQ of the *Luftwaffe* C-in-C, 'Air Fleet West'. There, for the first time, they were informed of their objective: 'The proposed offensive will start from the Eifel and be directed on Antwerp.

---

[2] In the end von der Heydte found a former regimental comrade, the local chemist, who knocked up his fellow citizens to find accommodation for the freezing paratroopers.

It will be carried out by Model's Army Group and the parachute force will be under the orders of that headquarters.'

In the end both Erdmann and von der Heydte left in disgust, driving off to see Field-Marshal Model, who had set up his HQ for the forthcoming offensive in the little town of Euskirchen. They arrived late on the night of 14 December, to be received by Model's Chief-of-Staff, General Krebs who, like his master, affected a monocle.

Krebs filled them in. The parachute force was to help clear the way for the 6th SS Panzer Army, one of the three involved in the new offensive. Thereafter it was to block the road along which the advance of the 6th SS Panzer, commanded by the veteran SS man, Sepp Dietrich, might be threatened by the sudden appearance of new American units.

Again both von der Heydte and Erdmann objected that they were not ready. Krebs, a smooth staff officer who had served as German military attaché in Moscow and was soon to commit suicide in Hitler's Berlin bunker, shrugged and led them to see Model.

Model, one of the most competent and aggressive of Hitler's marshals, who was also to shoot himself in four months' time, was roused from his sleep to see them. He was clearly terribly overworked and at the end of his tether, but he had not lost his old habits of precision. After listening to the Baron's protests, he asked bluntly: 'Do you give the parachute force a 10 per cent chance of success?'

'Yes.'

'Then it is necessary to make the attempt, since the entire offensive has no more than a 10 per cent chance of success. It must be done, since this offensive is the last remaining chance to conclude the war favourably. If we do not make the most of that 10 per cent chance, Germany will be faced with certain defeat.'

Von der Heydte gave way to the unassailable logic of that statement and tamely accepted his assignment to Dietrich's 6th Panzer Army, although he disliked the former First World War sergeant-major and Munich bully-boy intensely. He left almost immediately to report to the latter.

The Baron found his new chief at his HQ at the medieval

Eifel township of Muenstereifel, reputedly one of Hitler's favourite places. (In 1940 his HQ had been located close by.)

The stocky SS man, who had built up the *Waffen SS* from one
regiment to a private army of some twenty-odd divisions, gave
off a faint odour of alcohol. But it was not the smell of drink
alone which made his fellow Bavarian so offensive to the aristo-
cratic paratrooper; it was Dietrich's contemptuous attitude.

His first words as von der Heydte walked in were, 'What can
you paratroopers do, anyway?'

'Give me the mission, General, and then I can evaluate the
feasibility,' the Baron replied.

'All right,' Dietrich said, slapping a map on his desk. 'Take
the places marked X.'

Von der Heydte countered with a request for information
about the American reserves. Angrily Dietrich answered, 'I am
not a prophet! You will learn earlier than I what forces the
Americans will employ against you. Besides, behind their lines
there are only Jewish hoodlums and bank managers.'

The two commanders then haggled with General Fritz
Kraemer, Dietrich's chief-of-staff. In the end, however, they
established von der Heydte's objective—he was to drop at the
crossroads near Baraque Michel, an isolated wind-swept plateau
north of the little border town of Malmédy.

'You will go there and make confusion,' Dietrich said.

Again Kraemer interrupted his chief, whom he did not greatly
respect: 'It's not von der Heydte who is to make the confusion,'
he explained. 'You have mixed it up with Skorzeny's Operation
Greif.'[3]

Dietrich grunted and allowed von der Heydte to fix a boundary between himself and Skorzeny. In addition, he grudgingly
granted the paratroopers a guide in the shape of an observer
from the 12th SS Panzer Division, who would jump with von
der Heydte, carrying a radio. But when the Baron asked for
carrier pigeons in case the radio were broken, Dietrich exploded
angrily: '*Pigeons!* Don't be stupid!... Pigeons! I'm leading my
whole damn army without pigeons. You should be able to lead
one *kampfgruppe* without a damn menagerie!'

[3] Skorzeny was to infiltrate his Panzer Brigade 150, made up in part
of captured US vehicles with crews dressed in American uniforms,
through the US lines to the south of Malmédy.

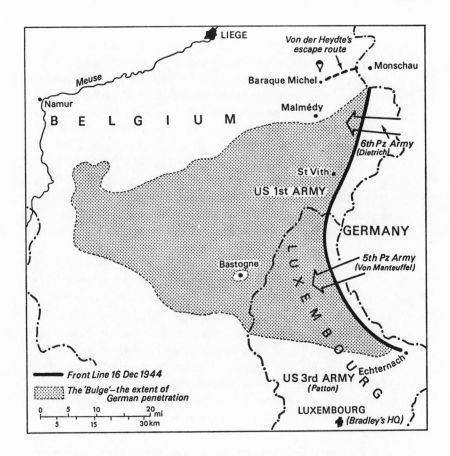

On this unpleasant note the interview ended. But worse was to come for this ill-fated last drop of the 'Hunters from the Sky', on which the 'Father of the *Fallschirmjaeger*', General Kurt Student, had set such great hopes.

*   *   *

Back at Oerlingshausen, von der Heydte, with only twenty-four hours to set his objectives and orientate his men, was pleased to find that Student had personally sent him a captured Russian parachute, the only one of its kind in German hands. It was triangular in shape, without the usual parachute vent at the top. Its design was apparently calculated to reduce the usual oscillations which took place during a drop so that the parachutist would have little problem in controlling his chute. For von der

Heydte it came as a godsend; but he did not let his pleasure at the gift blind him to the enormity of his task. His men, mostly conscripts and half-grown boys, were expected to jump, some for the first time, from transports flown by totally inexperienced crews under the worst possible conditions—*at night!* If that were not bad enough, he lacked exact details of the terrain into which they were to drop. In vain he hunted through the 6th Panzer Army's files for information about the ground, which he knew from his map was mainly marsh and forest. He drew a blank. The fifteen miles that separated Baraque Michel from the existing front might well have been completely unexplored country; no one could tell him a thing about what type of opposition he might meet there. For all he knew he might come down right in the middle of an *Ami* position.[4]

It was, therefore, with a sense of relief that he accepted General Kraemer's telephone call on 16 December informing him that 'the offensive has not progressed as rapidly as expected in our sector. We have reached only a small portion of our objectives. The enemy is still resisting forward of Elsenborn Camp in anticipation of reinforcements arriving from the north.' Kraemer gave von der Heydte a moment to absorb the new situation, then added, 'You will therefore drop before dawn tomorrow morning. Hold on as long as possible—two days at a minimum—and do as much damage as you can to the reinforcements.'[5]

Now von der Heydte knew there was no turning back—for better or worse the mission was on.[6]

The 1,200 'Hunters from the Sky' assembled at their fields just outside Paderborn and Lippspringe on the evening of 16 December, the first day of the great offensive in the far-off Belgian Ardennes. A priest was brought from Oerlinghausen to bless the men and their ancient three-engined Junkers 52nd, the

---

[4] As the area was an old German Army training ground (today the Belgian Army uses it for the same purpose), it was conceivable that the Americans might be using the terrain for the training of their own troops on the 'Ghost Front'.

[5] Kraemer meant US reinforcements of course.

[6] On that same day Dietrich's HQ had sent a legal officer to von der Heydte's CP to enquire why he was delaying his operation and the latter was subjected to an interrogation which lasted till midnight.

trusted 'Auntie Jus'. One after another the pilots of the 'Stalingrad Squadron', which had gained its laurels supplying the surrounded German Army in the Russian city, took their cumbersome planes into the night sky to the accompaniment of the hoarse chorus of the paratroopers, singing their song: *Rot Scheint Die Sonne* ('Red Shines the Sun') with its fatalistic text:

'When Germany is in danger there is only one
  thing for us:
To fight, to conquer and assume we shall die.
From our aircraft, my friend, there is no return!'

And while they formed up in the starless night sky, an Allied agent far behind the German lines tapped out the following message to his listeners in US Military Intelligence: '15 Junkers-88 and 90 Junkers-52 to take off at 0145 Paderborn-Wahn. Destination ten miles south of Aachen. To return at 0530.'[7] Thus US Intelligence knew of von der Heydte's mission even before it had really started; all they lacked was exact knowledge of his objective.

Two hours passed. It was now about three in the morning on 17 December. Von der Heydte was making a last check of his chute and equipment when suddenly his plane rocked violently. They were passing low over the front and had been spotted by the waiting Allied anti-aircraft crews. On the German side of the line the guide searchlights snapped on. The inexperienced pilots, their planes easily visible because of their red and green flight-lights (which the pilots needed to avoid mid-air collisions) huddled together in a crude squadron formation. The flak grew heavier. The air was full of white and red tracer. Presently one of the Junkers to the rear of von der Heydte's plane seemed to stop in mid air as if held up by some invisible hand, then plummeted to the ground in a vivid orange dive. Von der Heydte's men were shaken. Of the ten enlisted men in his aircraft only two had ever jumped before. The remaining eight were not accustomed to the frightening chaos of an air-borne landing. He hid his feelings and scoured the ground for his landing signal

7 My own enquiries in the Ardennes area show that the Americans were much more active in slipping spies through the difficult terrain than the Germans in spite of the fact that the latter had recruited into their own forces some 7,000 men from the border area, which had belonged to Germany until 1919.

—a brilliant burning cross composed of three white lights and a red one pointing westwards.

A quarter of an hour later, he spotted it. They were exactly on time and target (von der Heydte's plane was probably the only one that was, but the Baron did not know that at the time).

At 3.15 precisely von der Heydte jumped, his men following in good order. The night was icy cold and there was a strong wind. Wind velocity on the ground was supposed to be twenty feet per second, according to the experts; in fact it was more than fifty feet per second!

A thick fir forest, typical of the area swung into sight. Then at the very last moment it slid away. Suddenly and unexpectedly there was the shock of impact. Von der Heydte scrambled out of his parachute and looked around for his men. They were very few and very frightened. By 3.50 he had collected four teenage privates, a young lieutenant and one sergeant with a twisted ankle. One hour later he had rounded up a further twenty. As dawn broke over the Hohe Venn Mountains, the highest and seemingly the coldest spot in Belgium, Baron von der Heydte realized that his mission had failed virtually before it had started.[8]

But the widely scattered drop, plus the 300 dummy parachutists which had been dispatched over a large area of the Ardennes, did encourage Allied commanders to believe that at least a division of German paras had dropped behind the front that icy December morning. (Student could have told them that there were no more than 3,000 trained paratroopers in the whole of the German Army at that particular moment). Coupled with the news of the arrest of several of Skorzeny's saboteurs who told their American interrogators that one of their tasks was the assassination of General Eisenhower himself,[9] the para drop

[8] Of the 106 pilots of the Stalingrad Squadron only thirty-five dropped their loads in the right place. The rest began scattering the paratroopers as soon as they spotted the Rhine at Bonn. Due to the galeforce wind even those who were dropped roughly in the target area suffered severe casualties.

[9] During the training of the Skorzeny force in Grafenwöhr, a young officer had come to the former to say that he knew the real purpose of their secret mission—to kill the American Supreme Commander. Skorzeny did not disillusion him and thus the rumour spread. But twenty-seven years later Skorzeny maintained he had had no such intention (in a letter to the author).

sent a wave of alarm sweeping through the Allied rearline areas.

An enormous anti-sabotage operation started, covering four countries and involving, according to General Bradley, 'half a million GIs playing cat and mouse with each other every time they met'. Ill-trained and worse armed French and Belgian troops were rushed up to guard rearline installations. British replacements were combed out of barracks and reinforcement units to man roadblocks and bridges; and at every crossroad, US MPs were stopping their fellow countrymen to ask them idiotic questions about local state history, football teams and filmstars' private lives in an attempt to uncover the paratroopers and saboteurs. Counter-intelligence even dreamed up phrases in English, such as 'vague Vera veered westwards' or 'Swiss cheese is obtained from the cashier', which they *knew* no German could pronounce faultlessly. Orders, reminiscent of the great British spy parachutist scare of 1940, were issued, to check every nun as a potential saboteur (for some reason the poor 'white swans' were suspect throughout the war) and details were given of how to examine the suspect's thighs and shoulders for the tell-tale red marks of a parachute harness.

But the great spy scare did not stop at the persons of harmless nuns. It reached right up to the top. Brigadier-General Bruce Clarke, the defender of the key road and rail centre of St Vith to the south of the dropping zone, was arrested and imprisoned by his own MPs for five hours. Protesting hotly and angrily, with thirty years of Army experience behind him to lend his words eloquence, Clarke was told by the grinning MPs, 'Don't make me laugh. You're one of them Nazi killers!' Finally he was released, but only after one of the MPs had had the nerve to ask, 'May I have your autograph, General?' General Clarke obliged!

General Bradley, Clarke's commander, fared little better. During the course of a visit to a subordinate, he was stopped time and again, although his olive-drab car bore the three stars of an army group commander, and was asked to prove his identity, 'the first time by identifying Springfield as the capital of Massachusetts (his interlocutor held out for Chicago); the second time by locating the football guard between the centre and tackle on a line scrimmage; the third time by naming the current spouse of a blonde named Betty Grable!'

As for the Supreme Commander himself, he was confined to his own HQ by the local provost marshal and was a virtual prisoner for three days. As his secretary Kay Summersby described those anxious days in her book, *Eisenhower was My Boss*, 'Security officers immediately turned headquarters into a virtual fortress. Barbed wire appeared. Several tanks moved in. The normal guard was doubled, trebled, quadrupled. The pass system became a strict matter of life and death instead of the old formality. The sound of a car exhaust was enough to halt work in every office, to start a flurry of telephone calls to our office to inquire if the boss was all right.' In the end it was all too much for Ike. He simply walked out of his office, snorting to Miss Summersby, 'Hell's fire, I'm going for a walk! If anyone wants to shoot me, he can go right ahead. *I've got to get out!*'

*   *   *

But while this unexpected result of the drop at Baraque Michel was taking place way behind the lines, what of von der Heydte and his small band of paratroopers, located in the vague no-man's land between the advancing 6th SS Panzer Army and General Hodges' battered 1st US Army, fighting desperately to hold the Germans?

As dawn broke on the morning of 17 December, the German paratroopers crouched in the ditches at the crossroads were startled by the sound of truck motors. Before they could go to ground, the first of a long convoy of American trucks, loaded with troops, came out of the mist. But the *Amis* did not fire. Instead they waved at the surprised Germans. Obviously the enemy took them for their own troops. When the first batch had passed, the paras took cover, but for the rest of that morning they were constantly on edge as convoy after convoy of the US 7th Armored Division, pulled out of the line in Holland, sped towards embattled St Vith. The watching Germans could do nothing to stop them and in the end von der Heydte withdrew from the crossroads with the 125 men now at his disposal. After marching two miles, he bumped into another group of paras who had been rallied by a war correspondent named von Kayser, who had once been an army officer. Thus reinforced, he halted his men at the edge of a marsh and while his men formed a perimeter, he sent out patrols into the surrounding countryside. They came back a little later with a dozen scared American service troops, whom von der Heydte released the following morning—before setting off once more—giving them the responsibility of looking after those of his men who were too sick or too weary to continue.

Naturally the released Americans returned to their own lines with hair-raising, highly coloured stories of the large body of German *élite* troops doing apparently exactly as they pleased behind American lines. They, too, helped to contribute to the general air of nervousness prevailing at the front, in spite of the fact that General Kenneth Strong, Eisenhower's Chief-of-Intelligence, had estimated by now that 'enemy parachutists have been dropped behind the lines in an area not yet clearly defined but including Verviers. Their strength is estimated to be about 1,500.'

But the British intelligence officer's accurate information was not believed by most of the US senior officers in the line; they still preferred to think that large numbers of German *Fallschirmjaeger* were at large behind their front.[10]

Thus, tired, hungry and depressed, totally unaware of the indirect success of their mission, von der Heydte's 300 paratroopers wandered up and down the wooded, inhospitable terrain, hemmed in by the steep-sided valleys of the Soor and Helle. Time and again von der Heydte sent out messengers in the directions of the German line. None of them returned. Only once in those three days when the lost unit tried to fight its way back to safety did they make contact with their own forces in the shape of a lone Junkers 88 which dropped '*Essenbomben*' (food containers). But the containers were a disappointment; they did not contain food. Instead the weary paras found damp cigarettes and bottles of cheap *Kognak*.

This discovery took the heart out of the exhausted men and von der Heydte realized that they were at the end of their tether. He knew he had only one duty—to get them back safely to their own lines. It was no use trying to execute his original mission.

10 Mr Calvin Boykin, who was in one of the 7th Armored Division convoys, said that he and his comrades felt they were being 'shadowed' by German planes the whole time and that there were constant 'airborne' alarms during the course of their long and freezing journey south-east.

His men were completely broken. They would never fight now. He decided to make a final attempt to break out of the trap.

At dawn on the morning of 21 December, 1944, the 300 paras started to move eastwards, their breath fogging the air, their jump-boots sinking deep into the snow which had now fallen. They forded the freezing River Helle at chest-height at a spot where a little stream called 'Good Luck'[11] flows into it and started to climb the heights on the other side.

The exhausted Germans should have realized that the Americans would have been holding the ideal position on the top of the height which covered the Eupen–Monschau road, the only metalled highway through the *Hohes Venn*, but they were too tired. All they sought was an end to the eternal plodding through the snowy glare of the hillsides and the hunger which gnawed at their guts. The first ragged volley of US small arms fire woke them to their danger. They staggered back, leaving a couple of their number to bleed to death on the snowy hillside.

In spite of his overwhelming fatigue, von der Heydte reacted. He ordered his men to withdraw and, once they were under the cover of a nearby fir forest, sent out patrols to attempt to find a way through the American-held heights. But it was in vain. The enemy seemed to be waiting for him at every exit, sometimes covered by a Sherman tank or an armoured car. The news broke von der Heydte's will to resist. Mistakenly believing that his starving force was faced by Americans commanded by General Maxwell Taylor, he wrote a note in English stating: 'We fought each other in Normandy near Carentan and from this time I know you as a chivalrous, gallant general. I am sending you back the prisoners I took. They fought gallantly too and I cannot care for them. (He referred to his remaining thirty US prisoners.) I am also sending you my wounded. I should greatly appreciate it if you would give them the medical treatment they need.'

That done, he left the note with the wounded and the American POWs and ordered his men to break up into groups of not more than three. Thus, he felt, they might have a chance of breaking out of the American trap. Now it was every man for himself.

Waiting till his men had finally moved out, he crossed the River Helle once more with his adjutant and his orderly, making

11 In French it is called *Ruisseau de petit Bonheur*.

for the picturesque little Eifel township of Monschau, the pre-war rendezvous of honeymoon couples, which he believed was now back in German hands. For hours the three men staggered on, breaking through the US lines, heading steadily eastwards, ragged, starving and shivering in the bitter wind. Once they bumped into a small group of *Fallschirmjaeger*. They wanted to join up with von der Heydte, believing that his superior experience would help them to escape captivity. The Baron waved them away wearily: 'Each man must try his own luck at getting through,' he muttered. They went and the three plodded on.

In the grey light of dawn the three came down from the heights and saw the jagged outline of Monschau's ruined castle below in the valley. Von der Heydte, who had not eaten since he had left Germany—save for his iron ration—croaked hoarsely: 'I'm going straight to Monschau.' The other two protested. They were in better shape; they wanted to go on. But the Baron, who feared that both his hands and feet were frozen, could go on no longer. He sent them on their way and staggered into the little town.

Painfully he knocked at the door of the first house. There was no answer save the dull echo of his knock. It was the same with the second house, a half-timbered structure perched on the side of the rocky hillside, which was typical of the area. But at the third house, he was lucky. The householder, a schoolteacher, guided him gently inside. Gratefully von der Heydte sank down on a chair in the warm kitchen. 'Paper and pen, please,' he asked.

While he laboriously wrote a few lines, the teacher's fourteen-year-old son examined his camouflaged paratroop gear in admiration. 'I'm in the Hitler Youth,' he said proudly. But the exhausted officer had no time for his admiration. For him the war was over. The Americans had not been thrown out of Monschau after all. 'Take it,' he gave the child the note, 'to the Americans. I'm surrendering.'

Then, closing his eyes with a sense of infinite relief, Baron Dr Friedrich August, Freiherr von der Heydte fell sound asleep. His war was over; the last drop had been an utter failure.[12]

[12] After interrogation von der Heydte was passed over to the war correspondents, to whom he was a great catch. Someone asked him (and his reply went round the world the following day): 'What do you think of Sepp Dietrich? Is he a great strategist?' Von der Heydte's reply was, *'He is a cur dog!'*

Two

But von der Heydte's ill-fated force was not the only one that General Student had in the last great offensive against the West. Indeed he had two full divisions—the 3rd and the 5th Parachute —participating in the attack. Both were virtually inexperienced, although they bore the names of formations which had had their share of combat experience in the last couple of years. But now, filled out with reinforcements culled from the rear echelons and *Luftwaffe* ground crews, they were poorly led and were to incur heavy casualties. (The 9th Parachute Regiment of the 3rd Division was pulled out of the line in January, 1945, with three-quarters of its number dead, wounded or missing.)[1]

The 3rd Parachute Division became bogged down in the northern sector of the battlefield almost immediately and for the month or so it was in the line it played a wholly defensive role. However, its running mate, the 5th, which came under the command of ex-gentleman jockey and aristocrat Baron von Manteuffel, one of Germany's most aggressive generals, fared better. But the 5th was flawed by internal difficulties. Its staff and regimental commanders were direct appointees of Student himself and for some reason they formed a clique against their first divisional commander, who found he had great difficulty in controlling his units in action. On 18 December, as the Division made somewhat slow progress westwards to the River Meuse, the primary objective of Manteuffel's 5th Panzer Army, the divisional commander was removed and replaced by Colonel Ludwig Heilmann. Almost immediately the clique within the Division, which felt it owed a personal loyalty to Student and

[1] Dr Bouck, formerly of the US 99th Division, recalls the 3rd Para advancing on his position in the first hours of the offensive, as if they were on parade; and ex-SS Colonel Jochen Peiper virtually took over the 9th Parachute Regiment twenty-four hours later when he found, to his disgust, that they were resting instead of attacking. 'It was as if the front had gone to sleep', he said later.

the *Luftwaffe* and not the Army command, formed against him as well. Heilmann was not deterred. He tried to put some iron into his new command and forced them to speed up their advance. Soon he discovered, for instance, that a primary reason for the slowness of his paratroopers was due to their habit of attacking every small village on their march route in order to have warm billets for the cold nights. He speedily discouraged them and warned his battalion officers that they should also avoid making frontal attacks on defended positions. Moodily they complied, but all the same he confessed to Field-Marshal Model, the overall commander of the offensive, that the 5th was only 'a class four outfit'.

The Field-Marshal replied that he would succeed in reaching his objectives due to the paratroopers' 'usual audacity'. Heilmann did not know whether Model, who was noted for his cynicism, was being sarcastic or whether he really believed the paratroopers were still the *élite* formation they had once been. At all events he drew the conclusion that he would gain no help in his difficult command problem from that quarter.

As a result he decided to rely on the 15th Parachute Regiment, the 5th Parachute Engineer Battalion and the attached 11th Assault Gun Brigade, which manned some thirty ponderous self-propelled cannon, as his main source of strength. Thus it was that with this force he fought the Division's greatest battle of the campaign—to prevent the little Belgian town, now surrounded by Manteuffel's troops, from being relieved by American armour from the south. The town was Bastogne, held by the battered survivors of the 'Screaming Eagles', the US 101st Airborne. The armour was the premier US armoured division—the 4th Armored, the apple-of-the-eye of no less a person than the commander of the 3rd US Army, General Patton.

On 18 December the 3rd Army Commander had been summoned to meet the Supreme Commander at the gloomy former French barracks of Verdun. There, under the threatening heights which had seen such slaughter in 1916, a depressed Eisenhower laid down his plans for meeting the surprise German breakthrough in the Ardennes.

But if Ike was depressed, Patton, always eager for action, was not. After Eisenhower had said that he wished Patton to counter-attack into the Germans' southern flank, he asked: 'George, when can you start?'

Patton's answer was typical of the man: 'As soon as you are through with me.'

Eisenhower frowned: 'What do you mean?'

According to Sir Kenneth Strong, who was present, some of the British officers sniggered at Patton's boldness and even his fellow Americans were uneasy at such apparent unrealism. After all, in order to attack, Patton would have to withdraw his 3rd Army from their line in the Saar, swing round in a ninety-degree arc and then move thousands of vehicles over narrow, snow-bound roads. It was a very tall order indeed. Patton did not seem to think so. 'I left my house in Nancy in perfect order before I came here.'[2]

Eisenhower's frown relaxed. 'When can you start?' he asked.

'The morning of 22 December,' Patton answered.

According to Patton's aide, Lieutenant-Colonel Codman, the reaction was 'electric'. In his account of the campaign he writes, 'There was a stir, a shuffling of feet as those present straightened up in their chairs. In some faces scepticism. But through the room the current of excitement leaped like flame.' That particular flame seemed to leave Eisenhower cold. He retorted, 'Don't be fatuous, George!'

'This has nothing to do with being fatuous, sir,' Patton answered. 'I've made my arrangements and my staff are working like beavers this very moment to shape them up.' He went on to explain his intentions, concluding with the words, 'But I'm determined to attack on the 22nd with what I've got because if I wait I'll lose surprise.'

'All right,' Eisenhower said, 'start your attack no earlier than the 22nd and no later than the 23rd. And remember the advance has to be methodical!'

Patton nodded. 'I'll be in Bastogne before Christmas,' he boasted confidently, happy to be given his head at last.

The division to which Patton gave the difficult job of realizing

---

[2] Patton's HQ at that time. Prior to leaving for Verdun, he had told his staff to expect two or three versions of the same phone call from him, so that they could put his contingency plans into operation immediately.

his proud boast was the *élite* 4th Armored, which was the only tank formation of the American Army in the Second World War to be given the presidential citation for its whirlwind exploits in the campaign in North-West Europe.[3] During its first week of fighting in France the Division had covered nearly 200 miles, developing a style of fighting and a cocky attitude all its own. Fast and furious, it was based on swift aggressive fire with the Division's tanks being used as 'weapons or terror'.

In essence the Division's front was limited to the width of the roads down which its Sherman tanks rumbled, following behind the reconnaissance elements who would keep on going until they ran into enemy fire. Then the armoured infantry would swing into action, pressing in their attack under artillery cover, either breaking the enemy front or flooding around it on both sides. No one in the 4th seemed to worry about flanks, for as Sergeant Klinga of the 8th Tank Battalion put it once when his unit was again 'resting' miles behind the enemy lines 'They've got us surrounded again, *the poor bastards!*' By December, 1944, however, the 4th was not the Division it had been in France. Sergeant Klinga, the speaker of those immortal lines, was dead, as were close on 6,000 other members of the Division. General Wood, the divisional commander, in spite of his habit of rolling naked in the snow, had to relinquish his post after ninety days of combat. Now, the Division was commanded by a new man, General Gaffey, a personal friend of Patton's. Like Brigadier-General Herbert Earnest, CO of Combat Command A, he was a stranger to the Division and was not readily accepted by the closely-knit 4th veterans. Thus, on the same day that Colonel von der Heydte surrendered and the 5th Parachute Division prepared to meet the American armour in its bold attempt to break through to Bastogne, the two divisions—the German and the American—resembled each other in an uncanny manner; both were veteran formations, filled out with inexperienced replacements, and led by commanders who were distrusted by the veterans.

At six o'clock on 22 December the twin commands of the 4th stood ready at their start line which stretched from the villages of Habay-la-Neuve east to Niedercolpach across the

[3] The only other division to receive the award was the 101st which the 4th hoped to relieve.

poor, shell-pitted main road from the south into Bastogne. Under normal circumstances one of the Division's Shermans would probably have been able to cover the distance to Bastogne in half an hour. But the nervous replacements did not know that it would take their outfit four days to reach the besieged town and that many of them would not live to see their destination.

The plan was to send Combat Command A and Combat Command B into the attack abreast of each other, with the former working its way up the main Arlon–Bastogne road while its running mate advanced along the similarly battered and mined secondary road. In essence the two armoured groups, 'A' commanded by General Earnest and 'B' by General Dager, would be advancing on parallel ridge lines.

At precisely one minute after six the tank commanders gave their signal to mount up. Earnest's CCA moved out in two task forces of battalion size behind A Troop of the 25th Cavalry Squadron. Visibility was still bad and the ground was snow-covered, but in spite of the terrain and the weather the tanks and the following armoured infantry made good progress until they ran into older demolitions carried out at the beginning of the offensive by their own troops.

General Earnest, who had commanded an independent task force during the campaign in Brittany and had not had much luck since, fumed. This, he knew, was the opportunity for him to make his name, especially as Patton was giving first priority to the relief of Bastogne. But there was nothing for it but to accept an alternative solution for the advance: he would converge with CCB on the main Arlon road and the two groups would form a single column.

The American tanks rolled on, but shortly after midday the lead outfit struck Heilmann's waiting paras, the reliable men of the 15th Regiment guarding the demolished bridges outside the little Belgian town of Martelange. The battle for the road to Bastogne had begun.

*   *   *

On the 22nd Colonel Heilmann's 5th Parachute Division was holding a line eighteen miles long! In light of the actual situation on the ground and the fact that the textbooks recommended that a division should not hold much more than half that number of miles against first class troops, which he knew the men of the 4th Armored were, he had decided to concentrate his strength to cover the most important points. One of these was Martelange, which sprawled in a series of terraces rising from the River Sure. Accordingly he had placed his 15th Regiment in the town (their HQ was at the village of Warnach two and a half miles to the north), covering it with a battery of self-propelled guns.

The paras held their fire until they could not miss. Then they hit the advancing 4th with all they had and the advance stopped abruptly. The Americans could not bring their heavy cannon to bear because of the nature of the terrain and the fighting became an infantryman's battle which continued all afternoon. When dusk fell, it was still raging. Both sides took heavy casualties but the loss of armoured infantrymen was especially grievous for the Americans, since without infantry the Shermans alone would be of little use. After they had passed, and assuming that they did make a breakthrough, the German infantry could creep back to the road and cut it again.

Then, for no apparent reason, the paras pulled out of Martelange at about three in the morning, leaving the road to Bastogne free once more. The Americans did not wait for an invitation! A Bailey bridge was thrown across the Sure, and a task force from Earnest's CCA, composed of a company of armoured infantry, some light tanks and self-propelled guns clattered on in pursuit of the retreating Germans, whose comrades' bodies littered the shell-cratered streets of the burning Belgian town. Colonel Heilmann's own account of the 5th's operations in the Battle of the Bulge gives no reason for the strange withdrawal from Martelange. Perhaps his men panicked. But whatever happened, they were soon rallied once they had reached Regimental HQ at Warnack.

Hastily the regimental commander formed a firing line and waited until the American point reached the outskirts of the village. This time, as at Martelange, the Germans gave the enemy no quarter or warning (after all their artillery was down to seven rounds per gun per day and they could not afford to waste the precious ammunition). They waited until the Americans were only a mere hundred yards away before they opened up. Four US vehicles were hit at once. A Sherman, so notorious among tankers for the ease with which it could be set alight that it was nicknamed 'the Ronson', burst into a vivid sheet of flame almost immediately. Hurriedly the vehicles behind it fled for safety and the attack came to an abrupt end. The men of the 4th decided that they would wait for dawn when they could see their enemy. Perhaps, too, after a week of fog and low cloud which had kept Allied air down on the ground, the weather would improve and the fighter-bombers might be able to help them in their advance.

The weather had been worrying General Patton, too. Indeed he had gone so far as to order his chaplain, Father O'Neill, to 'pray for dry weather'. O'Neill had replied, mindful obviously of his duty not only to 'Blood and Guts' but also to God, 'Sir, it's going to take a pretty thick rug for that kind of praying.' To which Patton had snorted, '*I don't care if it takes a flying carpet. I want you to get up a prayer for good weather!*'

23 December dawned bright and clear. The battleground glittered with hoarfrost and the sun-covered fields dazzled the eyes of the men of the 4th waiting outside Warnach. General Patton told his deputy chief-of-staff that morning, 'Goddamit, Harkins, look at the weather! O'Neill sure did some potent praying!'[4]

Now the weary 4th tankers knew they would soon receive air support. With renewed energy they rushed the village from three sides, riding in on their tanks, while the divisional artillery pounded the place. But once they were in among the houses the artillery had to stop firing and the paras began to fight back desperately. The morning air was full of the rapid burr of the German machine-guns answered by the slower chatter of the US machine-guns. Foolhardy or brave young men slipped out of the shell-pocked houses and fired their *panzerfausts*. A shower of red-hot sparks flew through the air and more often than not there was the hollow clang of metal striking metal, as yet another Sherman was hit.

The fight swayed back and forth but slowly the Americans gained the upper hand. They worked their way down the cobbled

---

[4] A little later O'Neill was taken to Patton's HQ where the General pinned the Bronze Star on his chest, telling him, 'Chaplain you're the most popular man in this headquarters. You sure stand in good with the Lord and the soldiers!'

village, fighting desperately from house to house, five fiercely burning Sherman tanks marking their progress. In the end Warnach was cleared at the cost of sixty-five tankers wounded or killed and 135 dead paras. The advance could continue to the next obstacle.

Now it was the turn of General Dager's CCB to take over the lead towards the village of Chaumont. So far Dager's command, which was highly experienced and was regarded by Patton as his best armoured formation, had been subjected solely to small arms fire. Perhaps it was for that reason that Dager grew over-confident and failed to see that he was walking into a trap. Soon after midday when the last of the Lightnings had zoomed away after straffing the village, light US tanks loaded with infantry charged the village. At the same time Shermans moved in from the west.

Almost at once the tanks came to grief. The good weather which Patton had prayed for turned out to be to the paratroopers' advantage. Cold at the sun's rays were, they did thaw the frozen fields and before they had gone a hundred yards, the Shermans bogged down. They floundered in the mud while the drivers revved their engines to no avail. The SPs of the 11th Assault cracked into action and one after another the tanks were picked off. There was nothing the Americans could do except bail out as soon as their vehicle was hit—if they were still alive—and flee to the rear. When the slaughter had ended, eleven Shermans were burning strongly.

The armoured infantry fared no better. They, too, ran into the concentrated fire of the German paratroopers. Men dropped on all sides and the advanced company simply melted away. When their commander finally ordered the survivors to pull back, the lead company had lost sixty-five men and every one of his officers was dead!

Patton, mindful of his promise to Eisenhower to be in Bastogne by Christmas and as always mindful of the publicity which would be gained by him and his beloved 3rd Army if it achieved its objective on time, did not pull his punches. When he heard that both Earnest's CCA and Dager's CCB were bogged down, he called III Corps HQ (to which the 4th belonged) and told General Millikin, the Corps Commander, 'There is too much piddling around! Bypass these towns and clear them up later. Tanks can operate on this ground now!'

The Corps Commander knew that he could not afford to fail. He got on to Gaffey and he, in his turn, threw in his reserve to clear a way through the *Fallschirmjaeger*. Gaffey ordered Colonel Wendell Blanchard to put in his Combat Command Reserve at the village of Bigonville and take the Germans by surprise.

Lieutenant-Colonel Abrams, the commander of the 37th Tank Battalion, who was one day to become the Commander-in-Chief of all US troops in Vietnam, led the way. He was an aggressive, unconventional soldier, who had gained a fine reputation in France. It was not the enemy, but the road conditions, which held him up now.

Diverting from the main highway at Martelange and turning right on to a secondary road which went off north-east, he and his slithering tank drivers found it 'sheer ice'. As a result he was forced to reduce his speed to a mere walk, in spite of the fact that he knew that the 'brass', ranging from Gaffey through Millikin right up to Patton himself, were breathing down his neck.

About noon on the 23rd, the point of the 37th Battalion came under fire from a group of paratroopers in a small fir wood near a crossroads. Abrams radioed back for artillery support. The 75s opened up almost immediately and plastered the wood with a will. For thirty minutes they flung everything they had at the small stretch of firs. Then when the sound of the firing had died away the armoured infantry headed for the wood. Resistance was almost nil. All the infantry found were a few dead Germans and a handful of unshaven, badly frightened *Fallschirmjaeger* in scruffy camouflaged suits who were only too glad, it seemed, to surrender. They winkled them out of their holes and returned to their White halftracks, happy at the ease with which they had achieved their objective.

Their happiness did not last many minutes for Heilmann's paras were smarter than the Americans. Their commander, a veteran of the Russian front, had withdrawn his men 500 yards as soon as the artillery bombardment had started. Now, while the American infantry strolled back to their vehicles, his men sneaked back to their old positions, ready for the real battle.

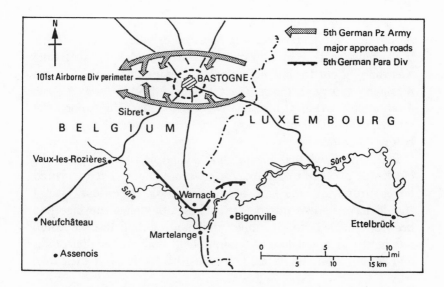

Just as the lead company was about to mount up again a German machine-gun fired a rapid burst into their surprised backs. A withering volley of rifle fire struck the Americans, totally unprepared for the German trick. Men dropped in agony everywhere.

Hastily the infantry called for tank support and Abrams' tankers hurried forward. They ran into a chain of mines. Irate tank commenders threw open their hatches and asked angrily what the delay was about. They never lived to find out. German snipers picked them off one by one as they leaned over the edge of their cupolas. Within a matter of minutes nearly all the commanders of one tank company were picked off. As dusk fell Colonel Blanchard called a halt. Just like its running mates, the CCA and CCB, Combat Command Reserve had come to a dead stop. It seemed as if Heilmann's inexperienced paras were winning all along the line.

General Patton was displeased! As he wrote later in his *War as I Knew It*: 'The advances for the day were not impressive, varying from two to five miles.' And it did not help one bit that his HQ kept receiving radio messages from the 'Battered Bastards of Bastogne' (as the Airborne troopers were now calling themselves) which hinted obliquely that the 4th Armored should get a move on. Thus, for instance, at the close of the day the Airborne commander General McAuliffe, who in spite of his brave reply to the German offer of surrender,[5] knew that time was running out for his men if help did not come soon, sent the message: 'Sorry, I did not get to shake hands today. I was disappointed.' One of his staff was less formal. He radioed the 4th's CP at midnight: 'There is only one more shopping day before Christmas!'

Patton realized that his original plan for attack around the clock was doomed to failure. As he wrote later: 'I remembered being surprised at the time how long it took me to learn war. I should have known this before.' Thus although a message had been intercepted from Colonel Heilmann stating that he could not hold out much longer without help and needed 'bazookas and ammunition', he decided to allow the 4th to do it their own way.

General Gaffey, who had felt Patton breathing down his neck for the last forty-eight hours—the 3rd Army Commander had even told him what type of tank he should use to spearhead his advance—was relieved that the pressure from above was off for a while. He knew that his men would invariably meet tough opposition if they were confined to the roads which must be the case if they relied solely on tanks as Patton had originally suggested. Indeed, even when the tanks did succeed in breaking through, the paras invariably slipped back into the villages 'taken' by the tankers and the whole mess had to begin once more.

In short, the whole 4th Division were opposed to any further head-on attacks by the weakened tank battalions, especially if these had to be executed at night (as Patton had originally insisted). Now the Division needed the footsloggers who were not confined to the roads.

Millikin asked for and got two battalions of the 318th Infantry to 'beef up' the 4th's infantry strength, while Gaffey requested

[5] His answer of 'nuts', which bewildered the German officers who asked for his surrender, has gone into the history books. More than likely, his reply was 'revised' because the original expletive would not have been suitable for the publicity releases. The inhabitants of Bastogne at first thought that 'nuts' had something to do with their own annual nut festival. Today, however, the little Belgian town is replete with 'nuts' museum, 'nuts' camping and even a 'nuts' restaurant.

Corps for fighter-bomber cover as the Division's 'Christmas present'; Christmas Day was supposedly going to bring good flying weather, and Gaffey could use all the 'flying artillery' he could get. Thus 24 December was spent by both sides in preparation for the battle on the morrow.[6]

CCR, commanded by Colonel Blanchard, which had finally taken Bigonville on the late afternoon of Christmas Eve, was resting, counting its prisoners, its own dead and wounded and consoling itself with the thought of the huge Christmas dinner it was to enjoy the following day, when a signal came in from General Gaffey.

It was brief and destroyed all their hopes of a quiet Christmas: 'Move to Neufchâteau at once.' There the Colonel received new orders telling him to take his command to support CCB, which lay south of Chaumont, and to protect the Division's left flank.

The mission was not as easy as it sounded. Blanchard knew almost nothing of the twelve miles of road that lay before him save that a lone company of US engineers were stationed at the village of Vaux-les-Rozières, preparing to make a last ditch stand in case the Germans attacked in that sector which hitherto had been relatively quiet. But in spite of the uncertainty and the fact that the CCR did not normally fight as an integrated combat unit, he knew that he was backed up by two outstanding fighting commanders—Lieutenant-Colonel Creighton Abrams of the 37th Tank Battalion and Lieutenant-Colonel George Jacques of the 53rd Armored Infantry. He gave the order to move. With a roar of tank engines and a clatter of half-tracks, the CCR moved forward along the icy road, heading into the unknown.

Meanwhile the infantry reinforcements from the 318th Infantry had arrived. They were in a sorry shape, having suffered heavy casualties in the first week of the offensive, and both battalions were understrength. (In the 1st Battalion all the officers from the battalion commander downwards were replacements.) In addition they had just experienced a freezingly cold six-hour truck ride, mostly in open trucks, which culminated in an uneasy few hours' 'rest' in the deep snow.

[6] One of the reasons for the initial success of the German attack in the Ardennes was bad flying weather which did not change—in the Allies' favour—until the offensive was a week old.

The 'rest' didn't last long. General Gaffey had told the 318th's regimental commander that he would probably have to fight for his departure line. The General was right. The departure line was a deep gorge and as soon as the frozen infantry began staggering up the opposite side in the hard snow, the paratroopers started pitching stick grenades down among them. All hell broke loose but still the infantry struggled on. Captain Reid McAllister, commanding the support company, exasperated by the attention of a heavy German gun which was holding up his men once they had breasted the heights, asked to take over the assault with the survivors. Permission was granted and air support was called for.

Eight fighter-bombers raced in at 400 miles an hour. Rockets burst from their wings. With a yell Captain McAllister's company assaulted the German positions and an hour later they had broken through. The gun and its crew were captured plus 161 demoralized prisoners. The advance could go on.

German headquarters now became worried. General Kokott, comander of the main assault division of Bastogne itself, the 26th Volksgrenadier, explained later: 'The action of the 5th Parachute was of vital concern to me for the American 4th Armored Division's drive north threatened my rear. It is an uncomfortable feeling to have someone launching a drive to your rear and I feared the 4th Armored. I knew it was a crack division.'

Accordingly he called General von Manteuffel and told him, 'I cannot watch two fronts, I do not think 5th Parachute can hold and I am in no position to prevent a breakthrough.'

Manteuffel's answer was in keeping with his character, but it was of little consolation to the worried infantry commander. It was, in Kokott's own words, 'The only solution to the problem was to attack Bastogne. He directed that I stop worrying and devote all my efforts to the attack from the north-west.'

Resigned to his fate, General Kokott obeyed. He planned to make his 'last desperate effort' to send an assault force, composed of a reconnaissance regiment, plus armoured infantry, to attack Bastogne from the north. The time of the attack was set for dawn on 26 December. Now everything depended on the ability of the 5th Parachute to hold back the 4th's attacks.

Meanwhile Colonel Blanchard's CCR, driving slowly into the

unknown, struck the first German positions. Naturally the worried Colonel, who realized how much now depended upon his mission, did not know whether the village—Remonville—contained German paratroopers. But he was not taking chances. He gave it what the 4th called 'the treatment!'

A company of Abrams' Shermans lined up on the hill facing the village and aimed its 75mms at the little group of cottages. Four artillery battalions close enough to hit Remonville were alerted too. Then at a signal Remonville got the 'treatment'—ten minutes of concentrated high explosive fire. Under its cover the attack went in.

While Shermans clattered into the main street, firing at the windows to left and right, armoured infantrymen leapt from their half tracks and began the grim business of house-to-house fighting. A burst of sub-machine fire at the door to keep the occupiers down. The door flung open. In with the grenades. The door clamped shut. The crump and screams from inside. Then the mad scramble inside, firing from the hip at those defenders who were still alive.

It was a bloody mess and casualties were high on both sides. Grimly the German garrison (3rd Battalion, the 14th Parachute Regiment) held on, doing better than Colonel Heilmann had expected it to do. But by dusk the battle was over and the weary armoured infantrymen began rounding up their equally weary prisoners—327 of them.

But Blanchard's success was short-lived. His point had only advanced a few hundred yards when it was forced to stop again. The road north was blocked by a large crater. To make matters worse, the para engineers had picked the site of the crater with care. It was bordered by a small river, which made it impossible for vehicles to detour.

Blanchard gave in. In spite of the torrent of abuse that would probably descend on his head from General Patton when he learned that the advance had had to stop once again, he was not going to risk a night assault. He was down to twenty tanks by now. So he called a halt for the day and set about planning the next day's assault.

Thus 26 December, 1944, dawned. It was a crucial day for both forces. In the north General Kokott launched his final assault on the besieged 101st, while to the south, Colonel

Blanchard would make his final attempt to break through to them. Time was running out for both commanders.

The morning was crisp and freezing cold. The ground was rock hard as Abrams' tanks clattered forward, making better progress than they had done in their summer dash across France. With the help of fighter cover they thrust rapidly through the paras' positions. The village of Remichamps fell to them easily. Abrams side-stepped Clochimont, where he expected to encounter the parachutists' main line of resistance, and closed with his objective, the village of Sibret.

The village was on the main road and would, in his opinion, be well defended. Could he afford to chance an all-out fight with the paratroopers? Not only was he down to twenty tanks, but also the 53rd Armored Infantry, which had been weak from the very start, was down to 230 men. For a while he paused and conferred with Jacques of the 53rd. Should it be Sibret, as Blanchard had ordered, or should they try to break through to Bastogne via the village of Assenois, straight to their fore? The time was 1.30 pm. Suddenly their voices were drowned by a great roar above them.

The first of the American supply squadrons of C-47 transports came into sight—289 of them. They were a sitting target for the gunners of the Hermann Goering Flak Detachment below. Anti-aircraft shells filled the sky. Here and there a C-47 broke apart and plunged to the hard earth. But still they came on. Hundred of supply chutes sailed down among the flak. Now the later squadrons, towing gliders, began releasing their burdens.[7]

The hectic battle above his head made up Abrams' mind for him. He doubled back to his tank 'Thunderbolt IV' and called Gaffey up on the radio, asking permission to attack straight north through Assenois. Gaffey said that he would call Patton and find out what he had to say.

Thus while Abrams waited impatiently, knowing that he did

[7] My informant on this part of the action, a nineteen-year-old glider pilot who later became a colonel in command of a fighter wing and saw much action in Korea and Vietnam, tells me: 'I was never scared again after that day. When they finally dug me out of the foxhole I buried myself in immediately we landed, I swore the next time I flew an airplane in action, it would have an engine and eight big machine-guns!' He lived to see his decision come true.

not have much daylight left, Lieutenant-Colonel Kaufmann, commander of the 5th Parachute's 39th Grenadier Regiment, still forced his men to face Bastogne. He was obeying General Kokott's order to have his troopers and their anti-tank guns cover the General's last desperate attack on the besieged town. Little did he realize that he, too, would soon face a similar assault—from the rear!

Finally Gaffey contacted Patton. It was now two. 'Will you authorize a big risk with Combat Command R for a break-through to Bastogne?' he asked.

'*I sure as hell will!*' was the prompt response.

At shortly after three, Abrams got Gaffey's message. He looked at the sky. It was already getting dark. If he were lucky he might have two hours of daylight left. He would have to act quickly. He radioed the 101st to keep a lookout for friendly troops breaking through. He called the three artillery battalions borrowed from CCB and asked them to support him with all they had. Finally he ordered Captain Dwight of his own 37th Battalion to take Company C of the 53rd Armored Infantry and his own tanks and break through.

At twenty minutes past four, everything was ready. Abrams gave the order to move and the tanks, armoured cars and half tracks jerked forward. In the lead thirty-three-year-old Charles Boggess, commanding nine large-size and more powerful armed Shermans—the Cobra Kings—pushed ever closer to the village of Assenois. Still all was silent. At thirty-five minutes past four, he called Abrams and told him that he was ready to attack. Would he inform the artillery? The Colonel would. 'Concen-tration Number Nine,' he radioed the waiting three battalions, 'play it soft and sweet!'

Almost immediately thirteen batteries—an unlucky number for Colonel Kaufmann's *Fallschirmjaeger*—crashed into action. Ten volleys rained down on the village. Boggess' nine tanks headed for the attack. Kaufmann's eight anti-tank guns leapt to the defence but they had little chance. The artillery and the fire from Boggess' machine-guns put them out of action at once. Within minutes they were in the village. The young tank lieuten-ant pressed on while behind him the infantry leaped from their vehicles as the surprised Germans started to react. A mixed group of paratroopers and infantry from the 26th

Volksgrenadiers recovered from their surprise and started to pour out of their cellars. Nineteen-year-old Private James Hendrix charged two cannon he saw vaguely through the smoke. 'Come on out!' he yelled. A paratrooper poked his head from a foxhole. At the double, Hendrix fired. The man fell clutching a wound in the neck. He ran on. Another foxhole and another German. Hendrix smashed at his head with his M-1. The enemy soldier disappeared as quickly as he had appeared. Hendrix paused and searched him, but found nothing save a box of US matches. As he advanced on the guns, the crews came out of the smoke, their hands high in the air, yelling '*Kamerad!*'[8]

But while Captain Frank Kutak, commander of the 53rd's A Company, directed the fighting in the village from his jeep, for he had been wounded in both legs, Boggess pressed on, followed by two other tanks. Behind him and the other two, there was a gap of 300 yards before the first of his other Cobra Kings made their appearance out of the gloom. The paras did not waste the opportunity. A couple of young soldiers ran out and flung several teller mines on the road. Captain Dwight, following in the first Cobra, drove on and ordered his men to clear the mines. Boggess did not wait. He charged forward with his small force into the unknown, heading for the woods to the north of Assenois. Below him his gunner Dickerson was using his 75mm like a machine-gun. The long barrel glowed a dull-red, as Dickerson fired round after round in rapid succession. The bow machine-gunner Kafner played his part too. His gun chattered incessantly. In the smoke and confusion, dim figures fell everywhere.

Suddenly Boggess saw a blockhouse. It was painted green. He snapped a quick order and Dickerson fired three quick rounds into it. It flew apart. Everywhere now there were coloured parachutes from the day's drop. Then they saw foxholes ahead, the brown of the new top-soil standing out in the snow. Boggess did not know who held them. Standing up in his turret—a dangerous thing to do if they were German—he called, 'Come here! This is the 4th Armored!'

There was no answer, so he tried again. Slowly several helmeted heads appeared over the ground. A white face rose

[8] Private, later Staff Sergeant Hendrix won the Medal of Honor for his exploits that day.

suspiciously. Then a single figure rose. It wore the uniform of an American soldier. The man advanced towards the waiting tankers. 'I'm Lieutenant Webster of the 326th Engineers, 101st Airborne Division.' He smiled and stretched up his hand. 'Glad to see you.'

Bastogne had been relieved and the 4th had kept its promise. The brave defence of the inexperienced 5th German Parachute Division had been in vain. Now the days of the Hunters from the Sky in the last desperate offensive were numbered.

1945—The End of the Hunters from the Sky

'If you have a map before you, you will take in the situation at a glance. My divisions are surrounded with the Rhine at their back.'

General Schlemm, CO 1st Para Army,
to Field-Marshal Rundstedt, 3 March, 1945

One

On the same day that the survivors of the badly battered 5th Parachute Division finally moved into second line position on the German side of the border to join the 3rd Division, which was already licking its wounds, Hitler held a major conference in the Reich Chancellery. On the afternoon of 27 January, 1945, the man who had once held almost the entire land mass of Europe was a complete physical and spiritual wreck, faced with tremendous political and military problems. Now after over five years of war, which had brought him some earth-shaking victories, not only was his Eastern Front being attacked by a 3-million-strong Russian Army, but in the West the combined American, British, Canadian and French forces were poised for the last assault against Germany's border from Holland to Switzerland. This was to be the year of reckoning and Hitler, sick and trembling, knew that only the most desperate of his commanders could help to delay the inevitable disaster.

After General Guderian had discussed the miserable situation on the Eastern Front, the West and the commanders there came up for discussion. The Führer showed interest for the first time. While Goering explained the need for retaining General Student as commander of Army Group H, located in Holland and on the Lower Rhine, he listened patiently, nodding his head occasionally when Goering made a good point in Student's favour. Student's critics, Goering explained, couldn't see that the former's slow speech was simply a mannerism. 'They think he's a fool because he speaks so slowly, but they don't know him like I do. I'd be happy to take him back because I know he can put the old spirit into his paratroopers.'

There was no response from the other members of the conference. The poor performance of Student's men in the Ardennes, from the failure of the last drop to the Bastogne action of the 5th Parachute, was well known to them.

Goering went on, 'I'll be happy to have him because I know that when there is a crisis you'll get angry and call him back. I'm looking forward to that day.'

'I'm not,' Hitler said drily. It was clear that his mind was now made up to remove Student.

Goering tried one more time. 'Maybe he'll learn to speak even more slowly later on, that's possible, but he'll also retreat a lot more slowly.'

'He reminds me of Fehrs, my new servant,' Hitler said. 'When I tell him to do something it takes minutes for him to get it. He's dumb as an ox, but he certainly works hard. It's just that he's so slow.'

There the subject was dropped. But Student's fate was sealed. His command was taken off him and given to General Johannes Blaskowitz. But although Student had to go, his paras remained to add one more page of self-sacrifice and futile heroism to their long record of these last five and a half years. And the man who was to be in charge of the last great action fought by the Hunters from the Sky was also one of their own, a survivor of the great days in Crete, General Alfred Schlemm.

General of the Paratroops Alfred Schlemm had been Student's chief-of-staff in Crete. Thereafter he had left the paratroopers and had taken over a regular army corps, fighting at Vitebsk and Smolensk during 1943, that decisive year in the Battle for Russia. Now in the last year he returned to his old love—the paras—to take over the 1st Parachute Army, which contained, in addition to *Wehrmacht* formations, the cream of the Hunters from the Sky—the 2nd, 7th and 8th Parachute Divisions.

In civilian clothes Alfred Schlemm would have made little impression on the casual observer. He was small and very dark-skinned so that with his broad face and large nose he might even have been taken for a foreigner, from the Balkans or Turkey. But his insignificant appearance concealed a man of strong personality and high intelligence, who could hold his own even with such men as Field-Marshal Rundstedt. In November when Rundstedt had briefed him on the task of the 1st Parachute Army, for instance, he had queried the former's estimation of the position. 'Very well,' he told Rundstedt, 'I'll do my best to hold on. The first thing I'll do is set up defence lines facing north-west.' Pointedly he added, 'Surely one day or another the

Anglo-Americans will have the idea of outflanking us in the north?'

'It's quite possible,' Rundstedt conceded.

His intelligence showed through at his first briefing with the new commander of his Army Group, Blaskowitz, in late January. 'Look out,' Blaskowitz told him. 'The enemy might attack you from the south.'

'No,' Schlemm said firmly, 'the attack will come through the Reichswald Forest. That's the ideal place for a surprise.'

And the paratrooper was right, for at dawn on 8 February, 1945, Montgomery's great offensive through the Forest, which he hoped would take him to the Rhine, started.

That morning Schlemm woke at the sound of the heavy guns. The volume of the permanent background music of the war had increased noticeably. At once he telephoned Blaskowitz: 'I feel that it's the big push', he informed him and without waiting for a decision from his slower-moving superior, he set about preparing for the Battle of the Reichswald.

The Reichswald (The Imperial Forest) is a thick fir forest, ten miles across from west to east and five miles deep. On its north it is flanked by the border town of Cleves and to the south by the railway and the key road junction of Goch. It was an ideal defensive position. The firs, as is often the case in Germany, were planted in thick regimented lines so that visibility was limited to a dozen yards and any fighting would be a hand-to-hand nature. If that were not bad enough the soil was sandy and it would be very difficult to operate tanks or heavy vehicles within the forest (and there were only two good concrete roads running through it). In other words, the advantages were all on the side of the defender and Schlemm had already made full use of them, siting his artillery on all trails and fire breaks, mining any glades, and planting picked paratroopers as snipers on all approaches. Energetic General Horrocks, commander of the British XXX Corps, which had the task of penetrating the dense firs, would have his work cut out. There would be no easy victories in the Reichswald.

After the 1,000-gun barrage ceased on that February morning, Horrocks' five divisions moved off. After the tremendous weight of explosive which had been flung at the unseen enemy, the cocky Scots soldiers of the Gordon Highlanders leading the attack thought they were in for a walkover. They were in for a great surprise. Their mine-clearing flail tanks bogged down almost at once in the rain-soaked terrain. One managed to clear a path, however, for the support Churchills of the Coldstream Guards, which did not take long to bog down too.

The Gordon Highlanders and the Cameronians pushed on through the mud and mire of the battered battlefield, and seized their objectives. Now the 6th Battalion of the King's Own Scottish Borderers took over and reached the outskirts of the Reichswald. And then the trouble started. A savage German artillery bombardment struck the Gordons. In a matter of minutes their command post was put out of action, with two officers killed, one wounded, and another eighteen 'other ranks' killed or wounded. Other troops of the same brigade ran into the first of the paratroopers. Wading through icy water to their waist, they were picked off easily by the fanatical young paras, conscious of their instructors exhortations at the training school that: 'You are the *élite* of the German Army. You are to seek out combat and be ready to endure hardship. Your greatest ambition should be to do battle.'

Horrocks now threw in a new division. The 43rd Infantry Division, which ended the war with more casualties than any other British formation, went into the battle at night. It was bitterly cold, the rain driving in sudden icy squalls over the flooded fields. They plodded forward through the wet misery, knowing that much worse was to come. The night attack became a nightmare. The British infantry fought a completely and cunningly concealed enemy who could only be located when a red stab of flame momentarily revealed his position. German mortars made the attackers' lives hell with their obscene grunts, followed by the thick bursts of explosives and the whizzing red-hot steel fragments as big as a man's fist. Mines completed the misery.

But advance they did, to be relieved the following morning—completely exhausted—by yet another brigade of infantry. One terrible day followed another and a desperate Horrocks, a man usually so full of bubbling optimism, flung in division after division. Later Eisenhower was to confess that those initial fourteen days were 'the worst two weeks of my life'.

General Schlemm kept his nerve. He knew his paras. He absorbed Horrocks' initial attack and held firm. Then he set about stabilizing his front and even managed to counter-attack on the road between Cleves and Kalkar. Indeed two weeks after the offensive had opened he was so satisfied with his position that even a surprise telephone call from the aged Field-Marshal in no way shocked him. Von Rundstedt, who was now relying on large quantities of alcohol in order to sleep at night, said baldly, 'The Americans crossed the Ruhr this morning.'

Schlemm knew what that meant. The enemy had wanted to advance between Duran and Roermond from the Maas to the Rhine right at the start of the great offensive. But by blowing the Schwamenauel Dam, the River Ruhr had been raised by three feet and increased to a broad stretch of water of several hundred feet. It had proved an almost impossible barrier for the Americans.

'The Americans attacked after a forty-five minute bombardment,' Rundstedt explained. 'They crossed the river on a front fourteen miles long covered by smoke.'

'That's bad news,' Schlemm said, his mind hurriedly examining the implications of this new threat.

On the next day Schlemm made his decision. Spontaneously he called his chief: 'At all costs we must prevent the junction of the enemy. [He meant the consolidation of the US–British bridgeheads.] My paratroopers are holding back the Canadians.[1] Have you enough men to hold the Americans?' Von Rundstedt said that he had not.

'Then I suggest taking two armoured and one infantry division away from me and sending them south.'

With as much enthusiasm as he could muster these days, the aged Field-Marshal accepted the amazing offer—an offer which indicated how sure Schlemm was of the fighting ability of his 20,000 young paratroopers.

The terrible battle went on. Whole villages disappeared in the shelling and bombing. Bitter little battles were fought on muddy islands, formed by the floods, between British infantry and the paras. Both sides returned from the line utterly exhausted, the men drenched to the skin, unshaven, red-eyed and 'beat'. The landscape came to resemble that of some strange planet, as visualized by a science-fiction writer. Shattered trees breasting

[1] Horrocks' Corps was under the control of the 1st Canadian Army —hence 'Canadians'.

the water, through which floated the disgusting debris of battle—
ration boxes, cardboard shell containers, khaki and field-grey
jackets—and the ultimate obscenity, a shell-torn body, nudging
up and down at the command of the tiny waves, blown by the
wind.

Schlemm started to give way. His losses were high. Perhaps
now he regretted his generosity to Rundstedt, for no reinforcements were forthcoming. On 3 March, the Canadian 1st Army
and the US 9th linked up at Geldern. He called Rundstedt and
told him, 'If you have a map before you, you will take in the
situation at a glance. My divisions are surrounded, with the
Rhine at their back. Under these conditions I can't do anything
against the enemy's superior forces. I'm asking your authorization to withdraw to the east bank of the Rhine.'

'I'll have to speak to Berlin,' Rundstedt answered.

Hitler did not like the request. He told General Jodl: 'I want
him (Rundstedt) to hang on to the West Wall as long as is
humanly possible. Above all, we must cure him of the idea of
retreating here.' All the Führer would agree to was the sending
of observers to the front. 'We have to get a couple of officers
down there, officers who are good men, so that we get a clear
picture.'

As Rundstedt translated the orders from Berlin: 'There can
be no question of General Schlemm withdrawing his troops east
of the Rhine. On the contrary, he must hold on to the west bank
at any cost with a bridgehead stretching at the very least from
Krefeld to Wesel.'

Schlemm obeyed. By the first week of March, he was forced
back and back, with only twelve miles of the river bank under
his control. Again he contacted Rundstedt, telling him, 'In my
opinion, the reasons for holding the bridgehead are outdated.
American artillery on the west bank, to both sides, covers the
river and shuts off all traffic.' He asked for authorization to
withdraw to the other bank but there was none forthcoming.
Under no circumstances was a bridge over the Rhine to fall into
enemy hands. They had to be kept open until the last moment
to allow the retreating German Army to cross; they were to be
blown only when there was an immediate threat of capture.
Failure to carry out these orders to the letters meant death. As
General Schlemm commented later, 'Since there were nine

bridges over the Rhine in my sector, I saw my chances of a long life getting slimmer and slimmer.' All the same when the Colonel in charge of the Homberg Bridge hesitated to destroy as the Americans came closer, Schlemm ordered that if the bridge was not blown immediately, he would personally shoot the colonel and 'anyone else he found near it.'

On 6 March, 1945, the Battle for the Rhineland entered its last phase. On a front no more than eight miles wide, a quarter of a million men were locked together in mortal combat. On the left, the centre and the right, two British and three Canadian infantry divisions pushed with all their strength in one final attempt to throw the paratroopers over the Rhine.

The 52nd Mountain Division, perhaps the freshest division left to the British (it had only arrived in Europe three months before) attempted to encircle the town of Alpen, and outflank it. They did so at terrible cost. It seemed as if nothing but violent death would move Schlemm's paras. The 6th Cameronians, for instance, their ammunition exhausted, lost four officers and 169 men. The Royal Scots Fusiliers of the same Division fared little better. Casualties were high, too, in the other infantry formations.

Now Schlemm started to evacuate everything and everybody left over the one available bridge at Wesel, covered by the remnants of four parachute divisions. His small bridgehead west of the Rhine was incredibly packed with men and material frantically trying to escape from the enemy. In one case, for instance, the staffs of three divisions were squeezed in the same sugar refinery! Schlemm knew that if he didn't clear his bridgehead soon, there would be the most appalling slaughter. He appealed to Blaskowitz: 'There is only one available bridge,' he told him. 'The Wesel. If an enemy spearhead reaches it and I have to blow it according to orders, we shall have no way of escaping. My effectives will then be lost to the command. And some of my men have had experience that would make them very useful in preventing an enemy crossing of the river.' It was the understatement of the year; the experience his paras had gained in these last few weeks was priceless!

'Berlin is dead set against any withdrawal, 'Blaskowitz answered.

'Well, please communicate what I have just told you,' Schlemm insisted. 'If Berlin does not believe me, or thinks I am painting too black a picture, let it send an observer. But there's no time to be lost.'

Indeed there was not. The sound of the guns was getting closer and closer. Both the Canadians and the British were pressing home their attack, fighting with the last of their strength to break the German's hold on the tiny piece of territory left to them on the west bank of the Rhine. The 2nd Canadian Division launched a full scale attack which was beaten back. Hurriedly Schlemm set up his command post near the Wesel bridge, covered by a formidable array of 88mm, belonging to the flak, which were now used in the ground role, and the survivors of his paras. Now it was the turn of the British.

On 8 March a brigade of the 43rd Wessex Division and the 4th Canadian Brigade tried again. It went in at dawn and despite heavy losses the British and the Canadians pressed home their attack. Fighting all day, the infantry finally penetrated the town of Xanten close to the bridge. Hurriedly flame-throwing tanks were brought up. The fearsome weapons worked their way from ruin to ruin, 'flaming out' the survivors of the paras. At last the remnants began to surrender. As they came out, the brigadier in charge of the British infantry ordered his staff 'to stand up in respectful silence' as they passed into the POW cages, for 'the German garrison of Xanten were very gallant men'.

Finally the representative of Berlin Army HQ arrived at Schlemm's CP—a dashing officer in a fine sparkling uniform. 'Come and inspect my lines,' Schlemm invited him, as they stood there in the CP which rocked with every new explosion. The officer accepted. He thought he would be driven out there in a staff car. He was mistaken. 'There's no point in it, because the front is quite near. We'll go on foot. If we're lucky enough not to have to crawl on our hands and knees,' he added with a trace of his old humour at the strange look on the suddenly pale face of the headquarters man. Naturally he saw to it that the Colonel had to crawl, through mud and mire. Time and time again the two men, one scared out of his wits, the other secretly enjoying the sight of this *Etappenhengst*, 'this rear echelon stallion', tasting a dose of the front line, had to drop into water-filled craters as enemy snipers spotted them.

'Well,' Schlemm asked when they got back to his CP, 'what do you think?'

'I agree that the situation's desperate,' the Colonel said, wiping his face, 'and the bridgehead must be withdrawn!'

Thus it was that early on the morning of 10 March, 1945, quiet descended suddenly on the battlefield. The exhausted Canadian and British infantry crouching in their slit trenches, waiting for the start of yet another terrible day which surely would see the death of some of their number, looked across to the German positions curiously. What was going on? What had happened to the usual daily 'hate'? When would the first long-haired German paratrooper in his camouflaged smock begin the inevitable sniping that would end as equally inevitably in his or their death?

Suddenly the calm was shattered. There was a tremendous roar, followed by another and yet another. It was the bridge at Wesel. As far as Schlemm was concerned, the Battle of the Rhineland was over. For over a month he had led the 1st Parachute Army in a masterly fashion. Finally, when he had lost 90,000 men (compared with 22,000 British, Canadian and American casualties), he had staged a disciplined and model withdrawal—the last German general to do so. But as the last of his weary paras slipped from the smoking ruins of the bridge and began ferrying themselves across the river to the tenuous security of the eastern bank, they must have known that General Alfred Schlemm had been forced to sacrifice the cream of the German Army in the West—its parachute divisions—to achieve that disciplined and model withdrawal.

Two

By the time the last German para had crossed the Rhine, General Student knew that the war was irretrievably lost. Soon the Allies would push across the last great natural barrier, protecting the belly (the Ruhr) and the heart (Berlin) of the Reich. The question remained whether he should stand and fight to the last, or should he put an end to it all with his service pistol, like so many of his friends and associates were now beginning to do? The world he knew was crashing about him. Last July it had appeared that he, too, was a suspect in the generals' plot. At nine in the evening on the 22nd, Student had been sitting on the terrace of his little house working at a pile of papers, clad only in his slippers and dressing gown, when the gigantic bulk of Otto Skorzeny had loomed out of the shadows. Skorzeny told Student that there had been an attempt to kill Hitler. Skorzeny had watched him carefully for a reaction. For his part he had jumped up, crying, 'No, that can't be possible!'

Later on he wondered why in this moment of crisis Skorzeny had come to visit him personally, bringing with him half a dozen of his best men, who had lurked somewhere in the shadows that night? There was no love lost between them. Would not a telephone call have sufficed? Or was there something more behind his visit?[1]

Personal tragedy had struck in these last months, too. His only son, who had followed his father into the ranks of the *Luftwaffe*, had been shot down and killed. Now he and his wife were alone, two elderly people, worrying about the future.

As the sound of the Russian cannon grew louder and louder, Student, still in Berlin, wondered what he should do next. If he

[1] Student's biographer, General Farrar-Hockley, states that 'he (Skorzeny) hoped to be able to arrest Student that night'. (Interview with author) Skorzeny, for his part, states that he was concerned solely with finding out 'who exactly was revolting in Berlin . . . Student's force just occurred to me'.

killed himself, what would become of his wife, left to the tender mercies of the Russians? Should he not try to obtain an active command, perhaps at the head of his own beloved paras? But there were not many of them left now. The remnants of the newly formed 2nd Para and the 3rd Para were trapped in 'Ruhr Pocket', Heilmann's 5th had vanished in the fighting on the Moselle, the 6th, 7th, and 8th Para Divisions, or what was left of them after the fighting in the Rhine, were reeling back before Montgomery's advancing troops. And then in the middle of April came the terrible news that one of his para divisions had run away. The 9th Para Division had fled before a Russian attack!

Colonel-General Heinrici, the stubborn old soldier who had been charged with the defence of the capital, had not liked the newly formed 9th Para Division from the start. As he told Hitler at a conference which Goering attended: 'The 9th Parachute Division worries me. Its commanders and non-commissioned officers are nearly all former administration officers, both untrained and unaccustomed to leading fighting units.'

Goering bristled at the attack on his troops. 'My paratroopers!' he said loudly. 'You are talking about my paratroopers! They are the best in existence. I won't listen to such degrading remarks! I personally guarantee their fighting capabilities.'

'Your view, *Herr Reichsmarschall*,' Heinrici remarked icily, 'is somewhat biased. I'm not saying anything against your troops, but experience has taught me that untrained units—especially those led by green officers—are often so terribly shocked by their first exposure to artillery bombardment that they are not much good for anything thereafter.'

Thereafter there had been bad blood between the two men. Heinrici's remarks about the paras rankled. A few days later Goering had telephoned Heinrici's chief-of-staff and said angrily: 'It is inconceivable to me that Heinrici should talk about my paras the way he did. It was a personal insult!'

On 15 April, 1945, the 9th Para Division went into action for the first time. Most of the young airmen, although they might have been in the *Luftwaffe* for several years, had only had two or three weeks' infantry training. But they stood their ground along a seventy-five mile front when 22,000 long-range Russian guns crashed into action. All night they withstood the bombardment.

Then just before dawn on 16 April, the artillery fire stopped abruptly. Up the Kustrin–Berlin road, which the paras were defending, hundreds of lights suddenly snapped on. Scores of Russian T-34 tanks, their lights ablaze, began to advance on the Germans' positions. In the grey pre-dawn light the first of the paras clambered out of their slit trenches in the outlying positions located in the flat marshy ground and started to run for the rear. 'The Russians are coming!' they yelled to the startled men in the main line.

It was a horrifying sight which met their eyes, as they peered over the tops of their pits. Russian tanks stretched as far as the eye could see! Behind them lumbered the first wave of Russian infantry, their long coats flapping about their ankles. Fifty yards further back came a second wave, and a third. Suddenly the *Luftwaffe* ex-flak crews who were using their 88s in a ground role opened up at the wonderful target. From the top of the ridge behind the front line trenches, hundreds of guns pounded the 'Ivans', as they called the Russians. Tank after tank came to a stop and went up in flames. The infantry came on, crying 'hurrah' in the Russian fashion. But without their armour they were easy meat for the paras. They were mown down mercilessly. By dawn the Russian attack was broken up completely at the cost of a handful of German casualties. The paras relaxed in their trenches, confident and cocky that they could take all that the Russians cared to throw at them. Little did they know that Marshal Zhukov, the Russian commander, was prepared to do exactly that.

Late that afternoon the Russians sent a single Stalin tank up the highway to draw the paras' fire. But no one replied. It got so close that the paras could see the commander's face as he stood upright in his turret, challenging them to shoot at him.

Finally the flak crews could not resist the wonderful target. A 88mm shell struck hard against the Stalin's track and the tank came to a halt. Hastily the crew scrambled out. The young paras tightened their grip on their weapons, but their officers ordered them to hold their fire. The command passed from foxhole to foxhole. The sun started to go down. The men grew increasingly nervous. In the blood-red glare they could see the Russian tanks begin to snake out of the nearby woods and head up the hill. A single 88mm fired and the column reversed and headed back the way it had come.

For over two hours there followed an eerie silence. Then at seven o'clock, the paras heard the roar of tanks again and the rusty squeak of their tracks. There must have been several score of them. They were advancing on the paras' positions on both flanks. The paras maintained their discipline and held their fire. One of the leading paras heard a gunner behind him say, 'I want those bastards in front of my guns before the first round is fired!'

A monstrous black shape loomed up out of the darkness. The din of the diesel motors and the rusty clank of the tracks was tremendous. Below the paras the earth trembled violently. The 88s opened up. The first tanks were hit and set ablaze. Red-shot shrapnel came showering down on the cowering Hunters from the Sky. Now the Russians started to appear out of the flames. There might have been a whole battalion of them. Screaming like madmen they rushed the German trenches.

The paras opened fire. More and more Russians dropped, but the rest came on, yelling 'hurrah'; then what was left of them fell back. But there was no rest for the frightened young para-troopers. Another wave of Russian tanks appeared out of the darkness. Now the Russians were everywhere. The paras' positions were filled with shouting Russian infantry. Desperate little individual battles swayed back and forth. The Russians seemed to know no fear and the paras began to waver.

And then, as if the six long years of fighting which their predecessors had undergone, had finally had their effect, they broke and began to run, clawing their way out of their holes, throwing away their weapons, streaming in panic to the rear.

Colonel Hans Woehlermann, the new Army artillery commander, who had arrived at the front that day, witnessed the rout. Everywhere, he reported later, soldiers were 'running away like madmen'. Even when he drew his pistol, the paras did not halt. He found the 9th's commander, Colonel Hermann, 'utterly alone and completely disheartened by the flight of his men, trying to hold back whatever there was left to hold back'.

Eventually the flight was stopped but the paras remained, in Woehlermann's words, 'a threat to the course of the whole battle'.

General Heinrici did not miss the opportunity to take his revenge on Goering. He rang him up at his palace at Karinhall, and said, 'I have something to tell you. Those Cassino troops of yours, those famous paratroopers—well, they have run away!'

The flight of the 9th Para was the end and Student knew it. One last time he reported to Hitler's HQ in the bunker under the ruins of the Reichs Chancellery. Surprisingly enough the first person he met in the confused mass of people in the dripping underground passages was his old chief, Goering. He was thinner and less confident than he had been but he had regained some of that old cynicism which had characterized him before he had attained such great power. Waving a well-manicured hand, he announced, 'You must remember, Student, that you are in Hitler's holy chamber.' With the toe of his highly polished boot, he pushed open the nearest door to reveal a pink-covered bed. 'Here sleeps Eva Braun herself,' he said like a tourist guide.[2]

Student left his benefactor to report to Hitler personally. The Führer's face was almost unrecognizable, yellow and terribly old; and he had to hold his arm to prevent it trembling. But still Student got the impression that 'Hitler felt he could defend Berlin, even if it meant dying there.[2]

'He believed every "golden pheasant" (party official) with whom he surrounded himself. They told him that Busse and Wenck, the two army commanders fighting to relieve Berlin, would be able to break through to him, Student remembered later. 'He clutched desperately at every rumour.'

In haste, Student reported his own position—an experienced soldier without a command at this moment of Germany's greatest danger. Hitler responded with surprising alacrity. He ordered Student to go straight away to the man who had relieved him three months before, Blaskowitz. There he was 'to collect all available reserves and break through to the capital at once!'

Student, a good soldier to the last in spite of the many blows that he had suffered in these last months, accepted the assignment at its face value. He reported to Colonel-General Jodl, Hitler's Chief-of-Staff, for further orders. The General, regarded as one of the cleverest men in the Army, looked at him as if he

[2] Student to the author.

were an idiot when he repeated Hitler's words. Jodl knew the game was up. 'You won't find any reserves,' was his only comment.

He was right. Student could not even reach his new command. Thus the General without an army spent the last few days of the war wandering from HQ to HQ, trying to find an assignment. Then he gave up and accompanied by his adjutant, his chief-of-staff and another general they had picked up on the way, he set off for the last German formation in the West offering organized resistance—Admiral Doenitz's troops.

Three times the little group of German officers broke through the lines of British and American divisions pushing towards the Elbe and beyond—thieves stealing through the night—until finally the one-time victor of Holland and Crete arrived at Flensburg, beaten and exhausted. There on 9 May, 1945, he passed into British captivity. The last of the Hunters from the Sky followed the many thousands of his surviving paras into the POW cage. It was all over at last.[3]

[3] But according to the divisional history of the 11th Armoured Division *Taurus Pursuant*, their war did not end then. 'In the Forst Segeberg', the history states, 'were a number of SS troops who had decided to continue the war on their own. The Germans, therefore, undertook to enforce their surrender and 8th Parachute Division, the enemy formation in the area, was ordered to operate against them. In due course the SS surrendered.'

Bibliography

K. Alman: *Sprung in die Hoelle*. Pabel Verlag.

R. Boehmler: *Fallschirmjaeger*. Podzun Verlag.

O. Skorzeny: *Wir kampften, wir verloren*. Ring Verlag.

R. Thompson: *Battle for the Rhine*. Ballantine Books.

C. Wilmot: *The Struggle for Europe*. Collins.

H. Ramcke: *Fallschirmjaeger*. Lorch Verlag.

M. Clark: *The Calculated Risk*. Harper.

D. Eisenhower: *Crusade in Europe*. Heinemann.

P. Leverkusen: *German Military Intelligence*. Weidenfeld & Nicolson.

H. Kippenberger: *Infantry Brigadier*. Oxford.

A. Kesselring: *Memoirs*. Kimber.

F. Majdalany: *The Monastery*. Bodley Head.

L. Moen: *Under the Iron Heel*. Hale.

B. Mauldin: *Up Front*. Holt.

G. Patton: *War as I Knew It*. Allen.